JC Redonnet

INDIA AND AFRICA

INDIA AND AFRICA

Edited by
R. R. Ramchandani

HUMANITIES PRESS
ATLANTIC HIGHLANDS, N.J.

First Published 1980 in the United States of America by
Humanties Press Inc.
Atlantic Highlands
N.J. 07716

ISBN 0-391-01796-9

Printed in India

Contents

Contributors

APPA B. PANT is former Indian Ambassador to Kenya and several countries, including India's representative from 1948 to 1954 to whole of Africa south of the Sahara and North of the Limpopo. His previous publications include *Tensions and Tolerance* and *Aggression and Violence: Gandhian Experiments to Fight Them.*

VIJAY GUPTA is Associate Professor, Centre for African and West Asian Studies, School of International Studies, Jawaharlal Nehru University, New Delhi. He was formerly Editor, *Africa Quarterly* (1973-78) and is the author of the forthcoming *Kenya: Politics of (In) dependence.*

SHANTI SADIQ ALI is a scholar of African affairs and is a member of Governing Body, Indian Council of Cultural Relations, New Delhi. She was formerly Secretary General of the Indian Council for Africa.

HOMI J.H. TALEYARKHAN is former Indian Ambassador to Libya (1971-77) and has been Minister for Food and Civil Supplies, Maharashtra Government (1962-65). He is presently Chairman of the Maharashtra State Financial Corporation.

SATYAVATI JHAVERI is associated with the Department of Politics, University of Bombay and is presently engaged in research on the geo-political and defence problems of the Indian Ocean. She has published *The Presidency in Indonesia: Dilemmas of Democracy.*

JAYANTI K. PATEL is Lecturer in Political Science, School of Social Sciences, Gujarat University, Ahmedabad and is the author of *African Politics.*

PADMA SRINIVASAN is Research Associate, Centre of East African Studies, University of Bombay.

R.R. RAMCHANDANI is Reader, Centre of East African Studies, University of Bombay. His recent publications include *Uganda Asians* and *Tanganyika: A Background Study* (co-author).

R.V. RAMDAS is Director, Shri Brihad Bharatiya Samaj, Bombay. His publications include *Indians in East Africa, Indians in Fiji, Indians in Sri Lanka, Indians in Guyana,* and *Mahatma Gandhi on Indians Overseas.*

A.S. KALA is Lecturer, M.D. College, Bombay, and was formerly a Junior Research Fellow, Centre of East African Studies, University of Bombay.

P.R. PANCHMUKHI is Reader, Economics of Education, Department of Economics, University of Bombay. He is presently on deputation as Chief (Financial Resources), Planning Commission, New Delhi. He has published *Education and Research in Economics* and *Major Educational Reforms in India: A Study of their Dynamics* (to be published by the World Bank, Washington).

PRIYA V. MUTALIK DESAI is Reader, Centre of East African Studies, University of Bombay and the Editor of *Economics and Political Development of Kenya.*

D.V. HEGDE is employed with Tata Economic Consultancy Services, Bombay.

RENU C. BHATIA is Junior Research Fellow, Centre of East African Studies, University of Bombay and is engaged in research on *India's Economic Relations with East Africa, 1947-1975.*

V.G. MUTALIK DESAI is Head of the Department of Economics, M.D. College, Bombay.

Foreword

I am happy to learn of this publication which is based on a number of papers presented at an All India Workshop organised by the Centre of East African Studies of the University of Bombay. I had myself the pleasure of associating with that workshop which attracted a wide participation not only from the University and college teachers but also some of our leading African specialists from other Indian Universities and from other walks of life—some foreign diplomats to African countries and renowned Africa watchers presented papers and effectively participated in the deliberations. The Centre of East African Studies, although recently established, did an exceedingly fine job for which it deserves praise.

Ever since its inception the Centre of East African Studies has done its best to promote and pioneer African studies at the academic level in this University. Despite limitations and constraints under which it has functioned, it is indeed heartening to mention that the Centre has already earned for itself a place in the higher academic life of the country and has now taken roots as one of the major Centres of Study and Research on Africa.

India and Africa belong to the old world and have had age-old contacts with each other. During the colonial period, such contacts were further intensified but the nature of relations between the two peoples suffered in some ways from several disadvantages. After national independence the colonial equation was naturally found to be a totally unsatisfactory basis for building up a sound framework for a lasting and mutually beneficial relationships. A new beginning has been made and today Indo-African relations are nearly completely free from the underpinnings of colonial overtones and bias. Several new avenues of cooperation have been opened up. However, much still remains to be done.

The contributors to this volume have delved deep into various aspects of socio-political, historical and economic variables that have direct or indirect bearing on Indo-African relations and cooperation. Some of them have been able to identify as yet untapped areas of cooperation. It is the first study of this kind in the field and I earnestly hope that the readers will find it useful.

I wish that the Centre will be able to undertake more such studies and dig deep into other areas of research pertaining to the field of African Studies.

PROFESSOR RAM JOSHI
Vice-Chancellor, University of Bombay

Preface

This volume is a collection of papers presented at the workshop on "India and Africa" held by the Centre of East African Studies of the University of Bombay, from 6th to 8th October 1977. The workshop attracted several academic specialists and diplomatic experts on Africa from all over the country. In all, seventeen papers were presented of which fifteen have been included in the volume. The revised copies of the remaining two were not received by the time the manuscript had to be sent to the publishers. We are, therefore, sorry that they had to be dropped.

The theme "India and Africa" was deliberately kept wider to enable the participants to discuss and deliberate in some depth on different aspects of Indo-African relations, the variables that influence the contact and cooperation between the two peoples and the relevance of the methods and modes of tackling some of their developmental problems, the factors underlying their approaches to international issues, and the compulsions and contradictions in the working of some of their socio-political institutions.

There has been in recent years growing interest in the field of African Studies the world over. In India, too, interest in this area has steadily widened. The enthusiastic attendance, at the workshop, by several University and College teachers and public men, besides those who presented papers, is an ample evidence of that. We, at the Centre, felt encouraged. As a small Centre, we are conscious of our limitations, but the tremendous response reassured us of the great potential for research and studies in this field. We are, therefore, very happy to announce the publication of this study. It was delayed a little as the authors wanted to revise the papers in the light of the discussions and comments at the workshop.

Now a word of thanks. We are indebted to so many persons and organisations in the holding of this workshop that we beg apologies if we do not mention by name everyone who has helped us in one way or the other. The major funding was done by the University Grants Commission, and we are much obliged to that body to extend to us every kind of encouragement in our functioning during the last few years of our existence. The Indian Council for Social Science Research (Western Region) also gave us a little grant by way of stationery and some secretarial assistance. We are obliged to Drs. Fereira and Karnik, the Director and Deputy Director of that organization for their personal interest in us.

As regards the operative part, we are most grateful to our Vice Chancellor Ram Joshi for his inspiring support all along. Despite his very busy schedule of work, he readily agreed to preside over the inaugural and the first sessions of the workshop, in order to be with us the entire morning of the first day. I am also thankful to him for being kind enough to write the Foreword to the book. To Mrs. Shanti Sadiq Ali, wife of our Chancellor Sadiq Ali, we owe our deep gratitude for her consistent interest in us, and providing an ever willing guiding hand in the organisation of the workshop. Mrs. Sadiq Ali is an Africanist in her own right. As a former Secretary General of the Indian Council for Africa, and free lance journalist, she has written much on Africa. She had accepted our invitation to write a paper and participate in our workshop much before she happened to move to the Raj Bhavan. Later, she also agreed to inaugurate the workshop and remain with us throughout the six sessions.

Our grateful thanks are again due to Mr. Appa B. Pant, who in his twenty-seven years of ambassadorial experience, had spent some of his most fruitful years in Africa, particularly Kenya during most crucial years of her struggle for independence. He not only wrote a paper and effectively participated in the deliberations of our workshop, but also presided over one of the sessions. To Mr. Homi Taleyarkhan, India's former

Ambassador to Libya, we are much obliged to contribute the paper at a short notice. He also presided over one of the sessions, and sat through all sessions to participate in the lively discussions. Our most sincere thanks are due to fellow academics from the Universities of Delhi, Gujarat, Jawaharlal Nehru University and from our Bombay University, who presented very useful papers and contributed so much to the successful conduct and organisation of the workshop. The person to whom we owe the most in the organisational efforts is Prof. (Miss) A.J. Dastur, Chairman of our Area Studies Programme at Bombay University. She was the moving spirit behind everything that had to be done and faced up in connection with the workshop. To her I pay my personal tributes and express my most humble gratitude. I must also thank all my colleagues, at the Centre, and our secretarial staff without whose full co-operation we could not have achieved much. Lastly, I must thank the University of Bombay for the grant towards the publication of the book and to Radiant Publishers for undertaking publication of the volume.

Bombay   R.R. RAMCHANDANI
27 July 1979

R.R. RAMCHANDANI

Introduction

THE INDO-AFRICAN CONTACTS go back to the earliest times. There is ample evidence of this in ancient Indian religious and secular literature in Sanskrit and Pali, archaeological finds, art, coinage and traditional lore. Much of that is corroborated by pre-Christian era accounts of ancient Egypt, Mesopotcmia, Persia, Babylon and the like. India's early ocean trade with Egypt and Mesopotamia is traced by some to go beyond 3000 B.C. It is not unlikely that the Indians might have also traded with the coastal region of Eastern Africa in those early times. The ancient Indians had developed a network of their mercantile trade. Much before the Christian era, sea-faring ships were regularly fitted on the shores of India to carry Indian merchandise to the lands lying on the western and northern shores of the Arabian Sea, to Persia, Arabian Coast, Egypt and the East African coastal region.

Richard Reush writes: "The coast of East Africa was known to the Ancient Indian centuries before our era."[1] Reush opines that the Ancient Hindus also seemed to have good knowledge of the interior of East Africa. In this connection Lieutenant Wilford's two long essays in the *Journal of the Asiatic Reseaches*[2] of 1792 and 1895 and Captain J.H. Speke's *The Journal of the Discovery of the Source of Nile* (first edition)[3] are the works of great interest. Captain Speke gives an impressive account of probable knowledge that the ancient

1

Indians might have had of the interior lake region of East and Central Africa. A recent book by Professor S.M. Ali, *The Geography of the Puranas*, further throws some fresh light on this subject.[4] The early Indo-African contacts, and the nature of relations that developed between the two peoples across the vast Indian Ocean, is a fascinating field of research indeed; and offers rich rewards to those social and other scientists like historians, archeologists, social-anthropologists, linguists and geographers, who would like to dig deep into this area of research.

For the purpose of this study, however, suffice it to say that much before the European contact, and way back to the beginning of the 1st century A.D., there was already a thriving trading activity between India and Africa. It is sufficiently well documented. The historical evidence also make it abundantly clear that the Indians were all along mainly a trading community who nurtured no political ambition in these parts.

With the expansion of Europe, and the coming of Europeans in Asia and Africa, a new era began, an era of Western dominance based on merchant capitalism, followed by industrial capitalism. As machine-made production expanded in the wake of industrial revolution, Europe sought outlets outside Europe through colonisation and conquest. India felt its impact, so did Africa. To fit into the mechanism of the new order—capitalist system—the colonial capitalism demanded full exploitation of cheap colonial labour. As the system advanced slave labour was replaced by contract labour. The scope of supply of cheap labour was thus immensely widened. India and China became yet other rich reservoirs of indentured labour. The Indian labour was employed on sugar plantations in South Africa, Mauritius and the West Indies. The subordinate and technical services, apart from labour for the well-known Uganda Railway, were again recruited from India. It may be mentioned that in the former British East African territories, Indians mainly supplied middle-level services —clerks and artisans, teachers and supervisors—and provided the channels of distributive trade. They opened up the interior region through merchanting and 'duka' trading. Over time, they became a significant factor in the economic life of the East African countries. But, it must be underlined that they had no hand in either devising the system or designing its objectives.

The friction between Africans and the people of Indian origin that was generated in East Africa during the colonial period was unfortunate. It was a product of the peculiar colonial capitalist pattern of development. Fortunately, it is moving into history.

The new collaborative links that are being forged between India and independent African countries are free from any friction or misunderstanding. On the contrary, they are based on immense mutual goodwill and clear understanding of each other problems. They are likely to be further strengthened because firstly, India, at its present stage of development has attained certain technological and manpower capacities whose supply price is generally much lower to that of the Western sources. Again, certain production processes, having been developed in labour surplus market, are comparatively more labour intensive. They are, therefore, likely to be found by the African countries to be of greater relevance to their present requirements. Secondly, in India, today, seeking a job or business opportunity in African countries, is totally free from any racial prejudice which might have influenced an Indian immigrant of the colonial perio dwhen the East African and Southern African societies had come to be socially stratified on racial lines.

India's ties with the African countries after independence are no more based on former colonial equation. Even before her own independence, the Indian leaders had consistently stood by the African countries in their struggle against colonial domination, racial discrimination, and human degradation. Since India attained independence, she lent full force of support, given her own her limitations, to the emerging African nationalist movements. In the words of India's former President S. Radhakrishnan: "Indian independence blazed the trail of liberation for many countries in Asia and Africa." It will be recalled that the great Indian leader, Mahatma Gandhi, had himself fought against the repressive racist policies of the South African government. He evolved and sharpened the technique of non-violent resistence—'Satyagraha'—while he still lived and suffered the impact of racial discrimination in South Africa. Under his dynamic leadership, and later under the leadership of Pandit Jawaharlal Nehru, a close affinity developed between the Indian and African nationalist movements.

India became the torch bearer. Gandhiji often pointed out
to the British imperial masters that "Indian independence. . .
will be a help to noble effort throughout the world and a promise of relief to all its exploited people." Not surprisingly, after
India's independence, the freedom struggles in Africa and elsewhere soon gathered god-speed. The colonial powers felt increasingly compelled to give up their political hold over Africa.
Between 1956 and 1971 almost all the African countries, except-
ing Rhodesia, Namibia and that citadel of white settlers, the
Union of South Africa, emerged as independent nation states.

India maintains most cordial relations with African countries
She is committed to help the cause of liberation movements
to the best of her ability. On several issues concerning conflict
situations in the world, India and most of the independent
African countries have often stood on the common platform,
strictly adhering to the policy of non-alignment and peaceful
co-existence. They also work hand-in-hand on the wider economic issues in the North-South dialogue. They are aware of
the tremendous prospects of their economic cooperation and
have already taken several strides in that direction. New
patterns of development are emerging both in India and
Africa, and a new economic order is taking shape before our
very eyes.

The new relationships, of course, will take time to shape up.
Traditional bonds are not easy to loosen. The new responsibilities and burdens are bound to weigh heavily on the leadership of recently born nation-states. There are new compulsions
and contradictions. To resolve them all at once is not going to
be an easy task. But, the beginning has been made. It is widely
realized that political independence without economic self-
reliance does not mean much to the peoples of the former
colonial territories. But, to achieve even some semblance of
economic independence, the old colonial dependent structures
have to be modified to serve new policy goals. Some new ideas
are already afloat. Social Scientists are probing anew into the
problems of underdevelopment and socio-economic change in
the countries of Africa, Asia and Latin America. Since the old
colonial pattern of development certainly constituted a major
hinderance to their internal development that pattern had to be
modified or given up in favour of a more meaningful model.

In that lies the significance of the North-South dialogue. This is what underlies the concept of collective self-reliance and closer horizontal cooperation between the under-developed countries themselves. In the matter of evolving a mutually beneficial relationship based on the principles of reciprocity, it becomes important to understand and get to grips with the nature and level of development attained in the past by the presently poor countries of the world. It has been recognised that all of them are not at the same level of development. There are bound to be differences. Some are comparatively more advanced than others. For the success of cooperative efforts between them it is, therefore, essential to continuously exercise one's mind and identify complemental areas of underlining mutuality of interests.

Indo-African relations have steadiy forged ahead and acquired greater significance, mainly because a number of areas have already been identified in which they share common interests. Their economic relations have also been further strengthened in recent years as a consequence of that. Let us take just India's external trade with Africa as a whole. It jumped up from about Rs.105 crores in 1955-56 to Rs.380 crores in 1975-76, almost a four-fold rise. In the field of industrial cooperation, there are about 70 joint Indo-African ventures at various stages of implementation. The cooperation extends to small-scale industrial sector too. The Industrial Development Bank of India sanctioned, in 1977, a loan of Rs.20 million to Small Industries Development Organisation of Tanzania (SIDO). The IDBI had, by 1976, given credits totalling around Rs.200 crore to more than 40 under-developed countries, a good part of which went to the African countries.

It may be mentioned that India provides technical assistance to Africa under two main heads: 1) Indian Technical and Economic Cooperation; and 2) The Commonwealth African Assistance Programme. India has always been prepared to share with the other under-developed countries the benefit of her own technological development and industrial capabilities which we believe are in many cases of greater relevance to the needs of African countries. In her industrial advancement India has taken several strides, and claimed the place among the top ten of the industrially most advanced countries of the world. She has achieved this through a judicious mix of indigenous and foreign technologies. Today, hundreds of Indian technical experts, artisans and other professionals like teachers, professors, doctors and engineers are working in several African countries, and the hundreds of Africans are undergoing technical and other high-level training in India.

India was the first among the third world countries to institute educational scholarships for Africans; way back in 1949. By 1965-66, there were around 2,000 African students in the Indian Universities and other educational institutions of higher learning. And, in 1976, from one country of Mauritius alone there were more than 1,200 students, and the total number from Africa added up to a few thousand. The African students come to India from several countries like Kenya, Tanzania, Zambia, Malawi, Uganda, Rwanda, Burundi, Nigeria, Ghana, Togoland, Dahomey, Senegal, Mauritius, as well as from meghrab countries of Libya, Egypt, Algeria and Morocco. More and more meaningful avenues of cooperation are opening up.

This book is a collection of papers presented at the seminar held in October 1977, under the auspices of the Centre of East African Studies, of the University of Bombay. A few Africa watchers in India have attempted to analyse and critically examine the problems and issues which either India shares in common with some African countries, or which she might find of some relevance in the framing of her Africa policy. The volume is broadly divided into three sections: 1)Historical and Political Aspects; 2) Indians in Eastern Africa; and 3) Economic Aspects.

The historical and political section contains seven papers; two pertaining to Non-alignment, two to Liberation Struggle, one to the Indian Ocean and its Littorals, one concerns Party System and Political Development, and the last one relates to Paramountcy and Indirect Rule

In his paper on 'Non-alignment', Appa B. Pant, with a fund of diplomatic experience, argues how Jawaharlal Nehru, the first Prime Minister of independent India projected a special image of Non-alignment as a policy to be followed by erstwhile colonial countries. Nehru knew that following an independent line was not to be an easy thing. Non-alignment may be a

good political philosophy, writes Pant, "but actually to be
totally out of this game (of big nations) economically, strategically, ideologically is extremely difficult, even impossible". Pant
explains how it was particularly difficult, for the new African
nation-states who, unlike India, had in the course of European
colonisation come to be regarded as the 'hinterland of Europe'.
May be it was not a happy situation. But, then, it takes time
to acquire the knowledge to exploit the natural wealth of one's
country, and the process generally demands foreign technology,
management skills, and even foreign behavioural patterns to
start on the path of 'progress'. The alternative to that,
according to Pant, would be strict disciplining in "ideologically
pure puritanism", which is "indigestible to the newly emergent
societies and their 'leadership' who want their enjoyment of
power, pleasure, and profit *now* without further sacrifice."
Under the circumstances, only those countries could earnestly
practice non-alignment "who have a self-sufficient, semi-
autarchic, socio-economic political structures like that of
China. Others proclaim it and live to compromise with it."

As societies in Africa and Asia develop their capabilities for
utilising their own resources and sustain their progress and
prosperity, non-alignment would become practical. Till then
dependence on the Soviets or Euro-American-Japanese system
will limit the influence of the so-called Third World in the great
game of power. "Non-alignment", in the words of Apa Pant,
can be defined as a refusal to be a satellite, client state of the
"big socio-economic-political system", and at the same time
evolve "a reasoned, rational, pragmatic approach for the
developiment of a new mutually profitable, and satisfying
relationship with them." Unfortunately, it takes time to develop
a new relationship. While the old order crumbles, there is no
easy solution to the problems of poverty, destitution and decay.
It is to help evolve a new order, that India, African and other
underdeveloped countries could join hands. India has attained
a certain level of competence and capacities which could be
availed of by the African countries strictly on the principle of
mutuality of interests, and thus they could cooperate in the
process of change without depending too much on the big
powers. However, Pant means that what India can do is but
little in this great drama of change in Africa. Today the

internal struggles and development needs have put African
countries in the lap of Western Powers, and to a negligible
extent the balance has titled towards the Soviet bloc. It is not
going to be an easy task to change this situation.

Dealing with a similar theme Gupta traces the evolution of
non-alignment as a political philosophy in a historical sequence.
In the post-World War II period, when European powers
became weaker, the nationalist movements in the former
subjected territories emerged stronger and decolonisation
became inevitable. The newly independent countries were
naturally anxious not to compromise their freedom by aligning
with either of the two power blocs, namely Soviet socialist bloc
or American capitalist bloc. "The basic aim of the newly
independent countries was to secure the right to make their
own decisions in domestic and foreign policies free from foreign
pressures." However, Gupta too, like Apa Pant, doubts
whether the former colonial countries could really hold an
independent position in the arena of international politics.
Gupta attributes this to the natuie of new leadership which
"belonged to either national bourgeoisie or petit bourgeisie
and not working class." Besides, the newly independent
countries were at a different level of political and economic
development. That, alongwith different alignment of class
forces, led them to follow different foreign policies. The
countries with anti-imperialist bias were opposed to participate
in power blocs. The principal manifestation of their foreign
policy was the policy of 'non-alignment'. Nehru and his
compatriots—Tito, Nasser, Bandranaike, Seokarno, Nkrumah
and Nyerere—felt that a policy of non-alignment was the best
means of achieving their rational and international objectives.
As Nyerere explained they did not want "to be sucked into the
orbit of one or other of the great power".

Gupta then goes on to discuss policy goals of the non-aligned
countries in the economic sphere. He writes : "The non-
aligned countries were perturbed by the glaring inequalities
and imbalances in the international economic structure and the
ever widening gap between the developing and developed
countries." It is for such reasons that the non-aligned countries
have increasingly stressed the urgency of economic self-reliance,
accelerated economic development and collective strategy by

promoting economic cooperation amongst themselves. Today the non-aligned movement has come a long way from its small beginning and raised its voice against present economic order which perpetuates inequalities. It pleads for a new international economic order in which the former subjected territories will have a larger breathing space. OPEC has shown that the situation is not hopeless if they acted together to improve their bargaining strength. The imperialist powers had in the past succeeded in excluding the developing countries "from decision-making process affecting their destiny." They realized that the change could only be brought about by their ability to move forward together. Thus, during the last 15 years, non-alignment has already become a potent force to challenge the prevalent structure of exploitative economic relationship.

Another important aspect of the non-alignment movement has been its persistent opposition to the forces of colonialism and racism. Caste, creed and colour have no place in the philosophy of non-alignment; and political independence on the basis of majority rule is the sacred faith with the non-aligned countries. While most of the African countries have obtained their independence with the African rule well entrenched, the citadels of white settlers—Rhodesia, Namibia and the Union of South Africa—have yet to see reason.

In her paper on India's support to African Liberation Movements, Shanti Sadiq Ali highlights India's policy aspects towards the liberation of this region of southern Africa, where the potent force of all white power rests in Pretoria. She writes: "South is the key to the whole power structure of the region and its role in resolving the burning issues in the area cannot be minimised." But, the solution does not seem to be a straight forward matter. The Western powers have traditional economic and strategic interests in Southern Africa. The strategic location of South Africa, across the Atlantic and Indian Ocean, its nuclear and defence capability and its possession of strategic raw materials like chrome, nickel, gold, uranium, vanadium, etc. have made South Africa indispensable to the West. Ethnically, the white settler rulers constitute a part of the Anglo-Saxon racial stock. If the West could help to maintain status quo, it would surely like to do that, but Africa and the Africans of the region would no more tolerate the position of subordination and the system of built-in exploitation. The collapse of Portuguese colonialism and the Soviet and Cuban intervention in Angola and elsewhere have fundamentally changed the situation in Southern Africa, particularly in Zimbabwe and Namibia. The Soviet support to Angola's victorious MPLA demonstrated its superpower status and its military capacity to influence events in a country as far off as Angola. The Russian presence startled the Western world. The Kissinger shuttle diplomacy of 1976, and the subsequent Western concern for the events in Southern Africa is a direct outcome of such a rapid change in the scenario there.

Shanti Sadiq Ali, however, underlines India's limitations to any major role in the process of decolonisation in Southern Africa, although her role has been useful in stimulating the march to African independence. Ever since India attained independence, she has fought many battles in the United Nations Organisation, at the Commonwealth conferences and in the other international forums like Non-aligned nations conferences for peaceful transfer of power to the colonial peoples and the upholding of fundamental human rights for all men and women, irrespective of race, colour or creed. With the expansion of Afro-Asian membership of the United Nations, and with the emergence of an Africa group in 1958, India was content with a quieter role. But, she has consistently supported the liberation movements in Southern Africa. As regards material support to the liberation movements, India has significantly stepped up her efforts. During 1977-78, she allocated some Rs. 30 million to aid the struggle for the liberation of Southern Africa. During his visit to East African Countries, in 1977, India's former External Affairs Minister Atal Behari Vajpayee stated that India would "definitely consider" any request for arms, as and when made by the liberation movements fighting against the white minority regimes in Southern Africa.

There is a deeper moral commitment that links India with Africa, writes Homi Taleyarkhan, India's former Ambassador to Libya. He refers to Gandhiji's sufferings in South Africa who fought against that government's racist policies. Under the leadership of Mahatma Gandhi and Jawaharlal Nehru, the Indian National Congress, much before India's freedom, "had repeatedly expressed its deepest sympathy and its fullest moral support for their (African) great cause which was so akin to our own in its patriotic fervour and dimensions." Taleyarkhan reminds, how after independence, India has been in the forefront to espouse the cause of African liberation through various international organisations, and how the historic Bandung Conference of 1955 had led to the formation of "great movement of non-alignment". The membership of this group has grown from 25 in 1960 to 90 by the time the Colombo Conference was held in 1976. The movement stands for 'togetherness' of the developing countries who would like to keep "free from the influence of or pacts with super powers or any other big powers, both politically and economically. . . ."

Taleyarkhan, then goes on to enumerate help that India has rendered to Africa in the economic, educational and other fields. He stresses Africa's confidence in India as she has stood by the side of Africans in all motions, actions and movements that press and aim at decolonisation of African countries and doing away with "settler colonialism".

Considering the question of Indo-African cooperation, it is important to have a clearer perspective of certain political and strategic forces that operate to help as well as hinder this process. The Indian Ocean littoral countries deserve special attention. Being neighbouring countries, bordering the Ocean, the potential for cooperation among them is great indeed. In this respect Satyawati Jhaveri's paper relating to some political aspects of the 'Indian Ocean and Its African Littorals' is timely. She underlines a competitive build-up of both the power blocs to gain superiority in different ocean regions of the world. "This tends", she points out, "to colour and influence the developments in the countries concerned." If the littoral and island states are newly independent countries who are engaged in achieving political stability and economic breakthrough, the interaction complicates the situation.

The Indian Ocean has a long tradition of peaceful commerce and navigatin. But, in recent years the withdrawal of Britain from the near monopolistic control of the Ocean and the entry of Soviet navy in the Ocean waters, have led to the conflict situation. The maritime powers have been vying with each other to gain the position of strength in the Ocean. Both super powers have vital interests to defend. The United States would like to protect shipping lanes to bring oil from West Asia to the Western Countries, including the United States, and to safeguard the Western sphere of influence against the Soviet intrusion; the Soviet Union would in turn like to protect its trade passing through these waters and safeguard its interests "in the Red Sea to maintain contact between its Mediteranean fleet and its squadron in the Indian Ocean. The big power persuit of their respective interests interact adversely with the economic, political and social policy goals of the littoral states which are caught up in a dilemma of reconciling their desire to safeguard national sovereignty and integrity with the compulsions of the dependent position. The complexity of this magnitude sometimes leads to a conflict situation as it obtains in the Horn of Africa.

If the Red Sea has been an area of big power attention in the North-western corner of the Indian Ocean, the Cape occupies the central place in their strategic moves in the South-western region. Apart from the Cape, the port towns of Mombasa in Kenya, Dar es Salaam and Zanzibar in Tanzania, Beira and Maputu in Mozambique and Simonstown in South Africa are again important to exercise control over the Ocean waters. The NATO powers' help to South Africa and the connivance of the UN resolutions demanding isolation of that country because of its apartheid policies, become intelligible in this context. On the other hand, the bordering black African dominated states, especially Zambia, Tanzania, Mozambique, Botswana and Angola are committed to the liberation of the black communities in Southern Africa. The contesting non-regional powers—the USA and the USSR—are concerned about the confortation to determine their Southern Africa policy. The US, for instance, has to contend with the pulls exerted at home by the Pentagon, the multinational giants and the believers in Whiteman's burden on one hand, and the anti-apartheid movement on the other. It has also to take into account the ever increasing investments of the Western world in the other African countries, who have largely followed free-enterprise or mixed-economy models. At the 1977 Untied Nations sponsored conference in Lagos, "the black states of Africa virtually told the Western powers to choose between the apartheid regime and the rest of Africa."

It is, of course, the Soviet activity in the region and the Ocean which causes the deepest concern to the Western powers. Their remarkable success in Angola and their presence in the Horn have now made them bold to extend further support to the Zimbabwe's liberation movements operating through Mozambique. The Cuban soldiers and the Russian arms had done the trick in Angola. Will that be repeated in Rhodesia and Namibia? That could mean yet another foothold to the Soviet Union, this time in the heart of White-settled stronghold of the West. The prospect is bound to be unpalatable from the Western angle. But it cannot be totally ruled out if the African majority rule is finally established through Russian and Cuban help. The Indian Ocean and its littoral states have, thus, become a hot-bed of East-West interaction.

While there is little doubt that this East-West global contest for power is not going to be settled soon, there are several other factors that influence the attitude and the working of the African and Asian countries. One such important variable is the functioning of Western political institutions as implanted on the Asian and African soil during the long lasting colonial rule. Patel in his paper is interested in the working of the party system and its role in the political development. He brings in focus the comparative empirical dimension to find out how this signifinant institution in the Western democracies affects and in turn is affected by the political developments in the African and Indian social environment.

Patel examines in some detail the formation, definition and functioning of a political party as it evolved in the Western system. Applying that criterion he discusses pre-requisites for the working of a sound party system in the Indian and African social environment. In India, he feels, the pre-requisites were largely satisfied which allowed the growth of a healthy party structure. In Africa, only the urge for freedom and mass support to achieve it prompted the leaders party. Hence, according to Patel what came into existence "was not a real political party but an instrument which utilized the masses to press the demand of a very small number of articulated elites who were seeking to dislodge the foreign rule." But, despite limitations, many African nations are trying hard to work out a fairly popular government and go to the people for sanctions. That is a good indicator in favour of democratic development. However, in the absence of real political parties in Africa, as Patel defines them, "it is easier for authoritarian rulers to terminate their activity, outlaw them or repress them."

Both in India and Africa, political parties have not grown from within. Rather they have emerged externally, in the sense that they started as a challenge to the alien ruling group, but whereas in India, after a period of four decades, the elite group widened its base, provided competitive leadership, stabilized and became an anchorlike internally created parties; in Africa, the externally created mass parties, committed to greater distributive demands, find it convenient to consolidate the policy in favour of a non-competitive system. In Africa, there was little attempt at laying down a proper foundation on which a democratic polity might develop; as against that India was fortunate to have "had a fairly developed socio-economic structure, a fairly protracted struggle of independence which allowed the process of colonial dialectics to get into full swing. . .and laid the foundations of democratic structures like Press, Elections, Party Machinery, etc." The main ethos in which Indian political parties developed was nationalistic, integrative and modernistic. This is where African leadership has to fight tribal factionalism and evolving a new national consciousness is greater in African countries than in India.

In Africa Patel does not find an evolutionary pyramidical structure. Then there is a question of tolerance of other parties by the dominant party which initially captures the mass attention in the wake of struggle against foreign rule. In India, apart from the Indian National Congress, "other parties were allowed to function. The long training in parliamentary democracy, conscious leadership and existence of numerous respected leaders, tradition of free press, large educated class and a country so vast and full of diversity created an image of a democratic society. In Africa, the leadership group was very small, generally one charismatic leader overshadowed the whole party." Alien settler influences in Eastern and Southern Africa also influenced the formation and functioning of a political party. Under the circumstances, Patel argues that in Africa various tribes living in a colonial territory were, around the time of independence, not yet integrated into a nation-state. Freedom resolved these crisis upto a stage. But, it continues to pose a problem. The modernisation has not yet reached the stage when restratification in society takes place due to industrialization, education and urbanization. The participation crisis will develop when these new groups advance and demand some share in the authority. How the leadership will respond to such challenges will have a deciding influence on the nature of African political systems.

The last paper in this section concerns 'Paramountcy and Indirect rule' by Padma Srinivasan. As she explains both, 'Indirect Rule, as applied by Lugard in Africa, and Paramountcy as practiced towards Indian states, belong to the wider phenomenon of indirect rule through indigenous institutions. Although there is no evidence of any conscious application of their Indian experience to their African dependencies, "There were large numbers of British officers who had seen civil and military service in both India and Africa. And not the least among them were F.D. Lugard and Lord Hailey. There were similarities in the administrative and judicial functions of the collector in India and Africa; and the great legal codes of India became, after a few strokes of pen, the basis of East African administration."

Padma Srinivasan examines some interesting points of comparison and contrast between the two approaches. In the Indian situation the British were groping for a policy that was rather more than political laissez-faire and rather less than direct rule. "In other words they were groping for Lugard's Indirect Rule". But, whereas in India, Paramountcy gave one the impression of empiricism, Indirect Rule started at the outset, in the twenties, as a definite ideology. In India the British kept up the legal make-believe of honouring their commitments given to the princes, but in practice intervened in their affairs at their will. In the African context, Mrs. Srinivasan approvingly quotes Lugard who, according to her, did not approve of direct rule because under that system the administration shirked the direct task of educating the common people for self-government. As regards Indirect Rule, the system was paternalistic to the core and Mrs. Srinivasan does not make any mistake about it. It was both initiated and expounded by the

rulers themselves. The initative in the matter of devolving responsibility upon African traditional authorities lay with the
District officers—an agency which was wholly committed to the
perpetuation of colonial rule. "Inspite of all their lip service
to help Africans grow and develop from their cultural roots,
Lugard, Cameron and Mitchel regarded African life styles and
cultures as savage and primitive and immature."

It is interesting to note that in East Africa, the whiteman invariably believed that he was the bearer of the burden of
civilising the 'savage' African; and always accused the fellow
Asian settler that he (the Asian) never shared that burden, and
as such played no role in the advancement of Africans towards
the adoption of the so-called 'civilised' life-style.

In the second Section we have three papers on the theme of
Asians in some countries of Eastern Africa. The paper by
Ramchandani attempts to relate major factors in the rise
and decline of Indian enterprise in East Africa. He underlines
time and space dimension in the colonial context, in the analysis
of economic ascendancy of Asians in East Africa; and stresses
structural parameter in explaining their expulsion from Uganda,
as also the declining tendency of their enterprise in Tanzania
and Kenya. This analysis is viewed to be crucial in the understanding of the future prospect of the thousands of Asians who
still live in these countries, and the thousands of others who are
moving out every day from India in search of jobs or business
opportunities to Africa and other developing countries.

It is suggested that during the colonial period, since East
Africa was opened up through Indian agency in the sense that
Indians supplied the crucial missing factor inputs like subordinate and artisan services and trading talent, Indian enterprise and
immigration was actively encouraged. The Indians soon constituted the vital integral part of the East African economies. However, as the entire East African society, in the years before the
Second World War, had been stratified on racial lines, the Asians
had come to occcpuy a middle-tier position. The African interests had received little attention from the cloonial masters who
had all along concerned themselves mainly with their own economic interests and the interests of the White settlers. In essence
Ramchandani believes that the development of the African

colonial territories had broadly followed the pattern of centre-periphery relationship. But, under the working arrangemen of the system in the East African situation, the Africans were unfortunately pushed down to the bottom plank of the three-tiered racially structured socieites in their own territories. A wide imbalance of wealth had grown between the Africans on one hand and the alien settler communities of Europeans and Asians on the other.

The racial friction was organically a build-up from such mounting tensions. It was particularly acute between Asians and Africans for the Asians mainly operated in the market place—holding distributive channels and providing artisan and subordinate services—the majot springboard in a free-enterprise economy for further forward thrust in the commercial sector. Could not the Africans, in independent East Africa, occupy this critically important sector to provide a framework for their own vertical mobility denied to them during the colonial operation of the system ? Ramchandani argues that the expulsion of Asians from Uganda is to be explained in the context of such an interaction between earlier colonial equation and almost bursting aspirations of African masses immediately after independence.

Ramchandani further believes that what has happened to Asians in East Africa could be a useful lesson for the present day Indian emigrants seeking service or business opportunities in African countries, or may be in the other UDCs. The Government of India will do well to take a note of it. After all, the present is built on the past, and the future is bound to be influenced by the present day events. The past, therefore, deserves our consideration in our present policies. For instance, during the colonial period, the migratory process was conditioned by the colonial system. The situation has now undergone a fundamental change. The imperial umbrella has become totally irrelevant. The new equation that is now sought to be a basis of cordial relations between India and African countries has necessarily to provide for a new basis of Indian immigration into those countries. A new guideline, therefore, becomes the *sine qua non* of our policy framework in this regard.

In the past, the Africans have often accused the Asians of East Africa of having played an inconsequential role in the

nationalist movement of those countries. Kala in her paper
however, argues that this is not the whole truth. Making a
study of the Kenyan nationalist movement, she writes that ever
since the Kenyan nationalist movement got off the ground,
it was inspired by such political activity of the Kenyan Asians
which they had earlier waged against the racial discriminatory
policies of the colonial administration. After discussing the how
and why of Asians' struggle for their rights, she writes that
when the 1923 *White Paper on the 'Indian Question'* pronounced
'paramountcy' of African interests, some Indian leaders worked
for bringing the Asians and Africans together in their joint
struggle against racial discrimination practiced by the colonial
government and the White settlers. She points out how the
Asians assisted in the printing of a newspaper, *Muiguithania*,
that was edited by the then young African leader Jomo Kenyatta on behalf of Kikuyu Central Association. After Kenyatta's
return from London to Kenya in 1947, when he assumed the
leadership of Kenya African Union "very few Europeans"
according to Kala, "sympathised with him but most of the
Indian leaders considered him to be a great leader and cooperated with him in various matters." Soon an intimate contact
was established between the EAINC and KAU. Both interchanged speakers at their annual meetings. A fraternal KAU
delegation even took part in the proceedings of the 1948 EAINC
session where Makhan Singh, a trade union leader of Kenya,
sponsored the resolution supporting the KAU demands.
Makhan Singh to this day is regarded a great trade union
leader of Kenya who strenghened the morale of African labour.
Kala, however, admits that in the later days of the colonial
period, the rapid growth of African nationalism led to the
declining political role of Asians who gradually moved into the
background. But, they continued to support the nationalist
cause. India's first High Commissioner to Kenya, Shri Apa B.
Pant whole-heartedly supported the African freedom struggle
and coaxed the local Asian population into merging their
interests with those of the Africans. Even the late Tom Mboya,
one of Kenya's foremost former leaders, acknowledged, writes
Kala that, "The overwheming majority of the Indian community in Kenya supported the African stand and wanted to
adhere to the standards set by Nehru and Gandhi as friends

and allies in the struggle for freedom and democracy. In March 1961, Ibrahim Nathoo, an Asian leader, resigned his ministership over the Kenyatta issue. Kala thus believes that "the Asians did play a role of some consequence when Kenya was ripe for independence."

In Kenya, Asians constituted a tiny minority element. There were, however, some other territories in the colonial times, where the Indian settlement flourished to become a majority element. Mauritius is an example. Ramdas in his paper traces how Indian settlement in Mauritius took roots. He speculates that the Indo-Mauritian contacts are much older than European discovery of Mauritius, but concedes that the land was uninhabited four centuries ago. With coming of the Europeans, several Indian artisans were recruited under the French regime. Some traders also went during the French period. Later, when the British took over the island from the French, some Indian convicts were brought. African slaves still outnumbered free Mauritians till 1835. With the abolition of slavery, thousands of Indian indentured labourers were imported to work on Mauritius plantations. By 1861, the two-thirds of the population was already Indian—the proportion maintained to this day.

The Mauritian economy of sugar plantation was thus built on Indian indentured labour. The sugar production jumped up from 11,200 metric tons in 1823 to 500,000 metric tons by 1953. But the condition of Indian labour was pitiable indeed. There were, of course, some traders and professionals, too. As the Indian population stabilised, a generation of Mauritius born Indians grew up. By 1898, they outnumbered those born in India. Presently in Mauritius there is a tendency for certain groups to be associated with certain occupations. The Chinese predominate as salesmen, Indians in agricultural pursuits, and Franco Mauritians in administrative service. The lower reaches of the economy continue to be the bane of the Hindu population. Now that the country's political rule has passed into the hands of the people of Indian origin, they are bound to infleunce the future course of events.

The third and last section consists of four papers. Panchmukhi is concerned with the instrument of education as a variable in the policy goal of equality, the pronounced objective of the most of the developing countries. He discusses under two heads the measures of 'equality of education' taken in India and some of the African countries, especially Tanzania. Under the global measures he discusses rapid increases in education enrolment during the 1960's and 1970's and the significant rise in the percentage of Gross Domestic Product spent on education. Panchmukhi, however, does not feel satisfied, and explains: "The measures of system expansion are partly useful for equity objective, they cannot be completely relied upon." This is because the privileged class generally benefits more under this system.

Panchmukhi, therefore, stresses the urgency of specific measures to help the cause of the really unprivileged. He would recommend protective discriminative measures for the groups, and in the regions, identified as backward in matters like access to education, participation in education, utilization of education in jobs, etc. It is only through such radical measures that one could hope to achieve some equity through the instrument of education. "Both in East African nations and in India such specific measures are introduced with greater or lesser degree of imaginativeness". He views that since neither global measures nor specific measures have achieved educational equalisation, education cannot be relied upon as ameasure of economic equalisation in the long run. The reason, in his words, is, "it is not simply the access to education but also participation in education which is an important criterion for social mobility, and both are the function of socio-economic status of the student and the family. Since the institutional structure is the determinant of the socio-economic status, manipulating education while holding the institutional framework is not likely to bear fruit as the Indian-African experiences have shown."

Mrs Desai's paper relates to transfer of technology as a rationale for economic cooperation between India and African countries. The situation of dependency in the underdeveloped countries as a result of colonial legacy is widely viewed to be harmful for the healthy development of UDCs. A call for a 'New International Economic Order' by the UDCs reflects their desire for economic emanicapation through recovery and control of their natural resources and means of economic development. The strategy involves the principle of 'relying first and foremost on themselves'. The transfer of technology among the UDCs themselves signifies a step in that direction, a phenomenon of collective self-reliance. Mrs Desai reviews the current thinking on transfer of technology as a catalytic agent in the development processes of the African countries which are burdened with asymmetry in the consumption pattern, trade bondage and technical knowledge—a burdensome colonial legacy. The technical transfer could remedy this situation if the techniques intended to be borrowed are properly selected to suit the abundant labour and scarce capital situation, typical for a UDC.

It is important to improve indigenous skills and education to absorb imported technology and modify it to its own resource endowment to create a suitable technological base domestically. To achieve that Mrs Desai underlines concrete steps to foster cooperation among the UDCs as stressed by the 1972 United Nations Conference of Trade and Development. Since their emergence as independent countries, a large range of complementaries have grown among the UDCs. For instance, countries like India have developed certain capacities—both in the fields of technology and manpower—where the degree and level of development would approximate to the needs and conditions of several other UDCs. In these fields there is much scope for cooperation. The supply of scarce skilled and professional manpower resources, and the working of joint industrial ventures are the indication of such cooperation. It is true that these efforts are still a drop in the ocean when compared with the activities of multinationals in Africa, but a more constructive approach supported by other work in different fields can strengthen their impact as a major plank in Indo-African economic cooperation. The other area in which India has extended some support is technical assistance under programmes like Indian Technical and Economic Cooperation, Colombo Plan and Special Commonwealth African Assistance Plan (SCAAP). The assistance falls under three categories: institutional infrastructural assistance, physical infrastructural assistance and consultancy services. Mrs Desai believes: "One of the positive contributions of the Indian consultancy profession to the industrial development has been its assistance

in finding solutions appropriate to the local conditions and optimisation of the use of indigenous technology, equipment
raw materials and human skill." In the long run sound political relations are rooted in the intimate economic relations
and prosperous trading links between the countries. The spirit
of collective self-reliance demands more positive efforts in this
direction.

Dealing with the theme of Indo-Mauritian economic cooperation, Hegde underlines the Indian investments in the industrial sector of Mauritian economy and attempts to find the
future trends in that regard to raise the tempo of development.
The small size of the Mauritian market and poor natural
resources have been the major constraints of the Mauritian
economy. The result is that sugar continues to be the sole life-
line of the economy. But, monoculture economies are ever
prone to the instability conditions of the world commodity
markets. Hence the urgency for the diversification of economy.

Until 1960, industrialization in Mauritius was mainly confined to sugar and sugar by-products. It was in the 1960's that a
positive industrial policy was initiated by the Government, when
a package of incentives was announced, and in 1971 with the
announcement of a policy pertaining to export processing zone,
Mauritius today offers incentives which are regarded as one of
the best available anywhere in the world. Hegde feels that
with the availability of those incentives, Mauritius "provides
an excellent outlet for the intermediate technology available
with the Indian industry...". Indian technical personnel working in Mauritius could in turn, provide the efficient vehicle
for transmitting such technologies.

Hegde spells out a long list of advantages which Mauritius
provides to an Indian enterpreneur, and all the benefits that
accrue from the complementarities in the technological base
and cultural affinities between the two peoples. Above all he
believes that Mauritius is a sophisticated channel for the
Indian manufacturer to penetrate the wider African markets
congested with the goods from a number of advanced countries. The quantitative restrictions by the countries of the European Economic Community could similarly be circumnavigated
through an operational base in Mauritius. He recalls the
handicaps experienced by the Indain industrialists in the past,

and advocates a planned approach, a systematic appraisal of
the market potential in Europe and Africa; the technological
mix which can withstand competition from their counterparts,
from countries like France, Hong Kong and the United
States.

The paper by Renu Bhatia is concerned with joint ventures
as a means of economic cooperation between India and African
countries, and points out that "Joint ventures were sought (by
UDCs) as a means not only of securing scarce resources but
also as a means for safeguarding their political independence. . ."
India adopted a specific policy of encouraging joint ventures
abroad in 1964, and by 1976 the number of joint ventures
approved for setting up abroad rose to 263, and those which
commenced production went up from 12 in 1968 to 68 by 1976
of which 18 are located in African countries. Among the
African countries, Mauritius and Kenya occupy leading positions indicating that Indian investments have tended to concentrate in the countries where a sizeable population of Indian origin has settled. However, compared with the African countries,
the other Asian countries account for a larger number of Indian
sponsored joint ventures for which the main underlying reason,
according to Bhatia, has been political and security considerations. She attributes another reason to the policy of the African
countries who have on the whole not yet offered any special
encouragement to joint ventures between the UDCs, although
they often pay lip-service to the cause of increasing economic
cooperation between the UDCs to get rid of the big power
burdens.

The last paper by V.G. Mutalik Desai outlines important
features of the urbanization process in the Third World countries, particularly Africa and India, with a view to identify some
burning problems of urbanization in those countries, and find
adequate solutions.

All in all, as fresh efforts explore new dimensions of reaching
political understanding, and establishing firmer economic
foundation, the old avenues of cooperation are ever widened
and the new ones lighted bright. Therein lies the hope of the
peoples inhabiting the two continental masses of India and
Africa to surge forward to achieve self-reliant autonomous
modes of development.

REFERENCES

[1] Richard Reusch, *History of East Africa* (1954), pp. 28-30.

[2] J.H. Speke, *The Journal of the Discovery of the Source of Nile*, 1st ed,, (London, 1863), p. 13, also pp. 84 and 264.

[3] Lt. Francis Wilford, "On Egypt and other countries adjacent Cali River, on Nile of Ethiopia, from the Ancient Books of the "Hindus", *Journal of Royal Asiatic Researches*, III (Calcutta, 1792), pp. 295-462; and the second paper, "An Essay on the Sacred Isles in the West with other Essays connected with that Work", *Asiatic Researches*, VIII (1895, reprinted 1908), pp. 245-367.

[4] S.M. Ali, *The Geography of the Puranas* (New Delhi, 1966), pp. 26-46. Professor Ali's account of the Puranas indicates further scope of research in this field. A few other interesting accounts in this field are: J.M. Kennedy, "On the early commerce between India and Babylon", *Journal of Royal Asiatic Researches* (1898); R.K. Mookerji, *Indian Shipping—A History of the Sea-Borne Trade and Maritime Activity of the Indians from the Earliest Times* (New Delhi, 2nd ed., 1957); Merrik Posnanski, "Bantu Genesis—Archaeological Reflections", *Journal of African History*, IX (1968), No. 1, pp. 1-11.

Part I
Historical and Political Dimensions

APPA B. PANT

"Non-Alignment" and India-Africa

"NON-ALIGNMENT", ESPECIALLY WITH the erstwhile colonial power is a normal, natural, sentiment in Afro-Asia. But Jawaharlal Nehru projected it as something special and very significant at a moment in world history when it was being divided into two distinct blocs, and when there was pressure on all countries by both the superpowers to 'belong' to one or the other of them, i.e. be subservient to their power and economic needs. Jawaharlal saw a great danger in all this not only for the freedom and 'identity' of the newly emerging nations but to world peace. That is why in Korea and Vietnam in the 1950,s Jawaharlal Nehru took the initiative to try and stop a world conflagration, and succeeded.

Some realities of the situation must, however, be understood. Non-alignment as a political philosophy, a sentiment, an objective, an ideal is one thing. Its realisation in practice is another. Not to want to take part in the game of power, of the so-called 'big nations' in the political sense is, feasable though not always practical politics. But actually to be totally out of this game economically, strategically, and ideologically is extremely difficult, even impossible.

Unlike India to a certain extent the African nations from the very moment of their birth have been in the front-line of

27

the 'big' game of power politics and economics. Africa for a century and more has been considered, and used, as the 'hinterland of Europe'. Since the 1940's it has been the supplier of primary raw materials to America also. All Europe depends upon Africa and West Asia for its prosperity. Without oil and other raw materials of Mediteranean Africa the so-called 'modernization' of Western Europe could not have taken place. All the European wars wherein during the last hundred years, 100 million people were killed were for the domination and control of primary raw materials and commodities of Africa-Asia. All the so-called civilizing mission in Africa were for the raw materials, markets and for the export of populations from Europe.

In all developing countries, including India the capacity to explore, exploit and use their own natural wealth above and underground and in the oceans, grows very, very slowly. After 30 years of independence our own vast resources under and above ground and in the oceans are barely utilised (11.5 per cent only). Technology, management, organization and education cannot be bought even if you have the money which you do not have.

Thus 'foreign' technology, management skills, designs, money and even men, not to speak of behaviour-patterns, i.e. culture, is, as it were, necessary to start the process of so-called 'progress'. It affords a new 'motivation'.

The alternative of 'disciplining' yourself for years in strict ideologically pure puritanism to build a free society of social harmony and equilibrium, of equal sacrifice and advantage, is hard and indigestible to the newly emergent societies and their 'leaderships' who want their enjoyment of power, pleasure, and profit *now* without further sacrifices.

Thus strict 'non-alignment' in practice in economic, strategic, and cultural fields is very difficult to maintain whatever be the proclamations of the 'leaders'. Personal pride and prejudice of these 'leaders' in Africa-Asia make it easy for those playing the power game to absorb, or at least try to (with often disastrous results, e.g. Egypt, Iran, Syria), some, if not all, of these developing countries into their spheres of influence. Nasser once confessed in 1968 that his 'non-alignment' had to be 'deferred' till the end of the Arab-Israel struggle. Is today Zaire 'non-aligned' or Angola? Can Uganda, Ethiopia, and Somalia claim to be strict adherents to non-alignment when their very existence is dependent on the flow of arms and money from one or the other of the big power contestants—and at times from both of them.

Not to take part in the big power game as a sentiment is admirable and logical, even rational. Non-participation by all the countries of the world in it would bring this mad, wasteful fruitless game to an end. As it is this rivalry in arms race is producing a strange 'mutuality of interests' between the so-called superpowers. On one hand they seem to be going right ahead to produce the most expensive, wastefully terrible weapons of mass destruction, and on the other to depend upon each other to keep a viable as well as a mutually profitable equilibrium all over the world in the economic, strategic, and political fields. It is a strange game of subterfuge, make-believe, stupidity, and illusion and sheer waste of human resources and energy. What people (and Nations!) will not do to keep up this illusion of 'Power'!! They try to keep up this illusion till the irrationalities and contradictions in their economic and social structure bring the society down in ruins, as has happened to many countries in the past. Unforunately the power game does not only wrap the socio-economic-political structures of the societies that play it but also of those who have to sell or buy from them or who depend on them for arms, aid, protection, or inspiration. Only those countries can be strictly 'non-aligned' who have a self-sufficient, semi-autoarchic socio-economic-political structure like that of China. Others proclaim it and live to compromise with it.

As societies in Africa and Asia become more capable of utilising their own resources, and, through hard, sophisticated work produce efficiently the goods and services required to sustain their progress and prosperity, non-alignment would become practical. Till then directly and indirectly the dependence of Afro-Asian societies on the Soviet, or Euro-American-Japanese system will limit the influence of the so-called Third World on the great game of Power. Today this influence is negligible.

The whole world, the superpowers, Europe, Asia, Africa, and Latin American states, except for the time being China, is

developing a very highly intricate complex pattern of interlinked interdependence. Raw materials and resources are spread
out all the world over and in the oceans. Their control and
utilization by the 'Big' powers to sustain only their own societies at a high standard of production and consumption will
bring intolerable strains on the world community. This was
evident during the oil crisis. OPEC has now become a force to
bring a more rational, pragmatic approach for the utilization
of raw materials by the world community. Before the emergence of the OPEC, the Euro-Americans were practicing sheer
robbery to build up their prosperity on cheap fuel. It is the
attempt of the 'third' world (raw material producing) countries
to bring greater rationality in the price and purchasing power
to the commodities they have and of the products of the
developed world which they have to purchase. This means not
only better prices for raw materials but transfer of technology
to process them. All this means a new retationship between
the developed and the developing communities.

Thus non-alignment can be defined as a refusal to be a
sattelite, client state of the 'big social-economic-political system',
and at the same time a reasoned, rational, pragmatic approach
for the developing of a new mutually profitable, and satisfying
relationship with them.

Unfortunately such a new relationship does not develop in a
day or a decade. The internal socio-economic, often irrational
and retrograde pressures, pride, prejudice, sheer ignorance
and stupidity together with personal cupidity and avarice delay
this process. In Africa especially the old order is crumbling
creating new compulsions and contradictions but no solutions
to the old problems of development, poverty, population
explosion, non-urbanization and others. India has a certain
range of capacities, a mutuality of interests, in participation in
this process of change in Africa. In Eastern, Central, and
Southern Africa the Indians have taken a very significant part
during the past one hundred years in the 'modernization' of
this continent. The Indian contribution in all this change is
grossly misunderstood and undervalued. It is a fact that an
Indian as an immigrant is a very efficient, cheap stable producer of wealth and services, anywhere in the world.

But what India can do in this great drama of change in

Africa is marginal. In what was then Congo, now Zaire, we did our best, through the United Nations, to keep this vast, rich area 'non-aligned'. Today most of Africa has to seek support and depend upon for the internal struggles and their programmes of development on America and the Western countries and to a negligible extent on the Soviet bloc countries in which one can include Cuba. In the struggle for power in the Horn of Africa, Somalia-Ethiopia, the part India can play is negligible. The process of rapid change in Rhodesia and South Africa will move with a momentum in which Euro-American and Soviet strategic and economic interests will be the decisive factors and not the sentiments or pious hopes of a good friend of Africa like India. After all it is the developed countries who need and covet the resources of Africa, can process them, and pay for them in armaments or unwanted consumer goods! At this moment this relationship between the developed and developing (i. e. those who cannot use or process their resources) is inequitable, and, down-right robbery. But on it is based the prosperity and the power of the developed world. It is not going to be an easy, or, quick (20 years!!) work to change this situation. After many conferences, confrontations and conflicts it may become inevitable to bring about a new equilibrium in the relationships of the developed and developing part of this 'one' world.

Thus, a new, inter-dependent, mutually advantageous, socio-economic relationship between all the countries and societies of this small, over-populated, polluted, conflict ridden world of ours has to be evolved. To expand all over the world and sustain the standards of life of the present-day American society with its waste is impossible. There are not enough resources, on this planet to do this. America-Europe-Japan-Russia (when they attain it, if they do!) will not be able to keep their 'rich' 'powerful' societies stable in a 'poor' world. The 'adjustments' are going to be painful, spasmodic, ad hoc, and obviously take a long, long time to mature. Existing privileges, profits, power are builtin the very structure of these societies. These can be dismantled only after many battles, hardships, suffering as is seen now in Rhodesia and will be seen tomorrow in South Africa. Only when the new equilibrium that is envisaged is seen to bring a new range of

security and prosperity on a long-term basis the present structure of power and advantages will be given up.

What are the new 'compulsions', socio-economic, cultural
and intellectual? This globe of ours is small, getting over-
populated and has limited and even diminishing resources. For
the utilisation of these resources, and for production-distribu-
tion of adequate 'goods and services' through the application
of appropriate technology, management, and social engineering
the stabilization of peace, security and contentment would
require great intelligence and compassion. The day-to-day
politics, pride, prejudice, sheer ignorance are working against
this normal, natural process. In this perspective the games they
play between nation states, and that of 'Balance of Power' is
irrelevant from the point of view of human happiness and
welfare. Intelligent people all the world over see this now
clearly.

Non-alignment in this context means a serious attempt to
weave methodically a new fabric of world peace on mutuality
of advantage and profit of the various socio-economic-cultural
systems which are at different stages of development. Nation-
states today, as in Europe under the Common Market, have
a different function to perform than what they did only a
couple of decades ago. The great 'compulsion' of utilising
the limited, ever diminishing resources of this small planet
rationally, intelligently, efficiently, and above all 'compassiona-
tely' without wasting them would require the 'Nation-states' to
dismantle some of their useless structures and get out of their
habits of playing at power, of bureaucratic stagnation in order
to face the new world that is being born. New institutions
with different type of managerial capacities shall have to be
devised to deal with a totally new set of problems that now
confront humanity.

India and Africa have a great part to play in this grand
drama of human evolution. As they solve their own internal
contradictions and conflicts of their respective societies and
increase their capacities to deal with their resources to stabilize
their life they can be of assistance in the birth of this new
world.

VIJAY GUPTA

Non-Alignment to Collective Self-Reliance: A Perspective

NON-ALIGNMENT IS ESSENTIALLY anti-colonialism. It is an acceptance of the principle of peaceful co-existence; a national assertion of independence based on efforts for self-reliance; an international approach to achieve just and equal economic relations for stable peace. Non-alignment stands against the creation of blocs and similar combines of nations that can be or are easily militarized.

In this essay we will try to spell out the concept of non-alignment and discuss some of the relevant questions as to how non-alignment is the objective necessity for India, Africa and other developing countries; how is it the product of new political and economic relations and how changing material conditions of the developing and developed world have necessitated the adoption of a non-aligned policy. We will study the development of non-alignment movement as a weapon of resisting imperialist and neo-imperialist diktat; and as a force of achieving a just and equal economic relationship. We will study how the non-aligned countries have kept themselves away from military blocs or power groups. How this movement became a 'Unity Forum' for anti-colonialism, new economic order and thus against continued exploitation of developing countries? We

33

will examine the attitude taken by Africa and India and see whether the concept of non-alignment has changed since its inception or not.

Non-alignment—A Concept: A Historical View

The only form of non-alignment, prior to the world's division and polarization into two blocs, was a stand of neutrality maintained by a country at the time of war between other countries. The neutral country maintains equal relationship with the warring countries.[1] This state of neutrality was defined as "the juridical situation of states that do not take part in hostilities."[2] In other words a neutral state was one which did not participate in hostilities, refused the use of its territories and resources for any of the warring nations.[3] "The permanently Neutral State as a particular figure in international law is a creation of the Nineteenth Century."[4] After the Second World War the concept of neutrality underwent some changes. Article 1 of the United Nations Charter enumerates effective and collective measures for the prevention and removal of threats to the peace and/or the suppression of acts of aggression. The position of a permanently neutral state, thus, becomes incompatible with membership in the United Nations.[5] Article 2, para 5 of the UN Charter endorses this view. It reads as follows: "All members shall give the United Nations every assistance in any action it takes in accordance with the present Charter, and shall refrain from giving assistance to any state against which the United Nations is taking preventive or enforcement action."[6]

In order to correspond with the actual reality existing in the present-day world this principle was not invoked to keep the neutral states out of the United Nations. If we look into our history we find that our ancestors preached neutrality not as wartime foreign policy but as the basis of all-time foreign policy. Kautilya assigns a well-defined place and role to neutral states in his *Saptanga* theory, a theory which explains the methods and measures of securing the safety and infringability of a given state by a planned and strategic positioning of the friendly, the neutral and the enemy states in such a way that the menace of the enemy states is minimized and the advantage and power of the given state over them is maximized by sandwiching and surrounding them by the friendly and neutral states.[7]

The Kautilyan foreign policy principle was effectively used

by Jawaharlal Nehru in his effort to secure peace, integrity and freedom of India. To meet Pakistani challenge Nehru tried to erect a wall of friendly countries around India by entering into agreements on the basis of five principles (Panch Shila) of peaceful co-existence. These principles were included in the Preamble to the Indo-Chinese Agreement of 29 April 1954. They were: (1) mutual respect for territorial integrity and sovereignty; (2) non-aggression; (3) non-interference in each other's internal affairs; (4) equality and mutual benefit; and (5) peaceful co-existence.

The Panch Shila became the basis of foreign policy of newly independent and developing countries of Asia and Africa. With the end of Second World War a qualitative and irreversable change had taken place in the world. The European colonial powers had become weak. The nationalist movements in the colonies had become "uncontrolable" and thus decolonization had become inevitable. The USA which had emerged as a great capitalist power, was capable of holding the strings of the purses of European countries and was also industrially capable and anxious to exploit the minerally rich lands of Asia and Africa. The USSR had emerged as a great socialist power with fast growing economy and a strong army matching the western military strength. Another change was attainment of freedom by many former colonies with nationalist leaders who had a bitter experience of colonial powers and their exploitation strategies.

As a sequel to these changes, there emerged two systems—capitalist and socialist—in the developed world. The newly independent countries who were struggling to clear the debris of centuries of foreign domination and were striving to give content to their freedom and independence did not align with any of these groups. Consequently some regarded these countries as a third force, or a Third World, allegedly opposed to both the capitalist and socialist world and others hailed the policy of these countries for positive contribution to international peace, decolonization and economic independence. The policy which the newly independent countries adopted was not merely a reaction to the Cold War, it had a much firmer and wider basis. It was a response to the aspirations of vast masses of people who emerged into freedom from foreign domination and were eager to attain the status of respect and

equality with other nations of the world. It was in line with the
basic aim of the newly independent countries to secure the
right to make their own decisions in domestic and foreign
policies free from foreign pressures. It was a policy of non-
alignment.

Jawaharlal Nehru explains the policy as, ". . .the pursuit of
peace, through non-alignment with any major power or groups
but through an independent approach to each controversial or
disputed issue, the liberation of subject peoples, the maintenance of freedom, both national and individual, the elimination of racial discrimination, elimination of want, disease and
ignorance which afflict the greater part of the world's
population."[8]

Tanzanian President Nyerere chooses non-alignment policy
because, "we desire friendship with the non-Western nations
as well as with Western states and on the same basis of
mutual non-interference with internal affairs. We shall not
allow any of our friendship to be exclusive, we shall not allow
any one to choose any of our friends or enemies for us."[9]

For Dr Nkrumah, non-alignment "is not indifference that
leads to a policy of non-alignment. It is our belief that. . .we
must be free to judge issues on their merits and to look for
solution, that are just and peaceful, irrespective of the powers
involved. In fact, perhaps, a "non-alignment is a mis-statement
of our attitude we are firmly aligned with all forces in the
world that genuinely work for peace."[10]

The new states inherited their basic position within the international community direct from the colonial relationship. In
strategic terms, this meant that they remained within the
Western orbit, and in economic terms, it meant that the
majority remained virtually client states on the periphery of
the Western economic system. The question was could they,
in these circumstances, hold an independent position in the
arena of international politics.

The socio-economic and political structure of the new states
and consequently their foreign policies emanated largely from
the circumstances, methods and actions through which independence was achieved. Historically most of the nationalist movements in Africa and Asia had been led by petty-bourgeoisie
or national bourgeoisie and not by the working class. The

colonial peoples had fought against their former colonial masters and had been aided, directly or indirectly, by socialist countries in their freedom struggle. During the national struggle for independence some leaders had expressed preference for the socialist development system and for delinking their economies with imperialist economies. But they found that their economies were intricately linked with capitalist countries and the link could not be broken without risking economic stability. It was also noted that in case of a shift of economic links from capitalist to socialist bloc the latter was not in a position to meet all their requirements. Besides, they had no experience of dealing with socialist countries,[11] and hence were afraid and thus not prepared to join them. Most of them chose not to break with the capitalist economic system and join the socialist system countries.

The varying levels of political and economic independence and different alignment of class forces defined the different foreign policies pursued by various countries of Asia and Africa. In countries where the anti-imperialist circles were in power, the governments refused to participate in power blocs and came out against the policy of neo-colonialism, and yearned for peace and security in their respective regions and throughout the world.

The principal manifestation of their foreign policy was the policy of non-alignment. The basis was their need of restructuring their backward economies, freedom of their countries from imperialist hold and marching towards faster socio-economic development. As these countries had diverse ideologies, economic and social structures and political institutions, they did not follow the same system for development and were not uniform in economic development plans.

Recognizing this reality Nyerere states, "The member countries have adopted different ideologies and pursue different internal policies. We even differ in our foreign policies and sometime quarrel among ourselves! Only in opposition to colonialism and neo-colonialism and racialism we agree, yet even on that issue we differ on the tactics which should be pursued. In other words we are not ourselves a bloc."[12]

In their zeal to achieve faster economic development, the diverse section in the newly free and developing societies pressed for adoption of different economic planning and desired closer relations with the system of their preference. But the ruling parties, to avoid internal conflicts and achieve broader unity, adopted a mixed economy approach raising the slogan of self-reliance. However, self-reliance did not mean denouncement of all aid. Aid, foreign investment and technical assistance was acceptable. "In so far these are essential to our development and cannot be replaced by a re-allocation of our internal resources, we each have to seek for them, and accept them on the best terms we can get. All that any of us can do, individually, is to try and avoid becoming dependent on any single big power for our total economic advance. . . ."[13]

Nehru and his compatriots, Tito, Nasser, Castro, Bandaranaike, Sukarno, Nkrumah and Nyerere, felt that a policy of non-alignment as described above was the best means of achieving their national and international objectives. Such a policy answered the needs of all the newly independent countries which passed through similar historical experiences and very similar material conditions. They suffered colonial domination and economic exploitation by the imperialists. They were faced with similar problems of poverty and disease and the need to consolidate their hard-won freedom and independence.

They pledged to follow an independent policy, be self-reliant and restructure their economy, so that their dependency relationship presently leading to exploitation may change to an equality relationship. This they found was possible by creating a powerful state sector capable of introducing accelerated development process.

To protect their freedom they thought of unity with other newly independent nations and a unified attack on forces of colonialism, racialism and neo-colonialism. For Africans, unity of African nations was an expression of Pan-Africanism. Their anti-racialism was an assertion of human dignity. And thus it was imperative for them to join only that group or bloc which favoured Pan-Africanism and was genuinely against racialism and colonialism. They found the socialist countries as anti-colonialist and anti-racialist but realized that complete switch-over to them could mean upsetting the economy, even though temporarily. These historical conditions demanded the adoption of an anti-colonial and anti-imperialist policy, a policy of not aligning with the Socialist bloc.

When the independent nations of Asia and Africa were born they found an extreme type of antagonism between capitalist countries with those party to military pacts.[14] The latter was aiding Vietnam, Algeria, UAR and freedom fighters of Africa in their struggle against the British, French and Americans.

The newly independent countries had no choice, they could either accept alliance with Western military blocs or remain out of them. They could not join pacts, which the socialist countries had formed to safeguard themselves against the Western imperialist forces, as it was open to only Socialist countries of Europe. Recognizing that their freedom was threatened due to the presence of army bases in Asia and Africa, most of the Asian and African nations decided to remain out of these military pacts. Afraid of imperialist re-entry and to root out colonialism they adopted an anti-colonial and anti-racialist policy. To be strong they decided to unite on regional and global levels. Similarly in the economic field they preferred to adopt a policy of self-reliance which meant breaking off the bondage of economic dependence on former colonial powers and seeking the status of equality.

They had realized that "it is poverty which constitutes our greatest danger, and to a greater or lesser extent we are all poor. . . .It is in these facts that lies the real threat to our independence. For in seeking to overcome poverty we each inevitably run the risk of having sucked into the orbit of one or other of the Great Powers."[15] The newly independent nations did not want to be sucked into the orbit. The new political and economic relations and the changing material conditions of the developing countries and the developed world necessitated the adoption of a non-aligned policy.

History of Non-alignment

The policy of non-alignment passed through a number of stages. The first covers the period following the beginning of the collapse of the colonial system upto July 1956, when Nehru, Nasser and Tito got together in Yugoslavia and laid the foundation of non-alignment. This period marked the termination of the war-time alliance between the Western

Allies and the Soviet Union resulting in the politics of bloc formation, arms build-up and the generation of the Cold War.[16]

Alignment of forces in Asia and Africa began to take shape in this period. Individual Afro-Asian countries voiced their refusal to participate in the Cold War. At this time a group of young independent states came out in Bandung jointly with anti-colonial and the Socialist world to condemn the arms race, racism and demanded the abolition of the surviving colonial regimes.[17] This period witnessed antagonism between imperialist and anti-colonial forces.

The second stage began after 1956 and ended with the first conference of the non-aligned countries in Belgrade in 1961. This stage was characterized by the establishment of Soviet-US nuclear parity and the politics of bi-polarity dominating the world scene, resulting in what was called the balance of terror. This period also witnessed the massive liberation of African countries and the phenomenal increase in the membership of the UN, increase in the number of countries pursuing a policy of non-alignment and seeking to work together on an organized basis. During this period struggle between the imperialist and anti-imperialist forces sharpened eventually further weakening the imperialists and strengthening the anti-imperialist forces.

The third stage was the period of transition from old to new order. It began with a meeting of representatives of twenty-two countries in Cairo in July 1961. With active participation of India, UAR, Ghana and Yugoslavia the meeting defined the concept of "policy of non-alignment." This definition stated that a country's policy must be independent, founded on the principles of peaceful co-existence and neutrality. A country must support the movement for national liberation and it must not join any collective military alliance, it must not enter in a bilateral alliance with any power and it must not permit any foreign power to build military bases on its territory.[18]

A few months later in September 1961, 23 Asian and African countries and Yugoslavia met in Belgrade to lay a firmer foundation of non-alignment. According to the Belgrade conference the non-alignment movement was an anti-colonial movement and it was an outcome of a historical situation in the period of transition from old to the new order. The conflict, that existed between colonial and anti-colonial forces was due to changing socio-economic conditions of the world. In the words of the Conference the conflict had its origin "in the transition from an old order based on domination to a new order based on cooperation between nations, founded on freedom, equality and social justice for the promotion of prosperity; considering that the dynamic processes and forms of social change often result in or represent a conflict between the old established and new emerging nationalist forces; considering that a lasting peace can be achieved only if this confrontation leads to a world where the domination of colonialism, imperialism and neo-colonialism in all their manifestation is radically eliminated".[19] The Conference clarified that non-alignment movement was not founding a 'third bloc'—because the existence of different social systems does not "constitute an unsurmountable obstacle for the stabilization of peace." The heads of the states who participated in the conference did not suggest direct conflict with the old order but recommended a peaceful transition. The conference emphasised anti-colonial principles, i.e. the right of peoples to self-determination, to independence and to the free determination of the forms and methods of economic, social and cultural development as the only basis of all international relations.[20]

The Belgrade Conference laid down criteria for non-aligned countries. It regraded only those countries non-aligned whose foreign policy was based on non-alignment and who followed an independent policy based on peaceful co-existence; who supported liberation movements; who were not members of any bilateral or multilateral military pact in the context of East-West struggle, who had not granted bases to foreign powers.[21]

It emerged from the above criteria that countries which refused to join the Western imperialist powers and their military blocs (Western bloc was not open to non-Socialist countries), i.e. who disassociated themselves with the programme of containing communism and stood for vacation of their soil of armed forces of former colonial powers, were eligible for admission to the non-aligned group. Peaceful co-existence also meant that the newly developing countries could develop

friendship with both capitalists and socialists. This stage emphasised the historical necessity of change to new international
relations guaranteeing national independence in economic and
political fields. The need for unity amongst struggling nations
also became a necessity.

The next stage in the history in the non-aligned movement
covers the period from 1st to 3rd Conferences held in Cairo
in 1964 and Lusaka in September 1970. During this period
a number of changes occured. Most of the African countres
achieved independence. The USA started open intervention in
Vietnam. Efforts to interfere in Congo's (Zaire's) freedom
were made by Western powers and Israel occupied Arab areas.
On the economic front the imperialist powers tried to stage a
come-back through neo-colonialism disguised under the cover
of multinational corporations.[22] Neo-colonialism attempted to
carry out the imperialist policy under the guise of aid. In the
process of change from colonialism to neo-colonialism certain
structural changes occured. USA, which was not a traditional
colonial power, became a partner in neo-colonial exploitation.
Similarly, Germans, who had lost all colonies during the great
wars entered the field through investments and aid programmes.
Through multinational corporations and other methods colonialism took the form of *collective colonialism.* The old colonial
powers involved other economically advanced countries in
keeping the newly independent countries under their economic
control. Another form of collective colonialism was the formation of monpolistic unions, for example, the European Economic Community and European Common Market. The
Common Market turned the newly free countries into agrarian
raw material appendages to a group of powers instead of a
single power.

These structural changes precipitated changes in the anti-
colonial camp too. In developing countries forces of unity and
cooperation were being strengthened. In spite of serious differences the radical and moderate states of Africa succeeded in
setting up the Organization of African Unity (OAU). This was an
important development because the OAU affirmed the "policy
of non-alignment with regard to all blocs"[23], and expressed
their determination to "provide a solid foundation for peaceful
and positive cooperation among states."[24]

At the Cairo Conference (1964) the non-aligned countries adopted an enlarged programme of struggle for peace and against colonialism and neo-colonialism. The Conference noted with satisfaction that ". . . the principles of non-alignment, thanks to the confidence they inspire in the world, are becoming an increasingly dynamic and powerful force for the promotion of peace and the welfare of mankind."[25] During this period there was a growing disappointment on the question of aid from the big powers particularly the Western capitalist powers. Historically speaking we find that in the fifties and early sixties there was tremendous optimism at the prospect of the developing countries "catching up" with the developed world. The development process was envisaged to proceed on an innovative path based on the historical experience of the developed countries. Foreign aid was presumed to assist in the endeavours for development. There was the belief that the increased participation in international trade brought nothing but benefits in terms of increased external resources to the developing countries.

During the late sixties the past experience had made the developing countries question the validity of these assumptions. The development strategies, as propagated by former colonial powers, failed to relieve, to any substantial extent, the poverty of the developing countries.[26]

The need to remove economic imbalance inherited from colonialism and imperialism was emphasized and demand for just terms of trade for the economically less developed countries was made. The non-aligned countries were perturbed by the glaring inequalities and imbalances in the international economic structure and the ever-widening gap between the developing and developed countries. More and more developing countries came to realize that their economic situation had continued to deteriorate and the resultant debt burdens on them had reached intolerable levels. These countries noted that if the deficit in the balance of payments rose at the present rate it wil reach the figure of $112 billion by 1980. (It was $ 12.2 billion in 1973).[27]

Recognizing the close inter-action between the political and economic relationship the non-aligned stressed the need of economic self-reliance, accelerated economic development for gaining status of equality with other nations and solidarity and collective action by promoting economic cooperation amongst non-aligned countries.

The Lusaka Conference endorsed this approach and pledged to actively cultivate the spirit of self-reliance through their collective bargaining strength. This approach was based upon the permanent sovereignty over natural resources, independent economic activities, the formation of producers' association and the proclaimation in the United Nations of the New International Economic Order. The developments in international situation, since the Belgrade Conference, demonstrated the growing impact of the non-aligned. The non-aligned nations played a constructive and progressively effective role in world affairs. They substantially contributed towards positive transformation of international relations and promotion of world peace.[28] The non-aligned contributed significantly towards the prevention of the division of the world into oppositing blocs and spheres of influence. The non-aligned succeeded in establishing themselves as an independent and vital force for the creation of a new and just system of political and economic relations and for combating unequal relations and domination arising out of neo-colonialism.[29]

To build a just economic system the Belgrade Summit had paved the way for the establishment of UNCTAD. The Cairo Summit called upon the international community to restructure the world economy in a manner conducive to the urgent economic development of developing countries. The Lusaka Summit pledged to actively cultivate the spirit of self-reliance.[30]

The non-aligned movement in a short period has become a strong weapon of resisting imperialist and neo-colonialist diktat. It has asserted its bargaining strength against collective colonialism and multinational corporations. The OPEC success in raising the price of oil encouraged other raw material producing countries to work collectively and bargain for better prices for their produce. The importance of cooperation and unity had been realized by developing nations. Consequently the 4th Summit Conference held in Algiers in 1973 highlighted these new factors. It laid emphasis on mutual cooperation among non-aligned and other developing countries

and its decisions and recomendations served as the basis for intensive international negotiations aimed at the establishment of the
new international economic order. It further affirmed the need
for collective bargaining strength among the non-aligned and
placed entire weight and influence behind the actions to be
taken by producer countries of raw materials to obtain a
remunerative price for their products.[31] According to Mrs
Bandaranaike, the then Prime Minister of Sri Lanka, "the
struggle shifts . . . to imperialism in its economic dimensions",
and the non-alignment movement, "has reached the stage at
which it is out to concentrate, more than once before, on lending economic substance to its political victories."[32]

"Since Algiers summit conference in 1973", President Kaunda
said, "majo reconomic changes affecting the developing count-
rieshad taken place. The expectation that Third World would
geta fair deal from the industrially rich countries had been
foiled. The developing countries faced a very grave and common
problem. They were linked with the international system which
worked against their interests."[33] The growing demand was
that the monopoly in decision-making by the developed countries had to be ended. There was a growing conviction that
"nothing short of a complete re-structuring of international
economic relations through the establishment of the New International Economic Order, will place the devloping countries
in a position to achieve an acceptable level of development."[34]

New International Economic Order

In view of the growing realization that the struggle for
political independence and the exercise of their sovereignty
cannot be disassociated from the struggle for the attainment of
economic emancipation,[35] a new international economic order
was propoeed as a system of collective bargaining against
collective colonialism. The new order was based on Nyerere's
concept of economic self-reliance and implied a firm determination on the part of the non-aligned developing nations to
secure their legitimate economic rights in international dealings through the use of their collective bargaining strength.
Nyerere emphasised the need for collectivity and cooperation.
He said, "Independent nations in any real sense will become

increasingly impossible for any of us unless we combine and cooperate together. Economic cooperation among ourselves is an essential part of the struggle to maintain our freedom. Without it we shall each beccme even more involved in the economies and thus in the power of the big states."[36] Adding further he says, ". . . the big powers will try to prevent us from forging a real united front and if we succeed they will constantly endeavour to break it up. . . They will even strengthen their control over our political freedom."[37]

Stressing the need for economic independence Nyerere said, "We must have economic development or we have no political stability; we have no political independence either, but become playthings of any other nation which desires to intervene in our affairs. The fact is that our political independence depends upon the degree of our economic independence, as well as nature of our economic development depends upon our political independence."[38]

The non-aligned countries' efforts, endorsed by the Algiers conference through the Declaration and Programme of Action led to the organization of the Sixth Special Session of the United Nations on raw materials and development. This session identified in this context the problems of under-development and the nature of present crisis which is shaping the world economy. The Lima Conference on industrialization and the Rome Conference on food defined the major objectives of a policy of redistribution of the world wealth based on the industrialization of the Third World and the full exploitation of all agricultural potential.[39]

The Paris Conference on International Economic Co-operation and UNCTAD held in Nairobi provided confirmation of the hostile attitude on the part of some powers towards constructive proposals, put forward by the developing countries concerning re-scheduling of foreign debts and the protection of the purchasing power of export proceeds from raw materials.

The leading Western powers, Japan, West Germany, the United States and Britain emerged as the hardliners, urging others to "dig in". The United States feared that a successful UNCTAD IV would mean a major shift of political power caused by the voting majority and financial control exerted over the commonfund by third world producers."40

The limited results of UNCTAD IV and the Paris Conference on International Economic Cooperation confirmed the differing attitudes of the developed and developing countries on the question of the new framework of international economic relations.

In spite of the hurdles put up by Western powers the most impressive development is the appreciation of common problem of inequality in the international economic system. The benefits of bargaining power had been clearly proved by the success of regional grouping of oil producing countries. The developing countries came to realize the necessity for increasing their bargaining strength for improving their economic assets and the quality of life of their peoples.

Expressing his views in support for a change in international economic relations President Kaunda said, "We of the third world have become increasingly aware of the fact that we share one common problem namely that we are linked with an inequitous global system of international economic relations which works against our vital interests. We are opposed to present system whereby the wealthier and industrialized countries retain the monopoly of making decisions affecting all other states. We believe in power sharing as an important guarantee for peace within the international comunity."41

By the time Colombo Summit was held there was greater clarity in the understanding of world forces. The non-aligned leaders had realized that "much of the present international economic relations are a carry-over from colonial relations . . . In some areas the old (relationship) have been replaced by new patterns of relationship which hide inequality and the essentially expoitative nature of the system and give a comforting feeling that a new era had dawned."42 The imperialist powers had excluded the developing nations "from decision-making process affecting their destiny". To free themselves, "the developing countries have to promote change in the international economic and social order," and to bring about this change they need "arouse conciousness and as well as a sharpened precise view

of our collective interests and the ability to move forward
together."[43]

This task could be carried out through collective self-reliance, through a non-initiative approach to development utilizing to the maximum the indigenous resources and mobilizing fully the collective potential and economic capacity to extract the best bargain from the developed countries.[44]

During the course of 15 years non-alignment has become a dynamic movement activating change; indeed becoming an instrument of change. Starting as a movement against imperialism and neo-colonialism it sought to change the prevalant structure of exploitative economic relationships.

INDIA, AFRICA AND NON-ALIGEMENT

The reasons which necessitated a policy of non-aligement in India and Africa are very similar. With a similar colonial past, we all were afraid of loosing hard-won independence. Our economy was intricately linked with the Western capitalist system. We were exporters of cheaply paid raw materials and importers of heavily priced industrial goods. We all wanted to improve our economic conditions and thus be less dependent on others. We wanted to be free within limitations. Our national struggle had taught us that even the armed imperialist could be forced to relent by determined united action. Thus we chose to unite, even though on limited issues.

Since its independence India based her foreign policy pronouncements on anti-colonialism, anti-racialism, non-interference in internal problems of others and for free hand to build up economic base for the country. India has also been against military pacts. In her actions she has largely adhered to this policy with two exceptions, first when attacked by neighbours she sought arms from big powers and entered into treaties which provide her greater security and second to win larger support on the Kashmir question she had relented in her anti-colonial militancy. Nevertheless, India has been continuously making efforts to avoid total economic dependence on the West and thus has not allowed imperialism to re-enter through the backdoor.

India has consistently opposed apartheid and racial domination since 1946. This she has done inspite of annoyance of Western powers. India, in recent years has shown a qualitative change in her involvement with African freedom struggles. From moral support she has now pledged full material, including military, support to the Africans.[45] India has given its active support for the estiblishment of a new economic order.

The fact that India's policy has not changed inspite of change in the government is evidently proved by the statement of the former Minister for External Affairs, Atal Behari Vajpayee, who asserts that "the foreign policy of India had come to be indentified with the policy of non-alignment. The new government had decided to emphasize non-alignment by qualifying as genuine and even-handed." Explaining further, he said, "the new government will exercise true independence of judgement and aim on a fearless search for the pursuit of international principles and beneficial bilateral cooperation.

"Our foreign policy will remain detached from the power blocs . . . we are not prepared to allow one set of our relationship to stand in the way of good relations with other countries,[46]

India's role in non-alignment movement is of great significance. India gave the movement an anti imperialist orientation and by cooperating, in the economic field, with Socialist countries it opened the way for other developing countries to reduce their dependence on former colonial masters. By adopting a policy of independent economic development India succeeded in turning the non-alignment movement into a weapon of resisting imperialist and neo-imperialist diktat.

Africa and Non-Alignment

Similarly, the African contribution to non-alignment is not only in terms of numerical preponderance but also in determination of not involving Big Powers in the solution of its internal crisis situations. The African unity has given a new strength to the movement. The African en-bloc voting in international conferences has become a force in itself. Africa also happens to be the worst sufferer in international economic relations and hence is foremost in its efforts to change the economic order.

Africa is the only continent which can be identified with the non-aligned movement. African presence in the non-aligned movement not only gives a numerical strength in the UN but also gives firm anti-racial and anti-colonial content to the movement. Every meet of the non-aligned countries has taken up African issues and discussed ravages of colonialism and racialism. As the continent with the largest number of least devoloped countries and one which suffered the enormous Sahel famine, Africa gave impetus to the demands for a new international economic order.

For Africans non-aligement is a source of strength for survival, preservation of freedom and self-reliance. The real and urgent threat to the independence of almost all the African countries comes not so much from the military but more from the economic power of big states. They are to a greater or lesser extent all poor and are trying to develop and be self-reliant. They lack capital and expertise which can be supplied by one or the other Big Power. Their problem is that in the process of seeking assistance to overcome their poverty they should not be sucked into the orbit of one or the Big Powers. To avoid becoming dependent on any single Big Power for their economic advance the African countries accept that they along with other non-aligned countries should act as a group and establish a new international economic order.

Africans believe that the struggle for political and economic independence for full sovereignty over natural resources and domestic activities and for greater participation of developing countries in the production and distribution of goods and the rendering of services and basic changes in the international division of labour assumes the highest priority. They recognize that the breaking up of the resistance to the struggle for the new economic order represents the primary task of the non-aligned and other developing countries.

As emphasized in the 25-member Coordinating Bureau and the non-aligned April 1977 meeting by Liberian and Nigerian foreign ministers, a new world economic order cannot be achieved without elimination of the evils of racial discrimination and colonialism. Africa is totally for war against these evils and therefore wants a united national patriotic leadership in Zimbawe to intensify armed struggle against Ian Smith's subterfuges and die-hard racism.

Africa has convinced the non-aligned nations of a need for the intensification of the struggle of peoples still under the direct domination of imperialism, colonialism, racism and apartheid. The racist regimes in South Africa and Zimbawe established by alien colonial settlers combine the ugly features of colonialism and racism as they all practice racism and subject the indigenous population, to every form of discrimination oppression, occupation and alien domination.

Conclusion

The bi-polar world power structure in which non-alignment was born fifteen years ago has gradually been replaced by new patterns of relationships in which many countries are loosening their military links with big powers, are asserting sovereignty and are exerting more control over the use and disposition of their natural resources. During this period a large number of countries, particularly in Africa achieved national independence. These countries, in their effort to advance economically, came in closer touch with international imperialism. They found that the Western powers' aid and trade, although proclaimed to develop newly independent countries, actually underdeveloped then. The former colonial powers, after independence, introduced neo-colonial machinery. The new system involved many countries in collective exploitation of developing countries through multi-national associations and corporations. The newly independent countries realized that in order to fight this collective imperialism they had to form collectives. As they had done on a national scale during the period of nationalist movement, they decided to bury their ideological differences now to form international united front overlooking diversity of ideologies, social structures, political institutions, and uneven stages of economic development.

Twenty-five years ago the primary preoccupation of the newly emerging countries was to avoid being a partner of military link-ups, set up by Western powers. Today, though not eliminated, the military alliances and bases, in view of the development of techonology, e.g. ICBM and satellite system, are not that important. The confrontation of yesterday has now been replaced by growing dialogue and spirit of detente. Detente recognizes peaceful co-existence and other principles of 'Panch Shila'. Detente has been interpreted by some as an instrument to obtain mutual recognition of sphere of influence, as acceptance of a balance of big power relationship. Such a concept is negative. As we have seen above, the prevailing structures of relationships are unsatisfactory, and to a considerable extent are a carry-over from the hey-day of imperialism, and are pregnated by new forms of unequal and one-sided dependency relationships.

We find that the non-aligned are seeking change towards a new economic order, towards a relationship based on equality, respect for sovereignty, self-determination, mutual interest and towards removing the causes of tensions. The non-aligned in every summit, have made it adundantly clear that, for peace and detente, they are not prepared to forego their right of armed struggle by the people under colonial or racial domination.

Besides struggling against racist regimes in Israel, South Africa and Rhodesia, the non-aligned have to fight against the politics of pressure and domination which are seriously threatening the independence of states, and also against measures calculated to cause disruption and destablization which threaten their internal security and create political confusion and economic chaos.[47]

REFERENCES

[1] J.B. Moore, *A Digest of International Law*, vol. VII (Washington, 1966), p. 860.

[2] Convention of Maritime Neutrality, 1928, 6th Text in Supplement to the *American Journal of International Law*, vol. 22, no. 3, July 1928, pp.151-57.

[3] C.C. Hyde, *International Law*, vol. III, 2nd ed. (Boston, 1947).

[4] J.L. Kunz, *Austrian Permanent Neutrality*, Editorial Comment, *Journal of International Law*, vol. 50 (1956), H. P. 418.

[5] Hans Kelsen, *Law of the United Nations, A Critical Analysis of its Fundamental Problems, with supplement* (New York, 1966), p. 94.

[6] Ibid., p. 480.

[7] R. Shamasastry "The Conduct of a Madhyama King, A Neutral King and Circle of States", *Kautilya Arthashastra*, Chapter XVIII, paras 318-21 (Mysore, 1960), 6th ed., pp. 345-49.

[8] Address to the University of Columbia, *New York Times*, 18 October 1949.

[9] J. Nyerere, *Freedom and Socialism* (Dar-es-Sàlaam, 1968), p. 369.

[10] Kwame Nkrumah, "African Prospects," *Foreign Affairs*, vol. 37, no. 1, October 1958, p. 49.

[11] Nyerere states, "Before Independence we had no direct contact with Eastern Bloc countries." J. Nyerere, *Tanzanian Policy on Foreign Affairs* (Dar-es-Salaam, 1967), p. 5.

[12] J. Nyerere, *Non-alignment in the 1970's* (text of the address given to the Preparatory Meeting of the Non-aligned countries) on 13 April 1970 at Dar-es-Salaam, p. 4.

[13] Ibid., p. 6.

[14] The North Atlantic Treaty Organization (NATO) in 1952, involving Turkey and Greece; SEATO: USA, Britain, France, Australia, New Zealand, Pakistan, Thailand and the Philippines (September 1954); the Baghdad Pact had Turkey, Iran, Iraq, Pakistan and Britain.

[15] Nyerere, n. 12, p. 5.

[16] Rasheeduddin Khan, "Non-alignment—Relevance, Challenges and Dimensions", *Secular Democracy* (Delhi) vol. IX, no. XIV and XV, July-August 1976, p. 73.

[17] G.H. Jansen, *Non-alignment and the Afro-Asian States* (New York 1966), pp. 20-28.

[18] Documents of the gathering of non-aligned countries 1961-1973, Belgrade, 1973, pp. 42-49.

[19] Ibid., p. 20.

[20] "Activities of Non-aligned Countries," *Review of International Affairs* (Belgrade), no. 488-89, 5-20 August 1970, p. 20.

[21] Yugoslavia, Cyprus and Tunisia were among those who participated in the Belgrade Conference. Yougoslavia at the time of the conference was a member of the Balkan Pact, a military alliance to which incidentally some members of NATO also belonged. Cyprus had a British military base on its soil. Tunisia had a base at Bizerta although President Bourguiba had challenged its legitimacy before coming to the conference. Ethiopia had a US communication station with America troops guarding it. Doudou Thiam, *The Foreign Policy of African States* (London, 1965), p. 81.

[22] Current inflow of foreign direct investment and outflow of income on accumulated past direct investment by region 1965-69 (in million dollars) is as follows:

Africa						
inflow	182.2	163.7	241.5	201.6	235.5	270.7
Outflow	380.8	318.8	708.6	963.7	924.3	996.2
Balance	-198.6	-555.1	-467.1	-762.1	-688.8	-725.5

Source: Vikram Nair and R. Kasbehai, "Multinationals," *The Economic Times*, Annual (Bombay), 1975, p. 123.

[23] *Charter of the OAU*, Principles, Article III, Clause 7.

[24] Ibid., Preamble.

[25] Documentation, *Review of International Affairs*, Nos. 488-89, 5-20 August 1970, p. 25.

[26] Non-alignment Conference, special supplement, *Ceylon Daily News*, 16 August 1976.

[27] UNGA. A/31/197, 8 September 1976. NAC/Conf. 5/S/3, p. 4.

[28] UN NAC/Conf. 5/S2, 1977. p. 12/5.

[29] Ibid., p. 15-17.

[30] NAC/Conf. 5/S/3, p. 15.

[31] NAC/Conf. 5/3, pp. 8-9.

[32] Speech by Mrs Bandaranaike reported in *Guardian* (London), 17 August 1976.

[33] Speech by Kaunda reported in *Africa Diary*, p. 8142.

[34] NAC/Conf. 5/S/3, p. 7.

[35] Ibid., p.8.

[36] Nyerere, n. 12, p. 11.

[37] Ibid., p. 10.

[38] Ibid., pp. 6-7.

[39] Some countries continued to oppose the effective implementation of these resolutions and thus expressed their reluctance to adjust to the changing situation.

[40] Abel Ndumber, "Focus on UNCTAD," *The Weekly Review* (Nairobi), 7 June 1976, p. 26.

[41] Kaunda's speech quoted by *Kuwait Times*, 17 August 1976.

[42] Address by H.E. Brig General Teferi Bante, Chairman PMAC Ethiopia, to the 5th Assembly of the Non-aligned Summit Conference, Colombo, August 1976.

[43] Ibid.

[44] *Ceylon Daily News*, 16 August 1976.

[45] Anirudha Gupta, "Non-alignment Summit and Liberation Struggle in Southern Africa", *Mainstream* (Delhi), Annual Number, 1976, p. 65.

[46] *Amrita Bazar Patrika* (Calcutta), 11 June 1977.

[47] NAC/Conf. 5/S/3, 1976, Political Declaration.

SHANTI SADIQ ALI

India's Support to African Liberation Movements

THIS ESSAY DEALS SPECIFICALLY with Southern Africa where, for almost 20 years or so, a relentless struggle is being waged against colonialism and racism. India's policy towards the liberation of Southern Africa, it is felt, can be better appreciated if the problem is first put in proper perspective.

South Africa, it is acknowledged, is the *de facto* colonial power in the Southern African region and the reasons for the mounting tensions in the area can be traced to the official policies of the racist regime in Pretoria. These may be summed up as: (i) a denial of basic fundamental rights to more than 80 percent of the people living in South Africa; (ii) South Africa's illegal occupation of Namibia and the extension of its policy of apartheid to the territory; (iii) the substance by South Africa of the illegal minority Government in Zimbabwe (Rhodesia) through critical military and petrol supplies and provision of commercial goods and transport for trade. Furthermore the crisis in this region has spilled over to the "frontline" states—Zambia, Botswana, Mozambique, Angola—and into the island hostage state of Lesotho, Zambia which has made heroic sacrifices ever since, in 1965, the rebel Smith regime unilaterally declared independence has been repeatedly threatened and invaded by Rhodesia. Mozambique is still reeling

55

from the shock of a series of armed incursions by the White minority regime of Rhodesia, destroying life and property indiscriminately. The flow of refugees from South Africa and Rhodesia into Botswana and Lesotho has strained their already fragile economics to such an extent that a major international effort amounting to over 150 million dollars is thought necessary by the United Nations to sustain their economies. In Angola, the members of the Movement for Total Independence of Angola (UNITA), are still waging a war of attrition against the People's Republic of Angola with assistance from South Africa and others. Clearly, then, South Africa is the key to the whole power structure of the region and its role in resolving the burning issues in the area cannot be minimised.

At the same time the Western powers have long regarded Southern Africa as an area of traditional interests, economic and strategic. The straddling position of South Africa across the Atlantic and Indian Oceans, its nuclear and defence capability and its possession of strategic raw materials like chrome, nickel, gold, uranium, vanadium, etc. have made South Africa indispensable to the West.[1] These nations' economic and investment interests in South Africa, Zimbabwe and Namibia are not merely restricted to mining and industrial activities but also cover agriculture and communtcations, etc. Ethnically also the Whites are considered an indivisible part of the Anglo-Saxon race. For all these reasons the West has been wary of upsetting its relations too seriously with the minority regimes in Southern Africa, in particular South Afrtca.

The sudden collapse of Portuguese colonialism in Africa, and more importantly, the Soviet-backed Cuban intervention in Angola in 1975, however, has fundamentally changed the perspectives for both South Africa and its allies. With their borders now dangerously exposed to independent Africa the White supremacists find themselves far from impregnable. More so as the Angolan experience—and in the case of Mozambique earlier—has strengthened the belief of the African majority in Zimbabwe and Namibia in the value of armed struggle. The Western powers have also suffered a set-back with the emergence of radical regimes in Angola and Mozambique; thus changing the balance of power in an area where they have significant stakes. Furthermore, their image has been tarnished in African eyes because they found themselves on the same side as South Africa in the Angolan crisis. The South African intervention in Angola, on its part, not only legitimized the Russian-Cuban support for the MPLA among African leaders but it also influenced a majority of member states of the Organisation of African Unity, which was earlier split down the middle on the issue, to recognise it as the legitimate Government of Angola. On the other side, the Soviet intervention in Angola was seen as an exercise by Moscow to demonstrate its Super Power status and its military capability to influence events in a country as far off as Angola. The MPLA's victory has certainly strengthened Russia's position even though the bitter Sino-Soviet rivalry witnessed during the crisis proved to be an embarrasment to several African states, in particular some of the "front-line" ones.

Nonetheless, it was the Angolan episode that startled America, as the leader of the Western world, into realising that black Africa could no longer be downgraded as the United States National Security Council in its special study in 1969 had attempted to do. The Kissinger shuttle diplomacy which followed in 1976 unfortunately revealed that the same objective of countering Soviet influence and advancing United States economic and strategic interests in Southern Africa appeared to have remained the strong current of official think-ing in the United States administration and they were not yet prepared to accommodate African national aspirations. It was thus understandable that the African reaction to the Kissinger initiative[2] ranged from open hostility to cautious scepticism. Still leaders like President Nyerere of Tanzania welcomed the diplomatic decision to start negotiations on Southern African issues because, in his words, "America has the power to apply political and economic pressure on the enemies of freedom and equality in Southern Africa." The Carter admini-stration, continuing the slow unfolding exercise, has gone a step further by repealing the Byrd Amendment which permitted the United States to import chrome from Rhodesia in spite of mandatory United Nations sanctions. Another departure from the cautious position of Dr. Kissinger on South Africa itself was evident in a speech by his successor, Cyrus Vance, on 1 July 1977 and earlier by Vice-President Mondale's 25th May press conference which reveal a much more committed attitude on the part of the present US Administration.

Vance in particular had argued for a fairly rapid change in the internal structure of South Africa and repeated in no uncertain terms America's refusal to recognise Bantustans as an interim solution.[3] It is recognised, however, that the situation in South Africa is qualitatively different from that in Zimbabwe and Namibia. The fundamental distinction has been realised by African leaders themselves and inscribed in the 1969 Lusaka manifesto on Southern Africa, which recognises the Republic of South Africa as "an independent sovereign state and a member of the United Nations."[4] Finally, US active support of the British initiative in Zimbabwe[5] and the US initiated moves on Namibia[6] testify to the continuing compulsions drawing America's attention to Southern Africa, namely, the threat of further radicalisation of this region by the Soviet Union—a threat further underlined by President Podgorny's visit to Tanzania, Mozambique and Zambia in March 1977—and the open revolt in the Shaba province in Zaire.[7]

To sum up, then, the present Western strategy in this part of the world appears to be aimed at arranging a smooth transfer of power and by assisting the new ruling elites in Rhodesia and Namibia they hope to retain some sort of indirect control or influence over these new countries. The new aggressiveness on the part of the US, and taking its cue from the United States, the UK, too, on the three southern African problems could lead to a quickening of pace of change in the region than envisaged for. The Western powers, however, can achieve their goal only to the extent the changes envisaged in Rhodesia and Namibia are acceptable to South Africa. Within South Africa itself the hope for 'liberation' lies in the increasing alienation of the non-White population from the White minority regime, the increasing consciousness of the black urban proletariat and from the tensions between the rural Bantustans and the urban Bantustans. An equally important factor in the direction of change in the Southern African region is unity among Africans in the three States and effective solidarity between members of the OAU.

II

In the light of the realities of the complex situation in Southern Africa, as outlined above, the limitations to any major role by India in the process of decolonisation are fairly obvious, especially when the large demand on her resources at home have been an added restraint on her capability to assist the liberation movements. Therefore utmost caution is called for in any assessment of India's policies in respect of this area. On other hand, to ignore or belittle the part played by India would be swinging to the other extreme. For, it is widely recognised that India's contribution, direct and indirect, has been useful in stimulating the march to African independence.

As one of the countries to gain freedom soon after the war, India actively engaged itself in the United Nations, Commonwealth conferences and other international forums in initiating diplomatic moves to create conditions for a peaceful transfer of power. India's whole-hearted identification with the emerging nationalist forces was most conspicuous in her assertive role at the United Nations from the time it was established and which synchronised with her own independence. Despite the bold assertion in the Atlantic Charter, the concept of self-determination had received very guarded acceptance at the San Francisco Conference where the atmosphere was marked by a preponderant concern for world peace. It was the Indian delegate, A. Ramaswamy Mudaliar, who striking a prophetic note, proposed an amendment to the provisions relating to peace. He suggested that due recognition should be given to the promotion of "fundamental human rights for all men and women, irrespective of race, colour or creed in all nations and in all international relations and asscoiations of nations with one another."[8]

India's endeavours to extend and consolidate the authority of the United Nations in the dependent territories came to the surface in the many legal battles fought at the United Nations on the question of decolonisation. Of special significance in the context of the situation in Namibia were the suggestions made by India to ensure that the Trusteeship system worked strictly for the interests of the dependent peoples. These included: (a) that in placing a dependent area under a Trustee, there should be no parcelling out of territories on the basis of strategic needs or outlets for surplus population; (b) that, besides the information required to be submitted by the Trustee, the Organisation should also get regular information on the measures taken, or proposed to be taken, to enable the Trust territory, in the shortest posible time, to achieve the objective of independence and also on the manner in which the wishes of the peoples were being taken into account and the period of time in which each trust territory would attain the objective of independence or self-government and more significantly; and (c) that the United Nations should make it clear that Trusteeship agreements did not involve annexation and that administrative and fiscal union between the administering authoriy and the trust territory should not mean incorporation of the one into the other as South Africa had done with regard to South West Africa (Namibia).[9]

Similarly, India made vigorous efforts to get world opinion solidly crystallized against South Africa. She was the first country to take up the question of apartheid and racial discrimination in the first session of the General Assembly of the United Nations in 1946 even before her own independence. Though the question arose from the treatment of peoples of Indian origin in South Africa, it exposed South Africa's discriminating laws as a violation of fundamental human rights. Jawaharlal Nehru highlighting the dangers inherent in the denial of fundamental human freedoms to certain races warned then that in their attempt to secure redress of the long-standing injustice against themselves, they (the so-called inferior races) might touch off a world conflagration of which no one could see the range of consequences.[10] As a result, the UN General Assembly in its resolution declared that the treatment of the people of Indian origin in South Africa should conform to the relevant provisions of the Charter and to South Africa's international obligations. Despite South Africa's refusal to accept the United Nations resolution, India's consistent stand helped stimulate a discussion of the issue of apartheid in its wider context. And as Dr Rajendra Prasad, the President of India, was later to explain in his address to the Lok Sobha: "This question is no longer merely one of Indians of South Africa; it has already assumed a greater and wider significance. It is a question of racial domination and racial intolerance. It is a question of the future of Africans (more than that) of Indians in South Africa.[11] Meanwhile, in 1954, India was again the first country to withdraw its High Commissioner in Pretoria and institute economic sanctions against South Africa, much in advance of the United Nations recommendatory sanctions. It is true India's trade boycott of South Africa was rendered ineffective initially by the re-export of products of Indian origin by countries like Australia, Kenya, Southern Rhodesia and Hong Kong and later by the breaking of the boycott by Pakistan, but it would not be denied that the loss of the South African market in which India had established itself earlier and where the demand for its products had been continuously growing was substantial.[12]

Again, when Portugual was admitted to the United Nations in 1956, India rose to challenge Lisbon's contention that it did not have any colonial possessions within the meaning of Chapter XI of the United Nations Charter; that according to its constitution which was unitary in character, an "overseas territory has no more and no less in its status than any other territory."[13] The controversy over the status of Portuguese colonies dragged on till 1960 when on the initiative of India, along with some other countries, a Committee was appointed and headed by India's Permanent Representative C.S. Jha, to go into the question. Finally, as a result of the Jha Committee's Report the General Assembly adopted a resolution in December 1960 specifying for the first time the territories in regard to which Portugal was under an obligation to transmit information under Chapter XI of the Charter.

As far as Rhodesia is concerned, India has throughout considered its status as a non-self governing territory as confirmed in the United Nations General Assembly resolution of 28 June 1962. Earlier, in 1953 India opposed in the General Assembly the idea of a Central African Federation comprising present-day Zambia, Malawi and Rhodesia, as it would have perpetuated White domination and extension of apartheid. On 7 May 1965 India again became the first country in the world to break off diplomatic relations with Rhodesia and was one of the first to impose a total embargo. The decision to withdraw the Indian mission in Salisbury was prompted by the series of

measures taken by the minority settlers government, especially
elections ordered for that day, indicating its determination to
take positive steps towards the unilateral declaration of independence. It demonstrated India's disapproval of the manner
in which the Rhodesian regime was persisting in the achievement of its illegal objectives and seeking to give a semblance
of constitutionality by the process of conducting spurious
elections. The decision to snap diplomatic ties was also considered a sign that India was no longer certain of Britain's ability
to effectively intervene in Rhodesian affairs to prevent a unilateral declaration of independence by the White regime.

Finally, India has been equally forthright on the Namibian
question and identified itself with the new forces (SWAPO)
which emerged in 1966. India's crusading role in the UN
Trusteeship Council to which it was first elected in 1954 has
already been described above. She is among the traditional
donors of the UN Trust Fund to provide relief, assistance and
education to persons persecuted under South Africa's discriminating legislation. India has regularly contributed to the
Fund for Namibia set up in 1970 and when the UN Council
for Namibia visited India in 1975, the Government decided to
further strengthen cooperation particulary for post-independence
construction of the territory by agreeing to provide training
facilities to 150 people from Namibia immediately. In addition,
India decided to send equipment and experts, professors and
lecturers to serve in the Institute set up in Lusaka for Nami-
bians.

Recognition of India's positive contribution at the United
Nations came in 1960 when the General Assembly adopted a
resoluton, without a dissenting vote, which proclaimed the
necessity of bringing to speedy and unconditional end colonialism in all its forms and manifestations[14] and India was
unanimously elected as Chairman of the Special Committee of
Twenty. The Committee was set up to examine and recommend measures for accelerating progress in the implementation
of the historic Declaration on the Granting of Independence
to Colonial Countries and Peoples.

With the rapid expansion of Afro-Asian membership of the
United Nations, India appeared to be content with a quieter
role. One explanation for this may be found in the emergence

of an African group at the United Nations in 1958, which naturally, assumed the responsibility of articulating the problems of apartheid and colonialism. This group became more vocal after the Organisation of African Unity decided to establish a semi-permanent group in 1963 to represent the African case on the liberation of Southern Africa at the United Nations. Nonetheless, there was some criticism of India's moderate role by the more militant African leaders, especially on the question of Algeria, where it was felt that the Indian Government's attitude was not in accord with its traditional anti-colonial policy. However, apart from the change of circumstances, other factors which affected India's erstwhile role was undoubtedly the 1962 Sino-Indian conflict and the realisation on India's part that a more pragmatic policy was essential. The priorities since then have shifted to exploring the practical options to it in respect of policies towards its own neighbours and the deployment of national capacities for dealing with basic economic tasks. India, however, continues to regard the United Nations as the most effective instrument of collective international action in the fight against apartheid and colonialism. And whatever the criticisms, there is no denying that political pressures at the UN forced Governments and peoples to recognise that the future of Africa had become a vital problem in international relations; that by encouraging African demands, the policy of gradualism advocated by the colonial powers and the White supremacists in southern Africa has been upset and, that the system of international accountability forced these powers, albeit reluctantly, to reappraise their policies. The latest tribute to India's constructive role at the UN is the reported move to involve her in the United Nations Peace Keeping Force in Rhodesia during the transition from White minority to majority rule as proposed by the United States and Britain.

Outside the United Nations, India has fully supported the policies laid down with regard to the liberation movements by the Organisation of African Unity founded in 1963. India in particular appreciated the OAU's endeavours to create conditions to find an African solution to an African problem—one of its cardinal principles—as it has been painfully aware of the enormous role external powers played to divide and weaken

Africa during the 1960 Congo (Zaire) crisis. More recently, in Angola the policies of some powers to consolidate and extend their leverage in the area have made them more suspect in the eyes of their African critics, calling for a complete reversal of their policies. India, on the contrary, strictly adhered to the policy of supporting the OAU in its efforts to form a Government of National Unity and it was only after the MPLA secured an absolute majority in the OAU that it officially accorded its recognition. Moreover, as India is anxious to sustain its relations with Africa on an entirely different basis, seeking no privileged position for itself and does not wish to take sides in the liberation movements, it has sought to channel its aid primarily through the OAU. By 1969 India had spent more than one and a quarter million rupees to assist the liberation movements.[16] By then the contributions to the OAU's Liberation Committee by the 35 Member states had reportedly dwindled from around 2 million dollars in previous years to less than a million dollars and only Tanzania, Zambia, Algeria and the Ivory Coast had paid their dues for the fiscal year 1968-69, according to the OAU Report. India's total assistance upto date has reportedly crossed the 5 million rupees mark. Evidence that India continues to stand by its commitments has recently been provided by the Tanzanian Shihata news agency, which reported during Foreign Minister Atal Behari Vajpayee's visit that India had allocated 27 million Tanzanian shillings (nearly Rs. 31 million) to aid the struggle for the liberation of South Africa this financial year.[17]

Of perhaps even longer significance than this gesture of full backing for the liberation movements is the drive initiated by India soon after the 1970 Lusaka non-aligned summit conference to share the burden of the "front line" states as any instability in these countries cannot but be unsettling from Africa's point of view at this crucial stage of the liberation struggle in Southern Africa. India recently offered to contribute a million rupees to the Lesotho Special Fund and half a million rupees for the Botswana Special Fund to be used at their discretion for Indian goods and technical services. Both these 'captive' states are critically dependent on South Africa which, until 1969, had toyed with the idea of incorporating them along with Swaziland and Rhodesia. It, therefore, goes to credit that these states have asserted the principle of human dignity and given refuge to young South African blacks and white radicals fleeing police persecution. It is in the fitness of things that India promptly responded to the UN appeal for financial help to ease their plight.

The high priority relations with Tanzania and Zambia have been accorded is evident from the fact that they are included in the neighbourly zone of countries which fall in the category second only to our immediate neighbours. These countries moreover are themselves beginning to appreciate the experience of a country like India which has been tested in a similar socio-economic background. But most important perhaps is the knowledge that relations with India are non-exclusive and absolutely free from any political overtones. Equally significant, the complementarity of our economies have lifted these relations to a higher plane qualitatively both in scope and dimension as reflected in the trade between our countries.[18] Last, but not the least, the opportunity provided for Indian technicians and experts to work alongside and under Africans will not only improve India's image markedly but the tendency to overplay African emotions against Asians can be tempered notably to the mutual advantage of both.[19] For Presidents Kaunda and Nyerere a successful experiment in racial partnership has a much greater significance as it could prove to be a most effective weapon in eventually eroding the foundations of apartheid in South Africa itself.

For all these reasons, speaking on the occasion of Vajpayee's last visit, the Tanzanian Vice-President, Aboud Jumbe, described cooperation between India and Africa as a model for Third World countries and a beacon of hope in the dark and troubled waters of economic exploitation and the rich-poor tussle.[20]

Finally, a new emphasis is noticeable in India's support to the liberation struggle in Southern Africa in the official statements made by former Foreign Minister Vajpayee during his visit to Tanzania and at the Commonwealth Conference. Renewing the pledge of support, for instance, he declared that India would "definitely consider" any request for arms made by guerrillas fighting against White minority rule in Southern Africa.[21]

Viewed from any aspect India can take pride in her Africa

policy which is as it should be, a balanced blend of idealism and enlightened self-interest.

REFERENCES

[1] For the strategic importance of South Africa to the Western bloc, see Sean Gervase, "South Africa under Nato Umbrella", *Africa Report*, September-October 1976; "Southern Africa. The Escalation of a Conflict," Stockholm International Peace Research Institute, 1976; and P. R. Chari, "The Military Balance," *Journal* of the Institute for Defence Studies and Analyses (New Delhi) vol. IX, no. 4, April-June 1977.

[2] "The Kissinger Plan," *Africa Research Bulletin*, vol. 13, no. 5, pp. 4004-5.

[3] For full text of US Secretary of State, Cyrus Vance's speech to the National Association for the Advancement of Coloured People (NAACP) on US-Africa relations, see United States Information Service, Official Text, 5 July 1977.

[4] For full text of Lusaka Manifesto of Southern Africa, see *Africa: Contemporapy Record Annual Survey and Documentation, 1969-70*, pp. C-39-C-43.

[5] The Anglo-American 7-point proposals for giving Rhodesia majority rule and legal independence by the end of 1978 called for Ian Smith's White minority Government to surrender power to a British resident Commissioner during the transitional period. The latter and his deputy would be assisted by a special United Nations' representative and a UN peacekeeping force. The transitional administration would conduct free and impartial elections on the basis of universal adult suffrage. An independant constitution would provide for a democratically elected Government, the sanction of individual human rights and the independence of the judiciary. A $ 1.5 billion development fund was to be provided to revive the economy. Ian Smith, according to reports, continues to be against the handing of power during the transitional period and was opposed to the disbanding of the Rhodesian armed forces as envisaged under the Anglo-American plan. *Times of India*, 3 September 1977.

[6] For the West's "declaration of principles" on Namibia see the *Guardian* (London), 9 April 1977. The aim of the five Western members of the UN Security Council—USA, Britain, France, West Germany and Canada—whose diplomats have been engaged in a dialogue with Pretoria after their meeting with the South African Minister—Vorster, on 7 April 1977, appears to be (i) to stop the Turnhalle constitutional process started on 1 September 1975 by South Africa in order to forestall action at the UN, and (ii) to

persuade South Africans to accept UN involvement for transfer of power in Namibia. The Afro-Asian Group in the UN, however, expects that the Western initiative on Namibia would be able to obtain the compliance of the South African regime to the Security Council resolutions calling for the vacation of the illegal occupation of Namibia and holding of free elections under the supervision and control of the United Nations for the whole of Namibia as one political entity.

[7] For background of events in Shaba province, see article by Bridget Bloom in *Financial Times* (London), 1 April 1977.

[8] Article 1, paragraphs 2 and 3 of the Charter.

[9] Swadesh Rana, "India, the United Nations, and World Peace," in *India's Foreign Relations during the Nehru Era*, edited by M.S. Rajan (New Delhi, 1977), p. 284.

[10] Nehru's address at Columbia University, New York, 17 October 1946, as cited by C.D. Narasimhaiah, ed. *India's Spokesman* (London, 1960), pp 75-76.

[11] Lok Sabha *Debates*, part II, vol. I, no. 3, 16 May 1952.

[12] India's then Education Minister, M.C. Chagla, participating in a Security Council meeting of 12 May 1964 strongly refuted allegations made by Pakistan on 5 March 1964 that India had trade relations with South Africa. "The small value of a few products shown in United Nations statistics as furnished by South African publications," he stated, "are presumably based on the country of origin of third country exports. Personal effects carried by travellers between India and South Africa may also account for the so-called exports."

[13] See U.N. Doc. A/AC.100/2, p. 37.

[14] See *United Nations Review*, vol. 8, no. 1, January, 1961.

[15] *Africa Quarterly*, vol. IV, no. 3, Quarterly Chronicle, p. 203.

[16] Surendra Pal Singh, "India and the Liberation of Southern Africa," *Africa Quaterly*, vol. x, no. 3, October-December 1970, p. 7.

[17] *Statesman* (New Delhi), 4 August 1977 and *Patriot* (New Delhi), 5 August 1977.

[18] Tanzania's decision to buy Indian machinery has gone a long way in rectifying India's adverse balance of trade, mainly because of its heavy reliance on supplies of cashew nuts. In 1973 Tanzania became the recipient of the first ever loan of 50 million rupees by India to the mainland of Africa and a trade agreement providing for the most-favoured nation treatment for each others exports and imports. The credit granted is not in soft loans, but this is more than offset by the lower capital costs involved.

[19] There are 600 Indian experts working in Tanzania, while in Zambia 3,5000 employed by the Government have gone a long way in lessening its dependence on White expatriates, many of whom were from South Africa and Rhodesia. The extent to which European hostility towards India exacerbated race relations in Africa should be a subject of special interest to scholars. There is moreover reason to believe that India's deep antipathy towards the colonial powers and

racist regimes resulted in its becoming a target of white antagonism and sinister attempts were made to prove that India had "imperialistic designs" in Africa which went beyond ideological support for African nationalist movements, and that Indians would fill the vacuum created by European withdrawal.

[20] *Statesman*, 4 August 1977 and *Patriot*, 5 August 1977.

[21] Ibid.

HOMI J.H. TALEYARKHAN

India and African Liberation Movements
and Economic Growth

THIRTY YEARS AGO, we came out of the throes of thraldom. We had to struggle hard and sacrifice a great deal before we could become independent. Gandhiji showed us the way by the invincibility of his faith in non-violence, the weapon with which he created the courage and forged the unity in the hearts of our people to withstand any blows in the quest of freedom, the most cherished ideal of humanity, in any part of the world, at any time of history.

Even in the midst of our own travails, we never forgot those of others. Gandhiji had seen the sufferings of Africans and of Indians in Africa for many years. He had suffered with them. Panditji's noble spirit had bled at what he had heard and read. The hearts of our leaders went out to all oppressed masses of humanity anywhere in the world, be it in Asia, Africa, Latin America, who were bent under the yoke of slavery and exploitation.

The plight of the great African continent immediately attracted their attention, from where Gandhiji himself had emerged, an eye witness and part of its sorrow and suffering, in South Africa, with its many countries and enormous

69

masses, all under the cruel heel of the colonialists and imperialists at the time, ruthlessly exploited as they were, its rich natural resources fattening the bellies of vested interests, has had a link of association and affinity with India which may be termed as ancient as its own glorious heritage, so contemptuously dismissed by the white foreigners as the Dark Continent.

But India knew better from historical experience. From the earliest times, Indian and African men of commerce and trade careered across the high seas doing business with each other. Scholars and learned men shared the exchange of culture. Even part of our flora and fauna can trace its origins to Africa.

India was among the foremost to come forward to share the aspirations of the African peoples in various countries of the continent where they were valiantly but for so long so futilely waging their heroic struggle for liberty and freedom from racial discrimination. Even before, it became free, the Indian National Congress under the leadership of Mahatma Gandhi and Pandit Jawaharalal Nehru had repeatedly expressed its deepest sympathy and its fullest moral support for their great cause which was so akin to ours in the patriotic fervour and dimensions. African freedom movements in various parts of its continent have as repeatedly expressed their heartfelt appreciation for India's outspoken expression and courage in their favour even in the midst of its herculean problems under foreign domination as it itself was then.

Bandung and Non-alignment

India wasted no time after becoming free to continue and renew and expand its support for the African cause through various international organizations, most notably through the United Nations, but earlier, also through the historic Bandung Conference and the five principles which it adopted largely as a result of the initiative of Jawaharlal Nehru. Bandung ultimately led to the formation of the great movement of Non-alignment in which along with President Gamal Abdul Nasser of Egypt and President Tito of Yugoslavia, Panditji was again one of the co-founders. The movement which held its first Conference in Belgrade, in 1960, five years after

Bandung, with only 25 members, held its latest conference in Colombo towards the end of 1976 with as many as nearly 90 members, showing the enormous growth of the popularity of the movement wtihin just a decade and a half.

Aimed as the movement was to keep all developing countries free from the influence of or pacts with super powers or any other big powers, both politically and economically as they can no longer be exploited, as a number of them still are inspite of becoming politically independent and by trying to create a climate of increased cooperation among its own members in order to encourage their growth according to their own lights, the non-aligned movement has been a boon to African countries. All those which have become free are already its members. The rest which are still struggling are deriving inspiration from it.

Opposition to Racialism

Non-aligned movement not only urges developing countries to be unfettered to any form of Western domination or superpower strings. But its ideal also is to stand for complete equality among men, irrespective of caste, colour, or creed. That is why right from its inception, even incorporation in the principles of the Bandung Conference, is the strong resolve to oppose racial discrimination in any form whatever, the one disease the poor black Africans have been so much subjected to, even to this day, in spite of the revolt of the rest of humanity in almost the rest of the world against this abhorrent practice.

It was India, which at a time when very few other countries of the world, had raised their voice against it, had been the first to break off diplomatic, and even economic, relations with South Africa. India has extended its fullest support to all African countries in their struggle for liberty, for race-wise equality and for economic opportunities. The African peoples had been totally kept in the dark about the potentialities for the development of their own personality in the political, economic and cultural fields.

Freedom for All

Right from the time of our own struggle, sacrifices and the

privations our people suffered, we never believed that independence was for our country alone. Even as we were waging our non-violent war for independence under Gandhiji, our thoughts were always also with those countries which were striving likewise, like those in Africa, and how much they were also suffering even as we were.

Panditji had said at the Asian Relations Conference way back in 1947: "The freedom we envisage is not to be confined to this nation or that or to a particular people, but must spread out over the whole human race. . . . It must be the freedom of the common man everywhere and full opportunities for him to develop."

At Bandung, Panditji had added: "It is upto Asia to help Africa to the best of her ability because we are sister continents. We are determined not to fail and in this new phase of Asia and Africa to make good. . . . I wish to speak ill of no one. . . . But we are no copies of Europeans or Americans or Russians. We are Asians and Africans. It would not be creditable for our dignity and new freedom if we were camp-followers of America or Russia or any other country of Europe."

Equality for All

Thus spoke Panditji way back in 1955. But India, even then, had made it clear that in its support for Africa, it was not only resolutions that would solve the problems facing both our continents. Only our practices and actions would bring success to our aims and ideals. And we believed that there was no friendship when nations were not equal and one had to obey and okay another's will and wish. In this connection, we had even invoked an edict of Ashoka who had said over two thousand years ago that we should respect the faith of others and that a person who extols his own faith and decries another injures his own faith. The dignity of faith and its tolerance beget the will to be free and to want others to enjoy the same freedom.

India always practised what it preached. Its leadership refused to be satisfied with merely being spectators as the screen began to rise on a vast theatre of events which was soon to engulf the world of colonialism which was till then enjoying the ill-gotten fruits of its unchallenged sway.

The Great Awakening

Encouraged by our support and of other freedom loving peoples of the world, extraordinary changes began to take place on the African continent. It began to wake up. The great awakening was on the threshold, within about a decade of the success of our great struggle in India.

Colonial ranks on the African Continent began to show cracks for the first time. In 1957, Ghana became free, followed a year later by Guinea. The colonial cracks became wider. The walls crumbled; the strongholds collapsed. Within one year, in 1960, as many as nineteen countries more became independent. It was like the unquenchable soaring flame or blaze of the light of freedom.

They were, Cameroons, Togo, Mali, Malagasy, British Somaliland and the Somali Republic (later to be known as Somalia), Congo (now Zaire), Dahomey (now Benin), Niger, Upper Volta, Ivory Coast, Chad, Central Africa Republic (now known as Central African Empire with President Bokassa styling himself as Emperor Bokassa), Congo (Brazzaville), Gabon, Senegal, Nigeria and Mauritania. Panditji was so thrilled by the advent of the year that he said that these countries which had remained outside the light of history had burst forth into the luminescene of liberty.

Several other countries followed in their freedom in the course of the next five years, that is, upto 1965. They included Algeria in the Maghreb in North Africa, while three other countries, viz. Libya in 1951, Morocco in 1953, and Tunisia in 1956, had become independent earlier. Yet the other countries that gained freedom were Botswana, Burundi, Gambia, Kenya, Lesotho, Malawi, Swaziland, Rwanda, Sierra Leone, Tanzania, Uganda and Zambia. The Sudan, the largest country in Africa, had become free in 1956; Mauritius in 1968, Guinea Bissau in 1973, Mozambique in 1975, and Angola in 1976.

Price of Freedom

These freedoms were not won without blood and sweat, toil and tears. Indeed a number of them were very bloody affairs and it had greatly distressed India to see some of them having to pass through such terrible bloodbaths, particularly in the Congo, created by the old colonial powers. Angola,

under the Portuguese, was indeed "the darkest chapter" of
Africa, and like the Congo, Angola, Mozambique and Guinea
Bissau had to wade through rivers of blood before reaching
their goal of liberty which years earlier Panditji had propheti-
cally declared they would attain. In Zimbabwe, Namibia and
South Africa, the struggle continues to this day. India has
been most deeply concerned about the racist policy pursued
by Southern Rhodesia. We have reiterated that national
independence must be territorially based and should include
racial and individual equality of citizens and must not give
any benefits to any racial group. Only then, we have rights
felt, the will of the majority can be established and made to
prevail through well accepted democratic processes.

So, there are now nearly 50 countries of Africa which have
achieved their political independence and have become
sovereign states after, as mentioned earlier, in many cases,
bitter bloody struggles, and in the case of some few still being
waged.

Beware of Neo-Colonialism

But there is another danger India has pointed out. The old
type of colonialism may be almost dead. But a number of
these newly free countries are tossing between two worlds, the
one dead, the other powerless to be born. They have their
own internal power struggles to overcome. Most of them
have done so. A number of them yet remain. They are all
fanned by the unrelenting efforts of neo-colonialism whose
forces try to destabilize well established Governments in
Africa, Asia and Latin America. India has repeatedly warned
we should be greatly on guard against such forces.

While our policy has always been to be friendly with all
those who wish to be friendly with us, without coming under
anyone's influence, we are in favour of developing closer
cooperation between Third World countries of which Africa
comprises such a big chunk, so that the Continent does not
fall again a victim to the exploiters.

Concrete Help

India had given concrete help in the shape of economic
requirements to several of these embattled zones during the

time of their struggle. Now, we have been providing them with a host of experts in various fields, technicians, and even skilled and semi-skilled labour. In a number of African countries, many Indians have been established for generations. They have helped the economy of these countries to flourish as the majority of them did not go there to exploit but to cooperate with the growth of the country.

What I have mainly in mind is the assistance we have given of late through our deputationists who have by their high qualifications, their experience, their skill, their ability to work hard and under difficult conditions, won for the majority of them the highest respect and esteem both among the local leadership and populace.

In addition to loaning our experts in the medical, engineering, educational, architectural, agricultural, industrial, oil, shipping, and water resources fields, we also encourage students from African countries to study in our universities. India provides special seats reserved for them in various faculties.

India is providing training facilities for a good number of Africans from various countries, including in the military field. These facilities are arranged mostly through the Indian Technical and Economic Cooperation (ITEC) programme, mainly meant for the poorer nations of Africa and Asia. The ITEC provides not only training facilities in India, but also for deputation of specialists abroad, assistance in feasibility studies and techno-economic surveys. In some African countries, it has also assisted in setting up development projects.

The African countries, which have benefitted by such assistance from India through ITEC in feasibility studies and techno-economic surveys, are Tanzania, Zanzibar, Senegal, Gabon, Zaire, Nigeria, Kenya, Sierra-Leone, Ghana and Zambia. ITEC aid is not necessary for oil-rich countries like Algeria, and Libya; though the economic collaboration with Libya is about the biggest in the Third World.

In addition to such economic cooperation, there has also been added cooperation in the cultural field. Nearly twenty African countries have sent over 250 scholars for study in India upto 1976.

High Level Exchange of Visits

This increasing cooperation in all these fields is due to our historical affinities, our innate sympathies with the aspirations of the African people and our equally innate desire to assist the development of their personality in all ways possible. It has been nonetheless due in recent years to the frequent exchange of visits of the highest level between India and the leaders of various African countries.

Our former Foreign Ministers have visited a number of African countries like Senegal, Sierra Leone, Guinea, Liberia, Nigeria and others. Our President himself paid state visits to a number of African countries, including Ethiopia, Tanzania, Zambia and others in recent years. Such visits invariably resulted in the build up of greater goodwill and, signing of economic agreements and issue of joint communiques. Such visits amply satisfied our African friends of our readiness to share our know-how, expertise and experience. More important still, they gave manifestation of our traditional interest in the larger African cause, namely, the final eradication of the remaining vestiges of racialism and colonialism.

These visits were not only from our side. But also from the African side. The President of Zaire in 1973, the Chairman of the Revolutionary Council of Zanzibar and First Vice-President of Tanzania, President of Senegal, President of Gabon, Prime Minister of Mauritius, a frequent visitor, who was also President of Organization for African Unity (OAU) in 1977, President of Zambia and of Tanzania, both of whom were awarded the Nehru Awards and a number of other African Heads of State and of Government were official visitors to our country.

Besides review of the general international situation, their visits resulted in signing of protocols of understanding, of cooperation in aviation and shipping, establishing common services centre and workshop in Tanzania; sending technical experts in small scale industries, fisheries, agriculture and irrigation to Zanzibar; and cooperation in railway projects and supply of locomotives and rolling stock, oil exploration, setting up joint commissions between India and the African countries concerned and a host of such and other types of cooperation.

We have not stopped short only at that. We have not

forgotten the humanitarian aspect as well. We have been giving aid and assistance in kind to drought and flood victims in Western Nigeria, cyclone victims in Mauritius, rehabilitation help to Zambia which was adversely affected by the sanctions imposed on Rhodesia. As far back as over a decade and a half ago, India sent thousands of woollen blankets and multi-vitamin tablets for Angolan refugees in the Congo.

Nor did India ever allow the struggles, which were still being waged over, lost from its sight. We sent aid, albeit token, to the MPLA in Angola, FRELIMO in Mozambique, PAIGC in Guinea Bissau, ZAPU and ANC(Z) in Zimbabwe and SWAPO in Namibia.

India was happy with the latest event when Djibouti, formerly the French territory of the Afars and Issas (TFAI) in the Horn of Africa became a free country, with a referendum having convinced the French that they were no longer wanted. Of course the severe fighting between Ethiopian and Somalian forces over the question of the independence of Eritrea in the Horn, greatly saddened India, as such quarrels lead to weakening of the scope of solidarity among the African peoples.

Economic Collaboration

Believing as we do that freedom is only the starting point, we have further extended our hand of help to the countries on the African continent in the shape of economic collaborations which are to the mutual benefit of both our country as well as theirs. We have been able to satisfy them about our capabilities and to win their confidence.

In the Maghreb, in Libya, we have therefore succeeded in securing some of the world's biggest contracts in consultancy and in construction for a five million ton capacity major steel plant in the former and a major Rs.1025 million worth power project in the latter; both won in the teeth of the severest competition from top companies of the most industrialized countries. In addition, also in Libya, India is constructing the world's most sophisticated airport in an arid area. We have also just been entrusted with a massive Rs.1000 million worth of housing and hospital construction programme in different parts of Libya, as well as a Rs. 720 million worth project for building an irrigation dam. India had already completed a turnkey project for a textile mill complex, another for transmission lines which are still being further extended contract after contract, now touching Rs.1000 million in value in aggregate, a consultancy for a mini steel plant, etc.

Again in the Maghreb country of Algeria, we are gradually gaining in weightage there also, albeit it is as yet nowhere on the scale as in Libya. The SAIL are just opening their offices there. A films delegation recently visited there. Also in the Maghreb countries, including other Arab countries, the IDPL have just become consulting engineers for pharmaceutical plants in 13 Arab countries by an Arab company for drugs industries and medical appliances.

Besides in North Africa, there are a number of other projects our companies both in the public and private sector have won in the rest of Africa, notably in Tanzania, Zambia, Nigeria, Ethiopia, Uganda, Zanzibar and elsewhere.

A very fine example of a consortium approach has been the formation of a consortium of nine leading textile manufacturers who have secured an award from Tanzania, for supply and erection of textile machinery and technical services on turnkey basis.

Besides this, India has extended its cooperation for supply and erection of transmission lines and electrification projects in Zambia; diesel, steel, locomotives, wagons and coaches, sugar plants for Tanzania; buses for Zaire, Libya and Uganda; and sugar plant for Kenya and Uganda. There is considerable scope for the spread of consultancy services also in Africa. So far, half-a-dozen African countries have availed themselves of the services of our top consultancy companies.

Other projects in Africa include a textile mill in Ethiopia, a jute mill in Uganda, management of a paper mill in Nigeria and also in the same country the construction of transmission lines and HV sub-stations, oil exploration agreements reached between our ONGC and the Government companies in Libya and Tanzania, establishment of a paper and pulp industry in Zanzibar, Tanzania, a comprehensive consultancy for feasibility of the new capital of Tanzania at Dodoma, and so on.

Trade and Joint Ventures

To Guinea, India is sending cassava (tapioca) seedlings. Our exports of both traditional as well as non-traditional items like engineering goods to African countries are on the increase. They prefer to buy from India because they know that India believes in cooperation and not in exploitation with the intention of assisting these new sovereign states in their development programmes. To at least thirty African countries, the exports of our engineering goods have increased from Rs.2653.42 lakhs in 1972-73 to as much as Rs.6553.87 lakhs by 1975-76, an increase of 248 per cent. These figures indicate the highest exports to Nigeria, followed by Tanzania, Egypt, Kenya, Libya, and Zambia.

India has gone beyond supplying the finished products that the African countries require for their development. We have offered them joint ventures in various fields. Government has already approved those in alluminum sheet rolling mill, a malt processing project, sugar and jute mills, radio assembly unit and rubber factory. Still more are on the way. It can be said with confidence that no developing country, while still in the process of its own developmental problems, has offered so much to its African brethren as India has done in a spirit which is symbolical of India's desire to meet the African urge for progress with the help of our own growing technical know-how and which would be to the mutual advantage of both India and the countries in Africa.

African Confidence in India

The African confidence in India stems from the fact that India has always been in the forefront of all motions, actions and movements pressing for decolonization of African countries. We have initiated and chaired UN Committees on Decolonization. India was in the front rank of the Afro-Asian group in the United Nations when during its fifteenth session, the resolution on decolonization was adopted by a massive vote of 89 for, with none against and 9 abstentions. Among the seven principles of the operative part of the resolution was included on our insistence that inadequacy of political, economic, social or educational preparedness should never serve as a pretext for delaying independence; all armed action

or repressive measures of all kinds directed against dependent
peoples shall forthwith cease, and immediate steps be taken in
trust and non-self governing territories to transfer all power to
the people of those territories without any conditions or reservations in accordance with their freely expressed will and
desire without any distinction as to race, creed or colour so
that they could enjoy complete independence and freedom.
Even though the forces of colonialism were now in full retreat,
we had the foresight to warn against the dangers of what we
described as "settler colonialism", that is colonialism under
new cloaks, namely, by the exercise of extreme economic and
other forms of pressures on the decolonized areas. Namibia
and Zimbabwe were two typical tragic cases in point.

Population and its Problems

India believes that, like her own masses of 600 million, for
nearly 400 million souls or about 10 per cent of the world's
population, who comprise the population of Africa's 50 countries, including Egypt, just the political independence achieved,
though the first and principal step, is not enough. Freedom
does not connote merely that, but also economic welfare,
social justice and a renaissance of the spirit. And we recognize
that as at home, so also in Africa, a number of revolutions are
afoot—political, economic, social, intellectual, technological—
all concurrently, but unfortunately not untrammelled by confrontation and crisis, from which we have been singularly free.

Population densities in Africa which vary greatly, reflect
vividly the economic contrasts of the continent, ranging from
about 500,000 in Gambia to about 80 million in Nigeria. Only
three countries have a population of over 20 million, over 30 of
them still have a population of less then 10 million and about
25 countries, even less than 5 million. Africa's population is
expected to reach about 800 million by the end of the century.
Its annual growth rate way back in the fifties was second only
to that of Latin America. It is constantly rising owing to continuing fall in mortality rates also.

Although Africa has been known to be the least urbanized
among the major regions of the world, today Africa's urban
rate of growth is among the highest in the world, touching

over 6 per cent, almost the double of the world's average. The demographic profile also appears to reveal that about 50 per cent of its total population may be just about 18 years of age, which is in striking contrast to that of the developed world. Much depends therefore on the shoulders of the younger and youthful generation of Africa to take up the responsibilities of building up the countries on their continent.

India's cooperation in its development may always be depended upon, politically, economically and culturally. India also helps to strengthen the exports from African countries which still mostly depend upon a little more than a score of commodities for earning three quarters of its volume and value in exports earnings.

They include crude in Algeria, Libya and Nigeria in particular,—all leading members of the OPEC, which also includes yet a fourth African member, Gabon; copper in Zaire and Zambia; coffee and cotton in Tanzania; diamonds in Sierra Leone; iron ore in Mauritania; cotton in Sudan; phosphates in Morocco; and now more of it with its part acquisition (Polisario calls it, seizing for squeezing, the phosphate resources) of Western Sahara recently quit by Spain; iron ore in Mauritania; sugar in Mauritius; coffee in Ethiopia, timber and manganese in Gabon; in addition to crude, cocoa in Ghana, allumina and bauxite in Guinea, coffee and tea in Kenya and some petroleum products too, phosphates in Togo, crude and phosphates from Tunisia, coffee and cotton in Uganda, live animals in Upper Volta and some more items here and there. Plenty is still to be developed with the vast natural resources at its disposal.

Safeguarding Freedom

This is where the Afro-Asian Group in which India is taking a leading part is trying to find ways and means of boosting up the African economy so that great continent with which we have so many affinities may also head rapidly towards the goal of economic emancipation by concentration on constructive activity with the cooperation of all but free from the exploitation of any and from the internal bickerings and quarrels which often mark the birthpangs of political freedom and which colonialists, fresh in their grief at having lost their loot of generations endeavour their best to sustain among the African peoples to prevent them from building the edifice of stability to achieve their righteous aspirations within the comity of nations of the world.

SATYAVATI S. JHAVERI

The Indian Ocean and its African Littorals

Introduction

The post-war years have witnessed a shift in the geopolitical concern from land to sea. Some of the factors responsible for this are: the end of an era of political empires, the growing self-assertion of the erstwhile subjugated people, and the possibilities of exploitation of the immense wealth buried in the sea-bed. But the most important single factor is a revolution in weapon technology.

Rapid changes in technology have contributed to the increasing importance of the oceanic regions. Floating anchorages for refuelling, repairing and replenishment, fleet trains providing supplies to the ships on high seas, aircraft carriers and nuclear powered missiles submarines have increased the opportunities for strategic maneouvres on the seas.

The military strategists now view ocean space as an area subserving the goals of strategic deterrence, of maintaining naval presence to assert one's own use of the sea and denying that use to the others, of maintenance of access to vital resources and of providing adequate surveillance capabilities. Attempts to achieve these objectives involve different naval powers in competition. The US had emerged as the strongest naval power after the Second World War and Soviet Russia too is

now the major naval power. These superpowers are now engaged in competitive build up to gain superiority in different ocean
regions of the world. It is possible for modern technology to
support deployments in distant waters, but the expenditures
involved are enormous and so the contenders seek basing facilities on islands and in coastal regions.[1] This tends to colour
and influence the developments in the countries concerned. The
ocean space and the littorals thus get so closely inter-related
that they almost form one entity.

This brings naval powers in regional politics leading to inter-
actions between land and sea powers. Where newly independent states in the coastal areas are involved, this interaction becomes more complex. These states are engaged in establishing
a national identity, achieving economic growth and moving towards political stability. In this process they come in conflict
with other regional countries and seek, where desirable, their
cooperation in economic development. In the newly awakened
continent of Africa such conflict and cooperation situations have
reached a continental level. These conflicts develop through the
attempts to redefine national boundaries, conflicting ideological
persuasions and political upheavals. It is in this complex situation
that the coastal states have to determine their adaptive policies.
This environment becomes more oppressive because of the entry of the non-regional powers and their rivalries. The outside
powers on their part judge the situation in terms of the adaptive
policies of the countries in which they are interested and the
capacity of the countries to sustain these policies. In the light
of these overall perceptions the maritime powers attempt to establish acceptable working relationships with the coastal states.
These include the right to retain bases with full soverignty or to
establish limited sovereignty through treaties.[2] Where this is
not possible treaties are concluded to have an access to base
facilities on commercial terms.[3] These non-regional powers
also seek to take advantage of the dependent position of the
coastal countries to create client states or client classes to further their (outside powers') strategic interests. These calcula-
tions and actions are continuously liable to change in the modern age of super technology, growing consciousness and
changing perceptions of rights and interests in the new states,
the shift of economic balance towards resource-rich countries

and the changing relationships between the maritime powers.

The Indian Ocean

The Indian Ocean, the smallest of the three big oceans of world, has a long tradition of peaceful commerce and navigation. It has emerged, however, in recent years as an area of importance for the policy makers of the maritime powers. The reasons given by the Western commentators for this development are two: 1) the withdrawal of Britain from the near monopolistic control of the Ocean, and 2) the entry of the Soviet navy on the scene. Due to inadequacy of resources and revaluation of its global interests Britain announced its decision to withdraw from the military commitments East of Suez. This withdrawal, however, was not complete. Even before the announcement Britain had carried out a survey of the Ocean jointly with the United States and Australia in 1964 to locate some islands with sparse population to establish their military presence.[4] As a result of this survey the British Indian Ocean Territory (BIOT) was constituted. It also entered into a treaty with the United States in 1966 to develop a communication base at Diego Garcia.[5]

It is also true that Soviet Russia has shown its flag in the Indian Ocean since 1968. In the Western section, in 1969, a Soviet squadron comprising of a missile cruiser, a rocket-launching destroyer and a tanker visited Port Louis, the capital of Mauritius. Four naval ships called at the port of Mogadishu in Somalia and an anti-submarine ship and a landing ship paid a goodwill visit to Sudan.[6]

But it must be remembered that the US presence in the Indian Ocean antedates the Soviet presence. In 1922 the United States signed Washington treaties[3] whereby it acquired the status of an equal partner with Britain in the control of the Indian Ocean. In the 1950's the US navy carried out joint naval exercises with the South African navy. The Anglo-American Agreement of 1966 also shows the US interests in the Ocean. It is, however, true that since the Soviet visits to the Indian Ocean ports, the competition in naval build up activities by the maritime powers have considerably increased. It is generally conceded that both the superpowers have vital interests in this area to defend. In the Western Indian Ocean the US interests are defined as the protection of shipping lanes to bring oil from West Asia to the Western countries including the USA and pressurising the oil producing countries in Western Asia to fall in line with the wishes of the United States in matters of oil production and prices.[8] The strategic interests of the USA in this region are: 1) It provides areas of deployment for Polaris missiles and Poseidon missiles which could be targetted on the nuclear facilities in Western China and large parts of Soviet Russia[9]; 2) Naval presence in the region might be used to lure the Soviet submarines in larger numbers to this region thus stretching its fleet in the Mediterranean.[10] The strategic objectives to be served might include unrestricted use of the Ocean ports and the airports; and to obtain a position of strength that can be of help at a time of decision in the area; or for exerting military pressures upon other major powers.[11]

The Soviet Union has the same objectives to serve by its presence as those of the United States. Further it has to contain the Chinese incursions against it in the area. Like the United States it has also to protect its trade passing through these waters, and safeguard its interests in the Red Sea. This Sea is important for Russia to maintain contacts between its Mediterranean fleets and its squadron in the Indian Ocean and to ensure that the USA does not use the Sea as a launching area for targetting long range missiles on its territory.[12]

The pursuit of these objectives form an important factor that interacts with the economic, political and social pursuits of the littoral states. In this process the littoral states are caught up in a dilemma of reconciliation between the desire to safeguard national sovereignty and integrity on the one hand and the compulsions of the dependent position on the other.

The major determinants of this pattern of interaction seem to be: 1) The degree of dissonance between the objectives of the littorals and the resources available to them; 2) The strategic importance attached by the maritime powers to the particular region in which they are interested; 3) The quality of leadership accepted by the states; and 4) The degree of acceptability by the international policy makers of the goals to be pursued by the littoral states.

This complex pattern sometimes leads to a conflict situation. Glaring example of this is the Horn. There is a triangular conflict in which each contestant is helped by the outside power. The non-regional powers involved are the USA, the USSR, and the Arabs. Each one of these powers has interests in the Sea and the Ocean waters washing the coastline of the Horn.

The Horn

The two corners of the Indian Ocean, one in the North Western Region located south of the Red Sea and the other in the South Western Region located near Southern Africa are important for the policy makers of the maritime powers. The interests of both the US and Soviet Russia in these regions as mentioned above are well-defined and generally accepted. This explains the anxiety for maintaining a naval balance here in terms of naval units and facilities.

In the North Western Region of the Ocean the USSR was strongly placed to control the southern end of the Red Sea. It had a barrack ship and tenders in Somalia.[13] Till recently it had for its use the base facility at Berbera in the Somali Republic. This port has a runway of 13,000 to 14,000 feet capable of accomodating any aircraft. There is an airfield, and storage, refuelling and maintainance facilities for ships and aircraft including surface-to-surface missiles and a floating dry dockyard.[14] The Soviet Union had also built a long-range communication facilities in Somalia which helped the Russian headquarters in Moscow to control the movements of Soviet warships throughout the Indian Ocean area.[15] There were reports that the Soviet Union had built an important naval radio station and ammunition depot at Socotra at the mouth of the Red Sea[16]; an old British built airstrip there had been refurbished. The Soviet Union had also anchorages in the Somali waters to serve the Soviet navy.[17]

The United States had an access to the Red Sea port of Massawa and Assab in Eritrea. They are connected with Ethiopia's capital and interior by highway truck transport. Massawa is described as "the most extensive and sheltered harbour on the African Coast of the Red Sea."[18] Till now the USA depended for its naval presence on the three destroyers with the US Middle East Command at Bahrein, with bunkering facilities available at Djibouti which is now independent. Djibouti has a

good airport, a harbour and a radio station. France had a sizeable fleet stationed here.[19] These facilities are available to
France even after Djibouti's independence. It has reserved the
right to station its troops there and has promised to assist the
Republic if requested in case of external danger.[20]

These naval facilities have to be supported through their
presence or influence in the lands surrounding the Ocean region. One of these areas is the Horn and at least the intensity
of the current conflicts there can be attributed to this rivalry
for securing a dependable political base.

The Horn is situated at the mouth of the Red Sea. As the
strategic importance of the Indian Ocean grows for the global
powers the strategic importance of the Red Sea and consequently of the Horn grows. With the changing manoeuvres of the
superpowers in the Indian Ocean the superpower alliances
with regional powers on the Horn also change.

At the moment the Horn is passing through a trying time of
internal tensions aggravated by big power presence. The area
of the Horn embraces in its fold people belonging to diverse
ethnic race, professing different religions and committed to different legacies in the form of territorial boundaries left by
imperial colonial power. All these have combined to encourage
forces of instability in the Horn.

At the end of the Second World War the whole of the territory came under British occupation. In 1952 a federation of
Ethiopia was created which later became a Union, with
Eritrea shedding its autonomous structure. This led to the
formation of a powerful liberation movement in Eritrea which
now wants to sever all connections with Ethiopia and become
an independent country. Eritreans are aided by some Arab
countries also. In this conflict besides religious and ethnic
factors, cultural differences are involved. The Eritreans have
imbibed western culture, have taken western education and
administrative training. They are traders and as such have
come into contact with the outside world. In all these respects
they differ from the Ethiopians.[21]

In 1960 the British and the Italian Somaliland got independence and the Republic of Somalia came into being. But the
Somali nationalism has remained unsatisfied. It lays claim on
the Ogaden province of Ethiopia, the former Northern

Frontier District of Kenya and Djibouti on the ground that all these areas have preponderantly Somali population.[22] But Ethiopia with historical memories of its empires extending upto the Red Sea has no intention to secede any of its territories which according to it are based on legal and historical rights. In June 1977 the Territory of Afars and Issas (Former French Somaliland) got independence and became the Republic of Djibouti.[23] This territory is of great economic significance for Ethiopia. Addis Ababa is joined with Djibouti by the Franco-European Railway and through this railway and the port of Djibouti is handled 60% of Ethiopia's external trade.[24] If Eritrea is separated from Ethiopia, Djibouti will be the only port left for Ethiopian trade with the lands across the sea. The Republic of Djibouti is plagued with tribal dissensions. At the moment Somali faction is in control. If it falls to Somali pressures Ethiopian economic difficulties will increase. Djibouti is a sensitive area where ethnic and ideological rivalries are strong. This provides a sufficient attraction for the big powers to meddle in the affairs of this territory.

The entry of the big powers in the region was heralded by the USA giving substantial help to its traditional ally, Emperor Haile Selassie of Ethiopia, in the fifties. Without the US help it would have been difficult for the Emperor to maintain his hold on Eritrea as a pacified province, though his personal charm and capacity too played a great part in this. The United States acquired permission to establish a communication centre at Asmara[25] which has now been abandoned. When Somalia became independent in 1960 it also received military and economic aid from the United States. But in 1969 there was a military coup and a government professing allegiance to socialism came into power. Thus started the big power rivalry in the region. Since then Soviet Russia became a major military supplier to Somalia and helped in building a military base at Berbera. The situation was further complicated when in 1977 there was a Left-inclined coup in Ethiopia. Soviet Russia was in an unenviable position of the supplier of arms to all the three contestants in the area—the Ethiopians, the Somalis and the Eritreans. With Djibouti becoming an independent nation it is likely to come under Somali pressures bringing in France as a possible contestant. The United States

is trying to woo Somalia by offering military help and a recent
visit of Lt. Col. Mengistu Haile Mariam, the Ethiopian Chief
to Soviet Russia has helped him in getting added military help
from Russia. The US has also given economic aid to Addis
Ababa. Attempts were set on foot by Castro perhaps with the
blessings of Moscow to bring the armed hostilities to an end
and to induce the three contending areas to form a federation.[26] These attempts have failed and Somalia has cut off
relations in November 1977 both with Castro and with Soviet
Russia. The facilities given to the latter in the two parts of
Somalia have been withdrawn.

   The Arab League in its recent meeting has turned down
Somali's demand for help, has admitted the Republic of
Djibouti as a full member of the League and has called upon
all outside powers to get out of the scene so that the people
of the area could settle their own differences.[27] Thus a number
of actors are busy in the Horn—each trying to get better over
others. This rivalry does not necessarily result in conflicting
policies pursued at a given time. As in other areas of interest
to the strategists here too the powers follow parellel policies.
In a recent article Mr. Dev Murarka from Moscow writes,
"The two super-powers do appear to have reached accommodation on the situation in the Horn of Africa, thus lessening
the danger of confrontation between them, directly or
indirectly, and increasing pressure for local accommodation.
By the very nature of things, neither Somalia nor Ethiopia
can wage a long war by themselves, without outside support."
But here too this is not the consideration of the big powers.
Their interests coincide in not allowing the Red Sea to be an
Arab Sea. To quote Dev Murarka again: "Now, in recent
times Soviet commentators have been repeatedly asserting that
the Red Sea should not become an Arab lake. On the contrary,
it should remain an international waterway." About the US
he has to say: "Perhaps it was a delayed awareness of the
security risks for Israel through Arab domination of the Red
Sea which was also an important factor in Washington's change
of mind. After all, the Arab countries have as a whole proved
to be very unstable partners of the big powers. The Soviet
Union has already discovered this at a great cost. The United

States too, would find it out in due course. These considerations, combined with some acceptable undertakings from Moscow may thus account for apparent moderation of Washington's escalating support for Somalia."[28]

The recent step of Somalia withdrawing the military facilities available at its ports to the Soviet Union, however, suggest that the intensity of rivalry between the two powers has by no means abated. The littoral states are still condemned to be the pawns moved to suit the aims of the big powers.

The great power rivalry and the internal dissensions in the Horn have resulted in an unsettled political situation, huge military expenditures and destruction besides shedding of blood. Unless a speedy solution to the conflict situation is found these developments in the Horn will have its implications for the strategic moves in the North Western corner of the Ocean.

South Africa and Tanzania

In the South Western region of the Ocean the Cape takes the place of the Red Sea as a main area of attention for the policy makers. The points that dominate the region are Simonstown in South Africa, Dar es Salaam in Tanzania and a chain of ports in Mozambique, including Beira and Maputo. The interaction between the maritime powers and the coastal states in this region is far more complex. It is an amalgam of the need for control of the ocean region, the racial conflict in Southern Africa, the attraction of natural wealth and cheap labour available there, some success reaped by South Africa in confusing African nationalism with communist threat to western civilisation and internal conflicts in some of the maritime powers between pro and anti-apartheid groups.

The headquarters of the South African Navy are located at Simonstown.[29] The facilities available there are substantial. They are: a truly modern communication headquarters, a naval dockyard and submarine servicing facilities, including nuclear power submarines. This base has got facilities to monitor ship movements over a large part of the Western Indian Ocean.[30] At other places in South Africa facilities have been established such as Commander Naval Operations at Silvermine, naval repair and maintanance facilities at Salisbury Island and a naval training centre at Saldahna Bay.[31] South Africa has fully modern air bases and supporting aircraft facilities all through the coastal areas. A tracking station at Silvermine monitors air naval traffic all the way to the Bay of Bengal—passing the information along to war-rooms in Washington.[32]

The importance of the ports of Beira and Maputo lies in their offering access to the Indian Ocean for Rhodesia and South Africa. But in March 1976 Mozambique has severed all rail and road connections with Rhodesia. South Africa still enjoys the facilities at Maputo for its exports. Besides these ports Mozambique has a chain of other ports conveniently placed for accomodating warships and fishing fleets on deep bays. It is alleged that Soviet Russia is using these facilities and further that the Soviet Union is establishing an air and naval support base on Bazaruto island within striking range of the industrial base around Johannesburg and the West oil route through the Mozambique channels.[33] Soviet Russia has floating buoys in the area to serve as anchorage and rendez-vous points for the naval bases.

The importance of Dar es Salaam lies in providing an opening to the sea to the landlocked countries like Zambia and the Central African countries. China is reported to have helped Tanzania to build a naval base near Dar es Salaam and has delivered a few Shanghai-type gun boats besides training Tanzanian marines.[34] The developments on the coastal lands adjoining this region have to be considered in the context of this complex network.

South Africa occupies a strategic position in the Indian Ocean commanding the sea routes that carry oil and minerals from across the ocean to the US and other Western countries. Besides this it has mineral wealth, including gold, diamonds and other strategic materials needed by the United States and Western Europe.[35] It has a large black labour force without any trade union protection which can be exploited to the full.[36] South Africa is the most industrialised nation on the Continent. Here the Western based-multi-nationals in colla-boration with the white African nationals are in control of production of minerals and expansion of manufacturing units. The Western powers have thus to safeguard their strategic and economic interests in this area.

South African white minority government is aware of this position and exploits it to the full, posing difficult problems for the policy makers of the Western nations. Their embarrasment arises from the insistence of the government of the Republic to cling to the apartheid policies to keep majority black population in perpetual political and economic subordination. It has launched a powerful propaganda claiming to be the only bulwark of the western influence on the African Continent. It has argued that if the white minority government lost its exclusive political and economic dominance the road will be clear for a communist attack on South Africa and through it on Europe and America thus destroying western civilisation. This propaganda has only a limited impact on the West. It tried to enter NATO and failing this proposed a South Atlantic Alliance including South Africa. Here too it has drawn a blank so far. In order to appease the opponents of apartheid, South Africa proposed a system of Separate Development. But this had proved unworkable. It attempted to acquire a dominant position in Southern Africa to exploit the markets in the black states by a proposal to form a common market or commonwealth of the states. It sought to open dialogue with African states on an arrangement in which South Africa would stick to apartheid but work in close cooperation with the countries ruled by the blacks. All these attempts have failed.

South Africa therefore decided to build its own military strength[37] to defend its position from external and internal attacks. In this the NATO powers, especially the US, France and Britain have helped South Africa inspite of the UN resolutions advocating an imposition of political isolation and economic and military restrictions on South Africa till apartheid ended there. The result is that the military hardware of South Africa includes French submarines and Mirage fighters with supporting equipment and British-built frigates and other ships and weapons.[38] From the United States it got enriched uranium. With this help South Africa has succeeded in acquiring technological nuclear energy capacity at weapons level and is reported to be making preparations for entering the nuclear club with a bang.[39]

The black States on the border of South Africa especially the frontline states, Zambia, Tanzania, Mozambique, Botswana and Angola are committed to the liberation of the blacks from the white minority regime in Southern Africa. South Africa has charged them with helping the black insurgents in the Republic. Some of these states, however, are economically dependent on South Africa and are not in a position to completely break economic ties with the Republic. This position is generally realised and a distiction is made between unavoidable economic connections and voluntary economic relations with South Africa.

Tanzania is a leading state actively helping the black liberation movement. Dr. Julius Nyerere, the President of Tanzania ever since its independence, is a practising Catholic. He is a strong believer in human equality and democratic processes. He vehemently opposes racialism, tribalism and exploitation of man by man. In order to fight tribalism and inculcate loyalty to the nation he uses the TANU party as an instrument of national identity. This is the only party permitted in the country. But this acœrding to the President does not affect his commitment to democracy which for him consists in discussion, equality and freedom. Through his experiment in Ujaama living he seeks to inculcate spirit of national consciousness and economic self-reliance.[40] Nyerere's incorruptibility and ascetic living combined with the commitment to the goal of economic self-sufficiency have helped Tanzania to remain steadfast to its principles and to maintain independence from big power interference.

Tanzania is an important member of the group of non-aligned countries. It has consistently followed the policy of disengagement from the past colonial links and has avoided moving too close to the Eastern bloc. In pursuance of this policy it has accepted in past both financial and military help from the western countries and at least for the first decade of its existence its main trade links were with the affluent states, especially with the Atlantic community. For five years from 1964 to 1969 Canada gave military assistance to Tanzania but declined to provide a military academy or jet fighters. Tanzania's open support to guerrillas in Portugal African territory embarrased Canada and so both the sides amicably decided to terminate this kind of assistance. Similarly, when Tanzania and Zambia decided to construct the Tan Zam railway they first approached the World

Bank, the US and the UK but they refused to oblige. Undeterred President Nyerere accepted help from China.[41] This shows his determination to follow his goal even if in the process he has to forego aid. True to his non-aligned policy he is prepared to take help from any quarter provided it did not interfere with the achievement of his goals.[42]

President Nyerere is a strong supporter of Pan Africanism and inspite of strong democratic convictions he has maintained relations with states under military dictatorship. He is a leading member of the OAU and belongs to the section which believes in escalation of the struggle for black liberation. The headquarters of the OAU Liberation Committee are located in Tanzania. Through its ports Russian and Chinese military aid could be funnelled to liberation movements of Angola, Zambabwe, Namibia, and South Africa. No wonder South Africa considers Tanzania a centre of subversion.

In the context of this confrontation between South Africa and the black states, contesting non-regional powers determine their South African policy. The United States has to balance the pulls exerted at home by the Pentagon, the multi-national giants and the believers in White Man's Burden on one hand and the anti-apartheid movement there on the other. Till recently American policy makers viewed the black liberation movements as insurrectionery and the US role as one of supporting the political stability and economic prosperity of South Africa. Its basic premise is expressed thus : "The Whites are here to stay and the only way that constructive change can come about is through them. There is no hope for the blacks to gain the political rights they seek through violence, which will only lead to chaos and increased opportunities for the communists. We can, by selective relaxation of our stance toward the white regimes, encourage some modification of their current racial and colonial policies and through more substantial economic assistance to the black states. . . help to draw the two groups together and exert some influence on both for peaceful change."[43] This policy of gradualness has so far not been modified. But the Carter administration has brought some pressure on South Africa to change race laws. This has been publicly resented by the South African Prime Minister Vorster who has characterised this pressure as subverting his government.[44] The Carter administration is following a dual policy of arms embargo and economic cooperation. This is clear from the recent US vote in the UN Council.[45] It can be easily explained in terms of the huge US investments in South Africa, its flourishing trade with it and substantial credits given by the American banks to South Africa.[46]

Britain is interested in South Africa because of the available military facilities, market for its goods and protection of interests of its nationals. The French interests seem to be purely commercial. At a recent UN sponsored conference in Lagos, the black states of Africa have virtually told the Western powers to choose between the apartheid regime and the rest of Africa.

China is interested in getting entry into Africa with a view to serve its global objectives. It has attempted this through military assistance and economic aid on easy terms and trade under liberalised conditions. Since Chou En-lai's visit to Africa in 1964 China's interest in this continent has increased. It was in 1965 that China offered help in building a railway from Dar es Salaam to Zambia. It relieves Zambia from its dependence on South Africa and Rhodesia thus administering a severe blow to South Africa in its attempts to create a common market for the whole of Southern Africa including Zambia. It also helps Tanzania to have an access to the mineral belt of Zambia and serve military objective of transportation of manpower, supplies and heavy weapons to the strategic banks of Zambesi. Both these are Nyerere's goals and he sees nothing wrong in accepting China's help to achieve them. China has also helped Tanzania in training its military personnel, in supplying surface-to-air missiles, in building a naval base and supplying a few Shanghai types of boats. The termination of the military help from Canada had left Tanzania with no option but to accept Chinese help. Thus China-Tanzania relations mutually helped each other in achieving their objectives. Of late, however, China's role in Tanzania is matched and surpassed by help from Soviet Russia, other Western powers, and multinational agencies. Tanzania has established itself as a truly non-aligned nation.

Soviet Russia has found an entry into this region through Angola and Mozambique. The MPLA victory in Angola was due to the involvement of Russian arms and Cuban personnel.[47]

Inspite of the knowledge of this involvement the US Congress refused help for the US intervention on a big scale perhaps because of the isolationist reaction at home, the result of the "shell-shock of Vietnam." Russians are reported to be training the blacks for guerrilla warfare and with its policy stance of championing the cause of black liberation it hopes to secure a foothold in South Africa if and when a majority rule is established there.

Conclusion

In this essay an attempt is made to view two regions of the Indian Ocean and their littoral states in Africa as a single entity. This is a case study of how the littoral states get interlinked with the political and strategic importance of the Indian Ocean caught up in interpower rivalries. Since the beginning of this decade the Indian Ocean has become a site of major power competition which has progressively intensified behind the facade of wait-and-see policy which these powers claim to follow. The main theme of this eassy is that this competition has overflowed onto the littoral states of the area considered here and the same moves are discernible in the developments in these states too. If this reading is correct it would mean that if for some reasons the competition in the Ocean further intensifies there will be a corresponding intensification in the littoral states. In a reverse situation the tempo of the competition on the land will decrease. It is in the light of this perception that the moves of the littoral states for the declaration of Indian Ocean as a zone of peace and proposals for the demilitarisation and denuclearisation of the Indian Ocean should be viewed.

These moves were provoked by the decision of the United States to establish its presence on Diego Garcia. At first it was envisaged as a communication base. But soon it was upgraded into a military base. Defending this President Ford said, "we must have this operating base so that we can co-ordinate our activities with our friends and allies in making certain no other nation seeks through military force to dominate the Indian Ocean or the lands that surround it."[48] Such considerations have prompted the United States to turn this small coral island into a lynchpin of Southern Hemisphere strategy. Diego Garcia is thus to be at the centre, linking bases from the Pacific to South Africa. Some observers believe that this may be a fore-runner to a three ocean navy and multi-billion dollar commit-ment.[49] The island could be thus a potential storm-centre affecting the Indian Ocean and its littorals.

United States has already sunk millions of dollars to develop Diego Garcia as a full-fledged naval operating base. It has a good harbour which is dredged to create a turning basin capable of accomodating submarines and aircraft carriers. Its lagoon is deepened to handle a dozen ships. The naval communication station has been built capable of maintaining communication with Polaris submarnies. It was reported that there was an expansion programme designed to accomodate, Polaris and Poseidon nuclear submarines and surface ships—in fact a major American naval squadron which can operate more or less continuously in the Indian Ocean. Diego Garcia will be in a position to send naval units to any region of the Indian Ocean in forty-eight hours.[50] There are also air base facilities on the island. Its 12,000 feet runway can be used by almost any aircraft in the world. Long-range anti-submarine aircraft are based on the island. The airstrip is used by P-3 reconnaissance long-range bombers and U-2 spy aircraft.[51] Construction, repairs and supply facilities are also available.

Diego Garcia will now be the principal centre of operation in the Indian Ocean, since the United States has abandoned Asmara communication installations and Bahrein as a base for the American Middle East Force. Under the concept according to which the Indian Ocean and its littoral states are viewed as a single entity this would mean that Diego Garcia will be a commanding centre to oversee the developments in the Ocean and in the littoral states. No other competing power has similar facilities under its exclusive control. If any one of them try to build a comparable centre of strength for itself there will be a conflict in the area which might involve nuclear weapons. This evolving situation with its changing correlation of forces and major power relationships in the Indian Ocean and in the littoral states thus would prove an integrated area of concern for students of international politics.

REFERENCES

[1] Ferenc A. Vali, *Politics of the Indian Ocean Region, The Balance of Power* (New York, 1976), p. 58.

[2] Ibid., p. 57.

[3] Barry M. Blechman, *The Control of Naval Armaments, Prospects and Possibilities*, (Washington, D.C., 1975), p. 96.

[4] *The Times* (London), 17 May 1966.

[5] Devendra Kaushik, *The Indian Ocean Towards a Peace Zone* (New Delhi, 1972), pp. 17-18. See also, the text of the terms of United States/United Kingdom exchange of notes of December 1966 published in April 1967, Command 3231.

[6] Kaushik, n. 5, pp. 35-36.

[7] Alvin J. Cottrell and R.M. Burrell, eds; *The Indian Ocean: Its Political, Economic, and Military Importance* (New York, 1973), p. 12.

[8] Blechman n. 3, p. 68.

[9] Cottrell and Burrell, n. 7, p. 67.

[10] Gen. Harbaksh Singh, "U.S. Strategy in the Indian Ocean," in T.T. Poulose, ed., *Indian Ocean Rivalry* (New Delhi, 1974), p. 6.

[11] Cottrell and Burrell, n. 7, p. 68.

[12] Vali, n. 1, pp. 180-83.

[13] Blechman, n. 3, p. 96.

[14] Institute for Defence Studies and Analyses, *News Review on South Asia and Indian Ocean* (New Delhi, May 1976), pp. 407-8.

[15] *Times of India*, 10 April 1973.

[16] *The Times* (London), 15 September 1970.

[17] All this has now changed but rivalry still persists.

[18] Herrick and Anita Warren, "The U.S. Role in the Eritrean Conflict", *Africa Today*, vol. 23, no. 2, April-June 1976, p. 51.

[19] *Hindustan Times*, 27 February 1976. *News Review on South Asia and Indian Ocean*, April 1975, p. 379.

[20] *Keesings Contemporary Archives*, 12 August 1977, p. 28499.

[21] For the details see, Herrick and Anita Warren, n. 18, pp. 39-49.

[22] For the review of the Somali claims see, David D. Laitin, "Somali Territorial Claims in International Perspective", *Africa Today*, vol. 23, no. 2, April-June 1976, pp. 29-38.

[23] For the background history of independence for the Afars and Issas see, Said Yusuf Abdi, "Independence for the Afars and Issas: Complex Background; Uncertain Future" in *Africa Today*, vol. 24, no. 1, January-March 1977, pp. 61-67.

[24] *Africa Research Bulletin*, vol. 14, no. 6, 31 July 1977, p.4325.

[25] Vali, n. 1, p. 132. Herrick and Anita Warren, n. 18, p. 45.

[26] *Africa Confidential*, vol. 18, no. 10, 13 May 1977, p. 1. *Africa Research Bulletin*, vol. 14, no. 4, 15 May 1977, p. 4396.

[27] *The Times* (London), 6 September 1977.

[28] Dev Murarka, "Moscow's Gamble in the Horn of Africa", *Commerce*, vol. 135, no. 3461, 1 October 1977, p. 608.

[29] Michael T. Schieber, "Apartheid under Pressure: South Africa's Military Strength in a Changing Political Context", *Africa Today*, vol. 23, no. 1, January-March 1976, p. 41.

[30] Patrick Wall, ed., *The Indian Ocean and the Threat to The West, Four Studies in Global Strategy* (Stacey International, 1975), p. 26.

[31] *Keesings Contemporary Archives*, 5-11 May 1975, p. 27105.

[32] *News Review on South Asia and Indian Ocean*, December 1975, p. 1233.

[33] *Africa Research Bulletin*, vol. 13, no. 10, 15 November 1976.

[34] Hendrik J.A. Reitsma, "South Africa and The Red Dragon: A Study in Perception", *Africa Today*, vol. 24, no. 1, January-March 1977, p. 49.

[35] James Barber, *South Africa's Foreign Policy 1945-1970* (London, 1973), p. 66.

[36] Frederick A. Johnstone, "White Prosperity and White Supremacy in South Africa Today", *African Affairs*, vol. 69, no. 275, April 1970, p. 132.

[37] For the details of the defence developments in South Africa, see Schieber, n. 29, pp. 27-45.

[38] Anthony Haringan, "Security Interests in the Persian Gulf and Western Indian Ocean" in Wall, n. 30, p. 26.

[39] See *Africa Confidential*, vol. 18, no. 14, 8 July 1977, pp. 5-7. Ronald E. Walters, "Apartheid and the Atom: The United States and South Africa's Military Potential", *Africa Today*, vol. 23, no. 3, July-September 1976, pp. 25-35.

[40] Herbert T. Neve, "The Political Life of Julius K. Nyerere in Religious Perspective", *Africa Today*, vol. 23, no. 4, October-December 1976, pp. 29-45.

[41] Reitsma, n. 34, pp. 55-56. On his return from London President Nyerere said, "I don't care whether I get communist or Western money. I want this railway link and I am not going to be stopped". *Guardian*, 3 July 1965.

[42] See Nyerere's speech at state banquet for the visiting Soviet President Podgorny on 24 March 1977.

[43] Neil O. Leighton, "A Prospective on Fundamental Change in Southern Africa Lusaka—Before & Beyond", *Africa Today*, vol. 23, no. 3, July-September 1976, p. 17.

[44] *International Herald Tribune*, 8 August 1977.
For Nyerere's reaction to the US policy towards apartheid and Southern Africa, see, Julius K. Nyerere, "America and Southern Africa", *Foreign Affairs*, July 1977, pp. 671-84.

[45] As for the arms embargo the position regarding enriched uranium is not clear in view of the 1957 treaty, snbsequently modified and extended between the US and South Africa on this subject. Walters, n. 39, p. 29.

[46] The lending of US financial institutions by March 1977 totalled $800 million. The lending by American banks and their overseas subsidiaaries had surpassed $ 2 billion. The US investment in the Republic

more than trebled during the decade 1966-1976 from $490 million to more than $1.6 billion. The profits of the US firms during a typical year 1970 was 16.3 per cent on direct US investment in South Africa, compared with an overall world rate of 11 per cent. In some years the rate was higher than even 20 per cent. Twelve major corporations account for three quarters of US investments in South Africa. South Africa imports annually $1.3 billion of American goods and exports $841 million worth of its products, thus showing a substantial surplus for the United States as against frequent American deficits in its international balance of payments. *Africa Confidential*, vol. 18, no. 5, 4 March 1977, pp 1-2.

[47] See Edward A. Hawley, "The People's Republic of Angola Joins the OAU", *Africa Today*, vol. 23, no 1, January-March 1976, pp. 5-11.

[48] *News Review on South Asia and Indian Ocean*, April 1976, p. 310.

[49] Robert Manning, "Big Power Rivalry in Indian Ocean, Why the U.S. Sought a 'Soviet Base' Threat", *African Development*, September 1976, p. 310.

[50] *The New York Times Weekly Review*, 2 June 1974.

[51] *Washington Star*, 27 December 1975; Poulose, n. 10, pp. 269-17.

JAYANTI K. PATEL

Party System and Political Development: A Comparative Perspective of Africa and India

A STUDY IN convergence and divergence of two political systems belonging to the third world, is essayed in the following pages. Both African and Indian politics present fruitful areas of comparison and contrast. In terms of historical context, process of transition along traditional-modern continium, problems of nation-building and economic growth and building a modern political system in a society undergoing fast pace of mass politicization, both India and African countries in general share large common area of experience. However, the response of their society, e.g. role of elites in a changing society to such phenomenon like participation, legitimacy and integration, differ in a substantive manner. African and Indian politics thus provide a fruitful area for a comparative study. As it will be seen, the framework of such a study could be built up around party system and political development in these two developing areas.

Rising out of indigenous background, how did various political party systems acquire special characters? What was the impact of different situations prevailing in various countries on the course of development? How did they respond to the problems of political development? And what possible

102

course may it take? These are pertinent issues. It would be fruitful to examine them analytically, rather than going into the details of each party or nation, and construct a casual matrix of the element, context and its impact, on the system under comparative study.

1. THE PARTY : DEFINITION AND PREREQUISITES

The dawn of party system is traced to a period which was marked by the eclipse of absolute monarchy and feudal oligarchy.

Classical theorists of democracy advocated the cause of popular participation; the days of hereditary rulers were over; representative system was in the offing. Many nations started entering the club of representative systems of government. With the new entrants, new types of party systems also came into existence with a variety in structure, role and functions of the party system. Totalitarian ideologies went further and advocated an alternative to the classical democratic pattern of competitive party systems by a one-class party systems.

With the end of the Empire System, many more nations faced the problem of founding a new order. Many had the experience of the representative government and they tried to model their system on the western legacy. However, their problems, the method of resolving such problems, orientation of the masses and cultural systems differed. They tried to reform, correct or substantially change the classical western pattern advertently or inadvertently. With the increase in variety of party systems, we were required to redefine, re-evaluate and correct our concept of party in general. A new understanding in the functioning of the party system as well contributed to the evolution of the concept of party system.

It is true that, if by the word "party" we intend to denote an institution which aims to win and exercise political power; we find its predecessors in ancient repiblics. But before 1850, no country in the world (except the United States) knew political parties in the modern sense of the word.[1]

Definition and Climate

The present-day party is adequately defined by the following

characteristics ennunciated by LaPalombara and Weiner.[2]
(1) Continuity in organization—an organization whose expected
life span is not dependent on the life span of current leaders;
(2) manifest and presumably permanent organization at the
local level, with regularised communications and other relationships between local and national units; (3) self-conscious
determination of leaders at both national and local levels to
capture and to hold decision-making power; and (4) a concern
on the part of the organization for seeking followers at the
polls or in some manner striving for popular support.

It is observed that the political party emerges when the activities of a political system reach a certain degree of complexity
or when the notion of political power comes to include the
idea that the masses should participate or be controlled. In
short, the political party materializes when the tasks of recruiting political leadership and making public policy could no
longer be entrusted to a small coterie of men unconcerned
with public sentiments. The emergence of a political party
clearly implies that the masses must be taken into account by
the poiltical elite either out of commitment to an ideological
nation, that masses have the right to participate in the determination of public policy, or the selection of leadership, or
out of the realization that even a rigidly dictatorial elite must
find the organizational means of assuring stable conformance
and control of the people. Hence both in democratic and
totalitarian systems, party is a must to organize public opinion, provide channels of communication, politicize the masses,
articulate and aggregate the interests of its followers, and
recruit political leadership.

One important factor which decides the nature and behaviour of political parties is related to the conditions of its
emergence. Western European parties largely came into exist-
tence when the parliamentary framework was already existing and some form of representation was in practice. Some
legislators came together due to several reasons. They formed
clubs and groups which later on, with the expansion of suffrage and need for winning the electorate were forced to
assume the nature and shape of a mass party. Thus a political
system was already accepted, the rules of the game and of
operating the system were not only known but accepted and

respected. Further an ideological climate was created which provided the motive force behind the working of the democratic competitive system. Also Western Europe had reached a stage of modernization which created and provided an infrastructure for a viable parliamentary democracy.

Prerequisites

Thus for the origin of a *real* political party, basic democratic institutions, ideology and a certain standard of modernization are prerequisites. That means: (1) a change in attitude of people towards authority and a belief that they have the right to influence the exercise of power; (2) an aspiring elite which seek to win public support so as to win or maintain power; (3) socio-economic changes creating specialized professional classes; (4) increase in flow of information; (5) expansion of the internal market, technology and transport network leading to spatial and social mobility; (6) a certain level of communication (as in India, and Congress was created after rail, post and press were reasonably well established; (7) growth of education and urbanization; (8) need to resist the increase in the power of the state or channel them into beneficial activities; (9) existence of voluntary organizations; (10) sufficient secularization which at least creates faith in the people that they are capable of affecting the world in ways which are favourable to their interests and sentiments, these are some of the major indicators. Thus, over and above the historical crisis and ideological impetus for the organisation of parties, it seems clear that parties will not in fact materialize unless a measure of modernization has already occurred.

We find that, in Africa, only the need for freedom and to organize mass support to achieve it prompted the leaders to organise a party. Otherwise a parliamentary super-structure was suspended from above and no infrastructure supported it; democractic ideology did not go further than the primitive tradition of the tribal system wherein representation, limited authority and collective responsibility were juxtaposed with tribal loyalty, respect towards the old and those who wielded authority. The modern concept of 'His Majesty's Loyal Opposition' was non-existent, the economy was simple and mainly based on subsistence economy, communication and education were very low, transport was a problem, the press was in the hands of the party leaders and mobility was very limited. Hence, what came into existence was not a real political party but an instrument which utilized the masses to press the demands of a very small number of articulated elites who were seeking to dislodge the foreign rule.

In India, on the other hand, most of the above prerequisites were answered, which allowed the growth of a healthy party structure with a reasonable infrastructure, to back and sustain it. However, we cannot simply dismiss African case on the ground that real political parties, as we define them, do not exist there. No doubt we must accept that these conditions limit and circumscribe the role of African political parties but, as instruments of popular support and mass mobilization, they act and function as parties. However, we should keep in mind these limitations before evaluating the role of political parties in political development in Africa. Naturally, their course and progress is different from many other modern nations due to these limitations. But, even with these limitations certain African nations, instead of reverting back to oligarchial, authoritarian or military systems, are trying hard to work out fairly popular governments and go to the people for sanctions. This is an encouraging indicator in favour of democratic development.

Suppression of Parties

Further, it should be noted that as no real political parties have emerged in Africa, it is easier for authoritarian rulers to terminate their activity, outlaw them or repress them. However, where there is a party, functioning even in name, an opportunity may develop for party politics at a certain point in a nation's history; while, where they are totally suppressed, the rulers have created conditions of great instability. When there are no adequate conditions for emergence of a real party system to look for the conditions for a competitive party system would seem futile. But competitive parties arise due to a historical situation like the previous existence of competitive groups, serious conflict within the existing party or parties, war, revolution, depression, policy paralysis or emergence of a new, externally-created ideological party. Thus they may be created due to pressure in the legislature, in the party or in the society; but they require to be incorporated in some degree, into the prevailing system and at the same time ensuring adequate socialization. This is again related to the manner in which salient historical crises are handled; the unresolved crisis of legitimacy or integration may initiate an extreme position which may support abolition of all parties. Similarly, externally-created mass parties, committed to greater distributive demands, find it convenient to consolidate the policy in favour of non-competitive systems. This is relevant in the African context in the sense of how the present political leadership is resolving these crises and what type of impact it may have on the future of party politics in Africa.

II. THE EMERGENCE OF PARTY

External Origin

Naturally the circumstances in which a particular party is born, the political culture and system of the society in which it is operating, the ideology and leadership as well as the support structure of the party and the functions it is expected to perform are relevant for evaluating the role of a political party. In the United States, Britain and many Western democracies party emerged from the house of representatives. Its origin was 'intra-parliamentary' and they developed with the extension of suffrage. No doubt "intra-parliamentary' emergence does not preclude the existence of external forces and factors completely. However, internally-created political party emerges gradually from the activities of the legislators themselves while externally-created party invariably involves some challenge to the ruling group and a demand for representation. In this sense political parties in Africa and India have emerged externally; the electoral and parliamentary struggle has been only one of the elements in the general activity of the party, one of the means, among others, that they used to realize their political ends. However, in India, though the praty emerged externally it functioned as a small elitist group and then developed into a mass movement well after a period of four decades; this allowed the elite group to stabilize and provide an anchor like an internally-created party. Also in

India the number of elites was adequately large to provide a collective-competitive leadership in the hierarchy of the party which had roots and local support too. Because of these differences African leaders emphasised ends rather than means or conventions, traditions and constitutionality, which brings them nearer to communistic analysis and strategy regarding parliamentary democratic system. Their concern is not with the game or rules of the game but with the aim, the objective.

Party as Movement

The second factor which consolidated this attitude is also related to the origin of the party in these nations. All these countries, except a few, came under colonial rule. Hence, the first purpose being independence and independence movement the prime concern, most of the parties grew as nationalist movements[3] and, in many cases hostile to whatever parliamentary framework that had been created by colonial governments.

Thus, African parties had some of the characteristics of Duverger's externally-created parties like: "less subject to influence from the legislative contingents of the parties and generally less willing to ascribe major importance to or be differential towards parliament, more aggressive in making demands on the system; they have not developed a vested interest in existing political institutions. They tended to be more centralized, ideologically oriented and disciplined." However, the movement part, being not ideologically comprehensive and spelled in detail (ideology being nationalism and not socialism, liberalism, etc.). Ideology could degenerate into populistic slogans and discipline could be replaced by sychophancy, in turn both supporting opportunism.

Accelerated History

This situation is further complicated by the rapid progress which is symbolically expressed by Hodgkin as 'Telescoping of Phases' or 'Accelerated History.' Most of the African countries have to face a revolutionary transformation instead of a stable dialectical evolutionary process. When freedom struggle is linked with the total overhauling of the society, the outcoming party is largely revolutionary in nature. New political system is a creation of the leader, the leader acquires charisma, a halo of superman—infallible and indispensable. The rank and file simply acquiesce in his leadership. While in a policy where the evolutionary process is stabilized, past leaders are not accepted as omniscient and infallible. There is a healthy acceptance of past, appreciating it, yet the knowledge about the mistakes committed or wrong decisions taken in the past imparts confidence in the present leadership regarding its capacity to rule alongwith humility and knowledge that they may be also mistaken,which is a healthy atmosphere for the flowering of an open society.

As developing nations are facing all the crises described by Pye in a small span of time, having all the revolutions on their hand at the same time it is difficult to maintain stability and balance in the system while maintaining the tempo of progress and development unless a self-conscious leadership and mature public life is available. From this point India was fortunate on many counts. We had a fairly developed socio-economic structure, a fairly protracted struggle of independence which allowed the process of colonial dialectics to get in full swing, gradual evolution into self-government which trained the bureaucracy, political leadership, army and laid the foundations of democratic structures like press, elections, party machinery, etc. However, in Africa, except South Africa, where power was transferred to white settlers, and countries like Ghana, Tunisia or Tanzania in some limited way, no proper foundations were laid on which the democractic polity might develop.

Stage in Development

Further, in India we had a developed society with national consciousness, a commercial economy and good communication system. While in Africa there was a tribal society, where relationship was based on kinship and in many tribes chiefly power was strong, simultaneously, compelling national consciousness and loyalty was arising. In some areas popular agrarian movements were developing with a nascent proletariat whose protest against the established social order was taking militant forms. In these societies a twentieth century phenomenon of universal suffrage with mass electorate and political leadership, whose power depends upon the use of

modern technique of propaganda, was ushered in, which created a complex context.[4] While India was free from most of this
context.

Other elements of the context are related to the socio-political heritage of African society. African society was largely a
primitive tribal society with subsistence economy. Hence, except
in some communities where centralized chiefdoms, monarchy
or State system evolved, the modernizing syndrome was lacking. Hence, a proper infrastucture was not available for the
functioning of the democratic polity. Further the prevailng
societal system influenced the nature of political parties. Also,
the colonial dialectics had not entered the third moment as
restratification of the society was at the lowest level. The
traditional structure, which was not completely replaced, could
influence the course of political development. Also a variety
of traditional structures and stages of evolution in society were
functioning at the same time all over Africa. They provided
a variety in the type structure and growth of parties in different
countries.

Feudalism and Reform Movements

Where societies were highly stratified and a broadly feudal
type of structure survived with little modifications, political
parties have tended at the outset to reproduce the traditional
pattern of authority. The Northern Peoples Congress Party in
Nigeria is a typical example of such party. Where party is
used simply to further the interests of this class while the
Democratic Party of Guinea led by Sekou Toure (which
derives part of its effectiveness from its connections with
Somory Toure's empire—actually the descendents of Somory's
warriors took the initiative in forming this party under the
influence of egalitarian ideology)[5] has influenced, reinterpret-
ed and reformed the earlier traditional system. Yet, broadly,
on the basis of the use of pre-colonial system for organization
of party and for obtaining a massive support in election, this
type of party successfully utilizes the traditional relationships
between ruling and subject castes, nobility and serfs; they are
led by pre-colonial aristrocracy. Hence, they may be labelled
as 'chief's parties', provided we remember that the role of the
chief varied from tribe to tribe.

Another type of party is the result of reformation or 'tribal renaissance'. However, unlike India, most of these movements were circumscribed to only some particular tribe like Yoruba, Ibo, Ashanti, Eve, Bakongo, Kikuyu. These tribes had their own traditional unity. This trend was described by Balandier as regroupment. It was an effort to reassert and reconstruct the tribal unity and create an identity against the disintegrating effects of colonial rule. In some cases these parties have tried to overcome earlier ethnic limitations.[6] In those instances, though the party secures the support of the pre-colonial aristocracy, it is generally led by the new elites. There are also well-known territorial parties and religious or messianic movements, outgrowing into political parties like Umma Party (connected with the legacy of Mehadi) and Nationalist Union Party (connected with the Khatmiyya sect) in Sudan.

In India even though there was pre-colonial monarchy and aristocracy, feudal structures, caste structures and religious sects, the traditional elites were either discredited by their collaboration with the colonial regime, or, no one king or aristocracy could claim national allegiance. The colonial dialectics[7] had progressed to the extent that the second movement of traditional revivalism and rfist movement of a ssimiliation could be synthesised into a positive identity—a radical outlook under the leadership of the new elites capable of getting mass support without any appeal to traditional authority. Even the Muslim League was dominated by new elites; though its appeal was based on religious identity it had a strong appeal as a party, championing the cause of a minority. However, the main ethos in which Indian political parties developed was nationalistic, integrative and modernistic. While African leadership faces the problem of national integration, it has yet to overcome the difficulties of tribal factionalism, having its roots in traditional tribal loyalties, and evolve a new national consciousness.

Colonial Rule

In Africa and India parties are essentially products of a colonial situation. Hence, naturally, the colonial system of government, economy and culture has affected its nature. First, we have to take into consideration the type of direct and indirect system of administration. In most of the British African colonies, there was an indirect system of administration. In India there was a direct system for British India and indirect for Princely States. In French, Portuguese, Belgian and German colonies the direct system of administration was tried.

The indirect system consolidated the position of traditional elites; during constitutional development they were given a major role, in the initial stage, in the legislative bodies. New elites had to make way aginst the traditional elites and supersede their authority. No doubt, where the hereditary ruler was attacked by the colonial ruler popular sentiment gathered around his traditional symbol of unity and authority in defiance of colonial rule: as in Morocco around Sultan Sadi Muhammad ben Yusuf and in Uganda around Kabaka of Buganda, through Istiqlal and Uganda National Congress respectively. Sometimes a recognition of common regional interests have produced more or less stable alliances between old and new elites, for example Action-Group in Yoruba region; Parti Democratique Unifie in Volta; even CPP in Ghana—a centralizing party—sought alliance with traditional chiefs of Brong against Ashanti. Even in India after independence, during elections, the Congress joined hands with certain princes. But the influence of princes was limited, new elites were dominant and capable of holding power without their support. While in direct systems new elites had an open field. However, in the direct system, new elites had to fight against colonial rule and old elites, whether supporters of the colonial rule or not, and evolve a national identity which might have had mooring in traditions yet could not be equated with the traditional system; while in indirect systems new elites struggle against the colonial rule and traditional elites could be easily combined while welcoming benefits of modernizing western rule. While the new elites of direct system had to make a distinction between modernization and colonial rule new elites' emergence and auithority was tied with colonial rule and yet in a classical dialectcal situation they had to negate the thesis, which could be done only by providing a new identity based on synthesis.

Conflict Situation

Further, in direct or indirect systems, the political elites had to occupy the political space created by the colonial rule. For this purpose they were supposed to think in terms of the whole nation. Also the national goal was one, namely freedom. Hence, it was natural that a national party or front should be organised. This urge for one front increased in proportion to the colonial repression. Algeria is a significant illustration in this direction. Though the elites were divided, primordial loyalties and mobilization pattern was divisive, colonial dialectics had not reached the stage of synthesis; FLN was created to fight the liberation struggle. However, the instances of Angola, Mozambique and Rhodesia (Zimbabwe) suggest that over and above the factor of repression, some other factors are required to cement unity. Further, the unity may be simply an expedient facade and not the reality (result of integration) which is evident from factions and warring groups within these fronts. It is seen that on the whole a non-violent conflict situation, charismatic leadership and single goal-consciousness foster 'Parti Unique' or front or congress.

Influences

(a) Ethnic Minorities

Sometimes multiplication of parties may be stimulated by colonial administration encouraging communal, religious or chiefly interest. Also, as the dawn of freedom draws nearer, minorities may get restless and clamour for special safeguards and autonomy. Ghana, Sudan, Nigeria, Kenya, etc. provide ample examples of ethnic groups advancing their claims. Communication, growth of press, emergence of middle class, development of representative institutions and franchise and an external stimuli also influence the emergence of political parties.

(b) Communication

In Africa communication was rudimentary which hindered the development of party organization and integration. The press' influence was circumscribed by the low level of education. However, the role of *West African Herald* in Ghana, Azikiwe's *West African Pilot* (formerly *African Morning Post* from Accra) Bourguiba's *L'Actions Tunisience* has played an important role in the cultivation of nationalism and

providing leadership. In Africa as independence drew nearer
the press provided a platform for relatively leftist ideas and
leaders, e.g. Senghor's *Condition Humaine*, Nkrumah's *Accra
Evening News*, etc.

(c) New Elites

Similarly, the African social structure was changing.
Chiefly powers or tribal authority was on the wane. In the
new age, leadership could be achieved by those people who
could organize their following from wider areas and had
capacity to realize desired political change in modern order as
against traditional order. Where this type of new middle class
elite was mobilized in fair size, as in general, Guinea, Ivory
Coast, Ghana, Togo, Southern Nigeria, Southern Cameroons,
Morocco, Algeria and Tunisia, some of the most effective
parties emerged. Albeit only economic development need not
be considered as the factor responsible for the emergence of a
middle class, otherwise it will not explain the retarded
development of political parties in Belgian Congo where an
economically dynamic society existed but opportunities for
higher education and essential civil liberties were lacking,
while in a static society like Somalia, where these opportunities were available, parties developed.

The composition and effectiveness of this African middle
class is illustrated by the membership of the House of
Assembly of Gold Coast (Ghana) one of the most advanced
societies. After the 1954 elections, included among its 104
members were 30 school teachers, 18 clerks, commercial
workers, accountants, retired civil servants, etc.; 18 members of
liberal professions (lawyers, academicians, clergy, journalists
etc.); 18 businessmen (i.e. merchants, contractors, traders, etc.);
7 professional politicians, 4 farmers and 3 Chiefs. Among
these 14 were university educated, 28 were certified teachers,
16 had obtained 'Senior Cambridge' or its equivalent, 10 had
some form of post primary education and 31 had received
only primary education.[8] While in India, in the first Lok Sabha
there were (percentage wise) 9.9 per cent teachers, 12 per cent
businessmen, 50.9 per cent from liberal professions (35.6 per
cent lawyers, 4.9 per cent doctors, 10.4 per cent journalists
and writers), 3.7 per cent from civil or military service. 22.4

per cent farmers and 1.1 per cent princes[9] were represented. This shows that the African elite class was not highly educated and in many African countries, on the eve of independence, the number of highly educated individuals could be counted on one's fingertips.

(d) Constitutional Development

Also, the progress towards independence was rapid and the constitutional evolution not stage by stage. African members were nominated on the legislative council since 1798 in Seirra Leone, 1862 in Nigeria, 1888 in Ghana, 1926 in Tanganyika, 1944 in Kenya and Uganda, 1948 in Rhodesia, and 1950 in Malawi. But they were mainly traditional Chiefs. Elective representation and African new elites came into the picture in most of the British colonies during or after Second World War. Similar was the case with French colonies even with their civilizing mission. In Portuguese and Belgian colonies popular representation was not tried until independence. Hence, trained leadership to handle the political system was not available in most of the African countries. Similarly the pace of constitutional reform during the last decade was so rapid that supporting political institutions lagged far behind and could not percolate down to the local level, which resulted in an infrastructure insufficient to sustain the democratic polity or party system.

Also in some countries like, Algeria, Angola, Mozambique and, for some period, in Kenya, political parties were prohibited. Hence, natural development of political parties parallel to constitutional development was not evident in these countries; instead we find a strong militant one-party system, which waged an extra-constitutional struggle and, thereby, they lost the chance of developing a participatory democratic party system. That is why Coleman observes that, "The really decisive factor—the precipitant—in the formation of political parties has been constitutional reform providing for (1) the devolution by the imperial government of a sufficiently *meaningful* and *attractive* measure of power to induce or to provoke nationalist leaders to convert their movement into political parties and (2) the introduction or refinement of institutions and procedures, such as electoral system, which would make it technically possible for parties to seek power constitutionally.[10] The Istiqlal in Morocco and the Neo-Dastour in Tunisia are, however, two exceptions to this rule. These two mass parties developed under semi-clandestine conditions. But south of Sahara this correlation has remained. Where such reforms were introduced, parties have developed an effective machine to contest elections and appeal to the electorate, proportionate to frequency of elections. Also , where parties were in alliance with traditional elites, like the AG in Nigeria, it worked through chiefs; where tribal reform societies or unions were the basis—like the NCNC in eastern Nigeria they utilized tribal unions, while National Unionist in Sudan relied on religious order, Ghana's CPP, Guinea's PDG, Union Sudanese relied primarily on their own tried militants. However, all mass parties even with an essential modern outlook are opportunistic in getting electoral support and would exploit local or traditional authority where it seems expedient. Also it has led to politicization of the masses and party leadership has had to evolve a programme which would interest the people and solve their problems. While facing this challenge, the new leadership had, alongwith the struggle for independence, to visualize and substantiate the new order. Thus, with the struggle for freedom, a concept of future and promise for things to come were offered. In many cases these promises were too idealistic, nearly populistic propaganda. It was not possible to substantiate them with performance, which enhanced the 'revolution of rising expectations', where a revolutionary gap is created between expectations and achievements. This results in a crisis for the new elites.[11] In countries adjacent to the south belt of Sahara from Mauritania to Chad (except Senegal, Ivory Coast, Ghana or Southern Nigeria) the initial effect of elections was to encourage the formation of small groups aiming at little else than filling the relatively lucrative new offices.[12]

External Stimuli

As to external stimuli (WesternE uropean, Soviet Communist, Asian) during and after the Second World War due to increase in communication and need for a national goal and specific programme, it induced various African leaders to borrow from the experiences of the external world. However the nationalistic stimuli came in the form of Pan-African sentiment and movement initiated by American Negros. Its Zionistic origins and narcism nurtured the first generation African leaders in Western Africa. Its Pan-African element did not allow the leadership to degenerate into narrow chauvanism. But its sentimental overtone, providing a nexus against whites and their domination hindered the pragamatic programme formulation in parties led by these leaders. CPP of Ghana, led by Nkrumah illustrates this point (with certain reservations); while, on the eastern coast, the impact of a mature Indian freedom movement through Indians residing in these areas, paved the way for an evolutionary freedom struggle coincident with party-building around specific issues. Harry Thuku, Nyerere and others[13] substantiate this point. In course of time, liberal and socialist thought influenced the formation of various parties; the leftist parties from imperial country encouraged and supported these parties and trained some leaders. Some of these leaders were connected with trade unions. These leftist leaders also influenced the young students who had gone to Europe to study and, thus, provided a broader perspective to African nationalist movements. French socialists helped to establish Gueye's Senegales Socialist Party which later developed into SFIO. Similarly popular front government in France and liberal coalition in Belgium affected the course of political development in their colonies respectively.

From the above settings we find that though colonial rule was a common factor, there were vital differences like type of foreign rule, stage of development in colonial dialectical process, socio-economic situation, concept and development of nationalism, growth of parliamentary institutions, elite structure and leadership, which have not only affected the course of party development but also its structure and working in later period.

Process of Origin

(a) Party a Mystique

Similarly, apart from these conditions in which political parties emerged in Africa, when we consider the process of the origin of African political parties, we find that they have an extra-parliamentary origin and many of them started as clubs or elite associations as in India. However, in India we find a continuous evolution within the National Congress as well as outside it, especially after independence (except the Communist Party and the Radical Democratic Party, who were established earlier but whose influence was negligible), while in Africa, we have yet to come across such an evolution. Also the origin of African parties was shrouded in legends, largely transmitted orally, which has given a mystical aura to the parties and its functions and functionaries, and the party members have more significance for the historical events of its establishments, e.g. for the RDA (Rassembliment Democratique African), the Bomako conference of October 1946, for the NCNC, Lagos meeting of 26 August 1944 called by Nigerian Union of Students, and for TANU Saba Saba the seventh day of the seventh (July) month.

(b) *Voluntary Associations*

No doubt, as in India, the origin of political parties in Africa was dependent on the voluntary organizations with specialized functions, whose leadership was in the hands of the new elites. However in Africa these associations mostly took up the role of political parties or created a specialized political instrument to deal with the political problems. Also the type and nature of these organisations differed from party to party and nation to nation. There were associations of servicemen (which were responsible for rightist parties) students, sports associations, tribal unions and improvement associations or religious bodies and movements.

While, in Guinea, young trade union leaders under Sekuo Toure transformed PDG-RDA into an effective mass party, in Ivory Coast 'Farmers Union' provided the nucleus for the PDCI-RDA; in Ghana Committee on Youth Organisation grew into Nkrumah's CPP; in Nigeria Azikiwe's Nigerian Reconstruction Group helped to prepare the ground for the NCNC; study circles and literary groups provided a similar impetus for RDA in some French African countries. It seems that the first type of organisations (servicemen, etc.) has led to the origin of conservative or rightist parties while the second type of organisations have contributed to the evolution of liberal or socialist (leftist) parties and they were more militant.

(c) Mass Party

However the organisation of a national political party required that this type of association should be transformed and reorganized to create a mass party which could unite or consolidate various segments into an integrated national party. These associations were primarily non-political. They were training grounds for the new elites. Their basis of loyalty was wider but not necessarily national. They enabled nationalist leaders to mobilize and manipulate important segments of the population and provided the basic blocks of popular support out of which the mass parties were constructed; Senegal's BDS (1948) is clear illustration of this point. Leaders like Senghor and Mamadou Dia drew into the party's direct and indirect hierachy leaders of ethnic and regional associations, while in towns the party was built round sections drawn from socially inferior or strangers (immigrants or outsiders).

In some cases, already existing associations were simply converted into political parties by attaching to them a party label and party functions without any significant changes, at least initially, in structure, leadership or ideology. For example, the Housa Jamiyyar Mutanen Arewa founded in December 1948 was hastily converted into Northern Peoples Congress during the general elections of 1951. Similarly, in the Yorubaland the Egbe founded in 1948 and the Action Group of 1959 had strong resemblance in regards to leadership basis of support and political philosophy in its initial phase. Same was the case with Association of the Bakongo People for the unification, conservation and propagation of the Kikongo language founded in 1949, which was politicized in 1956 into the ABAKO. In some cases the political party may form a working alliance with an association, e.g. the Ashiqqa party and its successor the NUP of Sudan allied with the Khatmiyya order and the cells of the order took over the functions of the party. This type of party has the advantage of a mobilized body of popular support and helped them in elections but it is liable to be sectarian, tribalist or fedual and hamper national integration. They were, fortunately, uninfluential in India, except in the case of the Muslim League. But, also in India, in many pockets and areas, feudal and caste factors did play a significant role after independence. However, during the freedom movement and afterwards also, the feudal system and caste structure were systematically attacked and undermined and they were denounced publicly.

(d) Basis of Loyalty

In India, during the independence movement, the Muslim League, Communist Party, Radical Democratic Party and some small parties did arise but the mainstream was the Congress, which continued to maintain the characteristics, of a united nationalist movement.[14] In Africa also, the elites in national movement in many countries could not embrace the entire population and, even where there was a national party, it largely relied on local groups or sectarian alliances, or one major tribe was the core group. Hence the nationalist movement which consolidated Indians and, thereby, cleared the ground for ideological, or interest-oriented parties to develop and compete for power, did not come to fruitition in Africa and the work of national integration is still the problem which African elites have to face.

Further, even now, most of the parties which are organized to compete for power in African countries fall back on tribal, feudal or sectarian alliances to mobilize support, though they may have ideological undertones and overtones. Hence, these parties are considered to be having a disintegrating effect and are frowned at; new ruling elites thereby get a convenient argument to curb them.

(e) Other Parties

In some African countries parties did arise during the course of national movement, due to a split in the movement. Sometimes 'dynamic' or 'progressive' leaders revolted against the leadership of the movement and established new parties. A typical instance of this type of split is Nkrumah's CPP from the UGCC and BDS in Senegal from the SFIO while in Sudan moderates broke away with General Graduate's Congress in 1945, to form Umma Party which opposed the union with

Egypt. Sometimes small parties or groups have also come out from the main party. In such cases a section of the leadership and the ranks go over to the new party but mass support is not easily transferred. However on the eve of independence they were either wiped out or were in a commanding position, with mass support to wipe out the parent body (e.g. in Ghana, CPP came to power).

(f) Regroupment

In short, on the eve of independence all nationalist movements faced the challenge of getting mass support, winning elections and procuring funds which compelled them to transfer themselves into a party and define their ideology in terms of a programme. But in Africa and India interest groups were not organized, nation building was the main programme, ideological controversy was not sharp and leaders tried to represent the whole nation as they did during the nationalist movement. People had a mystical regard for the leaders and identified the movement with the party and the leaders. This obstructed the growth of competitive party politics. However, in India other parties were allowed to function and long training in parliamentary democracy, conscious leadership and existence of numerous respected leaders, tradition of free press, large educated class and a country so vast and full of diversity, created an image of a democratic society. While in Africa the leadership group was very small, generally, one charismatic leader overshadowed the whole party. To meet this challenge, in some African countries opposition parties sometimes regrouped, e.g. in 1951 the formation of Ghana Congress Party, though it failed to transform itself into a mass party; but later on in Ghana the United Party was formed by former sectarian and tribal parties to circumvent the legislation barring ethnic or regional parties, But these types of unions usually do not prove stable, e.g. conservative Middle Zone League and radical Middle Belt People's Party in Nigeria united to form the United Middle Belt Congress to push forward the demand for a separate region; but they soon broke into two factions as it happened in India in many provinces during the agitation for linguistic reorganization. In some cases major party also absorbs such factions to consolidate its strength, e.g. the National Unionist Party in Sudan was the result of fusion between Ashiqq and other minor parties. In Senegal the BDS also expanded, reconstituted and renamed itself, after successive infusion of new elements, becoming the Bloc Populaire Senegalaise in 1958. This regroupment is not simply the swallowing of minor parties by the major party. The major party is also changed qualitatively. In India too the Congress absorbed the leftist groups and under their impact assumed a more leftist posture. In regroupment where three or four parties of almost similar strength unite, they continue to exist as separate blocs within the party for some period as is evident in the Janata Party. However, in course of time, issue-oriented leadership may weld them together or sometimes they may again tend to break away and form new parties.

(g) *Alien Influence*

In Africa, in some cases, colonial administration has also supported moderate parties (e.g. the NYP in northern Ghana). Also missonaries helped to form pressure groups, for example in Kenya the Anglican Mission helped in the formation of the Kavirondo Taxpayer's Welfare Association in 1923, and the Scottish Mission helped in the formation of the Progressive Kikuyu Party; while in Uganda Roman Catholics were responsible for the origin of the Democratic Party. Also alien settlers sometimes influenced the formation of Black parties as Indians in Kenya supporting Harry Thuku. Whites, through the United Tanganyika Party, tried to create a multiracial party. Besides some parties were formed as subsidiaries to metropolitan parties. Leftist parties were formed under the influence of western ideologies, e.g. SFIO in Senegal was formed in collaboration with the French socialists while RDA had connections with the French communists, though not in organic relationship. It is significant that this process is mostly evident in French and Belgian colonies where the policy of assimilation was favoured. While in the British colonies Socialist ideology did influence some leaders, as in India, where some liason was seen between the liberal leaders of both the countries, no significant ties existed between them.

III. POLITICAL DEVELOPMENT

The Crises of Legitimacy-Participation-Integration

From this discussion about the origin of political parties in India and Africa, we find that desire for freedom from colonial rule, which was alien and hence not legitimate, and which governed over various tribes living in a colonial space, not integrated into a nation, the natives being deprived from participation in authority, created three crises at one time: the crises of Legitimacy, Integration and Participation. But freedom resolved these crises up to a stage. Now, integration and participation crises may arise again if the new political systems fail to integrate the various ethnic groups, who feel that they are deprived from participation, or if new classes or leaderships feel that they are not admitted in the sharing of power and its benefits, they may then challenge the present leadership.

The resolution of these crises lead us further to one more crisis, viz. the distribution crisis. Power, welfare and freedom require to be distributed justly and properly. The Biafra and Katanga episodes are pointers in that direction while in India, except stray and small cases like the Mizo problem, these problems are largely solved and these tribes or sentiments are accommodated within the system; and they feel that there is the scope for achieving their goals within the existing framework. Emergence of the DMK Party and other parties of hill areas and their functioning within the political system illustrate this capacity of the Indian system. Similarly, class-based parties have also come to accept the democratic system and have reconciled to the parliamentary system, Communist rule in Kerala and West Bengal illustrate this point.

Looking at the African situation, we find that modernization has not yet reached the stage when restratification in society takes place due to industrialization, education and urbanization. When these new groups gather strength and become vocal a participation crisis will develop and they will demand some share in the authority, how the leadership will respond to these demands will have a decisive influence on the nature of African political systems.

If the response is repression, and violent underground resistance may start, resulting in instability for long period. If the response is to mobilize people or give limited admission, there may be a peaceful transformation towards competitive politics leading to fuller admission to the political system.

The Type

The African party system is mostly non-competitive. Also, the one party totalitarian system is entirely absent. Instead we find a one-party authoritarian or one-party pluralistic system. While the Indian system could be classified as one-party dominant-system upto 1976, with hegemonic power and a pragmatic programme[15]; even during this period opposition parties came to power in some states. Recently power passing over into the hands of the Janata Party has indicated that the system may change into a turnover-pragmatic system, a real competitive system with stability. This has indeed proved the maturity of the Indian political system.

The Roots

In the African context, we have yet to witness such a turnover. In the West and India also, when political parties came into existence a small group or clique controlled them; but, at that time, the power at their disposal was very limited. The tremendous power of the modern state machinery, which can be manipulated to curb the growth of the new contenders for power or repress them was available to them with the massive power of the modern state at hand and, where competitive system is not entrenched, democratic ideology and institutions are still in the budding stage and many crises like legitimacy, integration and distribution, make heavy demands, the leaders of the new emerging states are tempted to become authoritarian. Also, the opposition having no existence as a real party, which could be nourished on modernizing conditions, could not resist them and chances of its survival openly or clandestinely were minimum. In Africa, Ghana supplies an illustration to this point. In Ghana all the parties were banned but, the UGCC, having long roots in a parliamentary framework which existed for nearly two decades and a thriving economy which had created a middle class and a professional

class, could maintain a semblance of opposition against the
one-party rule of Nkrumah. The opposition continued its
struggle from bases outside Ghana under the leadership of
Dr. Busia.

After a military coup, the opposition provided an alternative
which again fell under another military coup. Now there is no
party, even an authoritarian one-party. In such situations it
becomes difficult to create a rationale for the party to establish
its legitimacy. While in India, during last two years of emergency rule, were some groups were banned and leaders of
various political parties jailed, however, the conditions for the
existence of parties remained; parties were not formally banned
and Congress as a party remained and its structure was neither
totalitarian nor authoritarian. Hence, when the time came for
providing an alternative to the existing rule, a group of leaders
came out of the Congress and people could choose an alternative party which was already existing formally and provided
a competitive alternative. Unfortunately, in most of the African
countries these conditions do not exist.

This background, emergence and context has decided the
pattern, role and nature of political parties in India and Africa.
Now its future course will be dictated by how they respond to
the problem of political development. We may discuss them
in regard to the issue of Participation, Legitimacy, Integration,
Conflict Resolution, Political Socialization and expected or
desired functions of the parties, known as 'Load'.

Response to Participation

Participation in competitive or open societies is open and
encouraged, while authoritarian systems either repress this
demand or limit the admittance or use the party as an instrument of mobilization only; creating an appearance of participation of the people but actually using them as tools; as in Egypt,
where Nasser used people either to support him or get a verdict
on his acts. In this situation control remains in the hands of a
small oligarchy and the party turns out to be a device to
recruit and get mass approval. But admittance of the mass
involves the risk of takeover; hence, the leaders resort to frequent purges and tightening, arguing that mass participation
threatens to destroy the revolution. However, if the process

runs through its right course, there is a possibility that at a
time of crisis a split may occur in that party which may evolve
later on, if care and conditions favour, into a competitive
system. Limited admission may also grow into a competitive
system if the overall system is not totalitarian and modernization, with democratic ideology, takes root. The repression,
which may be due either to the need to maintain a particular value system or restrict anti-system groups, or fear of
new claimants to power leads to a closed system and even the
overthrow of the regime that may be in power. But the overthrow does not automatically lead to a competitive polity. It
seems that, with the increase in modernization and development, government needs more and more power and may tend
to turn totalitarian, sometimes passing through frequent coups
and instability. In Africa, Ghana under Nkrumah, used the
method of repression and the result has been a military government. In Uganda, Amin is following the crudest forms of
repression; while Kenya, Tanzania and Egypt have followed
the path of mobilization. Further, if the governing party tends
to emphasise ideology, the admission and mobilization is
restrictive; while, where the party is an electoral instrument,
it tends to follow a pragmatic programme where modifications
are possible and participation demands could be accommodated.[16]

Response to Legitimacy

In emerging nations, at the initial stage, the party, which
headed the national freedom movement, has acquired a legitimacy to rule in the eyes of the people. However, they have to
evolve new and acceptable sanctions against religiously
sanctioned royalty or the longevity and pomp of aristocracy,
or the efficiency and order of colonial bureaucracy, or the
powers and charisma of the military; while modern party
systems have to resort to the sanction of popular government.
As all these claimants for authority would try to subvert or
dislodge it and the huge mass of participants, which has yet to
learn the rules of the game, itself creates instability and uncertainty. This instability or uncertainty is not the result of
rapid growth but the effect of establishing a new political
system that involves a new pattern of political participation. In

this situation, establishing legitimacy for a competitive party system is still further complicated due to lack of cohesion. This task becomes more difficult where competition is likened with disorganization and disunity and public attitude is not cultivated to the extent of accepting healthy opposition and change in authority.

Succession Test

If we look at the emerging system and test the legitimacy of the system, not on the basis of popular support it receives but, whether succession process or change in authority, from one leader to another in the same party or from one generation to the other or from one party to another is institutionalized or not, then, in India, we can say that the system has matured. The succession from Nehru to Shastri, to Indira and to Janata Party, was peaceful and within the constitutional framework. While in Africa we have yet to come across this process, where so far the transfer is affected or followed by coups. Experiences of Ghana, Zaire, Sierra Leone, and Algeria substantiate this observation.

Response to Integration

The problem of integration should be viewed from two points. One is national integration which is satisfied by a set of popular attitudes generally described as loyalty to nation above local or parochial concerns. While the second, the process integration, required regularization of structure and processes whereby the discrete elements in a given national territory are brought into meaningful participation in the political system. Africa has yet to affect amalgamation of disparate social, economic, ethnic and geographic elements into a single nation and create a capacity to control the entire territory and along with it achieve process integration. In India, at the time of independence, the new state (after partition) was accepted as a nation (with certain localized and limited reservation while we were definitely in a comfortable position) and process integration was possible during the days of a pluralistic pragmatic party system where largely homogenous elites could safely manoeuvre within the accepted system. Recent turnover has shown that process

integration has also made significant headway. While in
Africa, the fragility of nationhood and non-homogenous elites
and the centrifugal forces held in precarious check lead to the
advocacy of one party, rather than a competitive party
system. However in a one-party system the party becomes
governmentalised and its capability as an instrument of political
participation and recruitment diminishes. Further, as nation
and party become co-terminus, disaffection with the party may
endanger loyalty to the nation. Also, it lacks attitudinal integration. From this viewpoint the experiment of Kenya and
Tanzania, which have allowed factional conflicts within the
party, may serve the purpose of inter-party competition in some
limited way. However, it should be noted that a competitive
system really helps the process of integration, as parties have
to evolve a national appeal to capture power and each group
feels secure, yet tries to accommodate others, while evolving an
accepted formula through interest aggregation, thereby leading
to secularization which, in the end, creates a sense of political
efficacy and legitimizes the system. Indian experience proves
this thesis. In Africa, also, where parties are not narrowly
based on tribal, religious or regional foundations, they have
helped to bring about a sense of national consciousness at least
in urban centres and educated elites.

Conflict Management

Participation, legitimacy and integration have a long range
perspective but on day-to-day basis the essence of politics is
concerned with the ability of the political system to manage
constantly changing demand, that is to say, conflict management. Hence it is important to examine the role of political
parties in handling this vital situation. It is well accepted that
in a competitive system with pragmatic-turnover/hegemonic
systems conflict could be easier to handle. Also, where societal
cleavages are basic and intense or the cleavage is translated
into ideological or anti-system parties, conflict management
is difficult but may not be impossible; as for instance the
Nigerian example has shown that a federal structure may
facilitate national level bargaining and even toleration of hegemonic control at the level in exchange for political power
excercised by minority parties over territorial subdivisions. In

India also, we have seen acceptance of hegemonic centre by Mizos and Tamils, and also Communists, who relaxed their attitudes and accomodated themselves within the system. Similarly, in Austria Catholics and Socialists, and in Holland Calvinists and Catholics have evolved a working accomodation, while in Italy, even in a unitary system the communist Party had abaondoned its anti-system attitude when prospects of sharing power at national level was possible.[17] Hence, it may be concluded that, if some means is provided whereby power may be shared even when societal cleavage is basic or ideological, a nation may cope with this problem of conflict management. However, even in a one-party system, where other parties are excluded from a share in the power but pluralistic-pragmatic tendency is maintained and secondary association under the aegis of the dominant party are tolerated, the situation may be eased as in the case of Tanzania. In dealing with conflict, the attitude and skill of the leadership are also important elements. Nyerere and Kaunda seem to provide good illustrations of this type of leadership. Further, if the party is decentralized and the local units are capable of settling the disputes at local level as in India, the load on the party at national level is diminished.

Bureaucracy

Relationship between the ruling party and bureaucracy also requires a balance which may allow the party to influence the bureaucracy to place inputs, yet, its control might not be so much that it would degenerate into extension of the party, which may endanger the reliability of the bureaucracy and thereby create disaffection among other groups and parties. This type of threat of political-colonization of bureaucracy is greater in one-party or hegemonic systems. Also the legacy of colonial rule which was largely controlled by bureaucracy is not easy to forget and the new leadership may easily fall into the old rut perpetuating the old colonial tendency, which may create a situation where the government would be taken over by the bureaucracy. In Africa, where most of the educated elites are in the bureaucracy there is a potential threat of the bureaucracy usurping power or absorbing the party or the

single party may absorb the bureaucracy, but these may undermine the capacity of the party for handling conflict.

Further, one-party states usually tend to assert the primacy
of formal structures of government, which leads to "bureaucratization of society with an increased power position for
members of the formal bureaucracy."[22] While in India, we
have seen that bureaucracy was already settled and its structure
and working institutionalized, which provided against the
ruling party overrunning it.

Political Socialization

This four-fold role of political parties implies that the party
is an instrument for political socialization and much more so
in developing countries. Then, from this viewpoint, there are
two types of parties: mobilist and adaptive. The mobilist
party mainly assumes the role of a revolutionary agent and
tries to bring about attitudinal and behavioural changes within
the society while an adaptive party largely takes a pragmatic
attitude in quest of electoral support. The mobilist party
seems to be more conducive to the needs of a developing
society, where the party has to assume the role of a reformer
and bring about modernization through national integration,
secularism, economic development and a more national view
of life and campaign between elections to arouse the public in
achieving these goals, while the adaptive party simply provides
services or rewards during this period. In India, somehow,
political parties assumed the role of the adaptive party and
the problem of arousing the public was left to reformers and
social workers; this bifurcation of duties in a way helped the
political parties to limit their sphere of action and scope of
functions. While in Africa, the political parties have mixed
these two roles, which has pushed them towards a single party
system of the mobilist variety. However, some scholars believe
that the mobilist single-party systems may bring about national
integration but they inhibit effective participation and thereby
facilitate oligarchial systems primarily concerned with political
survival, national aggrandizement or personal gain rather than,
say, economic growth, social welfare or democratic values. But
here again it is difficult to generalise since a great deal depends
upon other variablesli ke leadership, elite structure, style of

conflict management, etc. Further, only exhortations and speeches do not lead towards the realization of goals unless a dedicated cadre of workers and a well organised party is at hand, which is conspiciously lacking on the African continent. On the other hand, there is evidence to suggest that electorally-oriented adaptive parties actually play an important role in affecting attitudinal and behavioural changes than the mobilist party. The adaptive party, in the process of winning support from different groups, while aggregating interests, brings about a more valid integration than the party which relies on coercion and exhortation. Further, adaptive parties provide a better two-way communication channel between the government and the people, thereby facilitating economic development which caters to the needs of the people. This has been amply proved by reports from the one-party West African states, which suggests a considerable gap between governmental claims and performance.[18]

'Load'

It is clear that parties are instruments of political socialization, but one more factor also in the context of India and most of the African countries has relevance. India was more developed from the viewpoint of education, newspapers and communication, and had relatively well established adult political attitudes, including many competing institutions concerned with affecting political attitudes than in Africa. Hence, the role of Indian parties in this direction was minor compared to that of their counterparts in Africa where they were allowed to step in and monopolize this field overarching the other socializing institutions.

The most important factor in shaping the role of political parties in developing nations is related to the 'Load',* which has increased due to two developments. One is the meaning attached to the concept of nationalism in the newly emerging nations and the other is the demand of the cluster of crises and functions which the leadership and the parties have to face in these countries.

It is interesting to note that, particularly in Africa, national-

*See Table II, Appendix 3.

ism has acquired more content than credited with the traditional concept of nationalism, which is satisfied by an accepted
identity. In Africa it includes Pan-Africanism, demand for
progress. Negritude and the ideal of 'just' distribution as the
dominant variable of the age, which has resulted in the demand
for welfare, development and progress in the internal sphere
and push towards economic independence in the context of
the outward world.[19]

African political parties have to function within this ethos.
While paying lip service to this ideal, African leaders know
that it is impossible to satisfy it and, to tide over the gap
between the ideal and performance they have to control the
opposition which may exploit these sentiments. Hence, many
African leaders veer round to single party systems.

This 'load' is further aggravated and reflected in simultan-
eous onslaught of the different crises in cluster, creating a
complex situation as well as all the various functions which
the party has to perform in the absence of other supporting
associations and structures, which may have handled them
like education, economic development, social reform and
politicization, distribution and so forth. In short we may say
that the elite resources at their disposal are very limited while
the jobs they have to do are varied and many.

The Legacy

Added to this, the traditional African society which was
communal in character and taken that the individual had no
identity apart from his group. The decisions were made only
after unanimity had been achieved through institutionalized
talking-it-out in a village palaver, which implicity rejected the
idea of a permanently organised opposition and considered it
alien. However, in Indian culture a large amount of tolerance at
theoretical and abstract levels helped in the formation of
parties championing different approaches. But Indian society
was also very elitist and confirmative within the group; hence,
even though within the party there might have been groups,
the leaders prevailed and were accepted as the *Panch-Maha-
jana* which is reflected in the one-party 'dominant-system'
operating by consensus.

Further, colonialism in Africa tended towards bureaucratic authoritarianism and exposure to pluralistic democracy was relatively brief. The masses and elites during most of their life time were under the authoritarian political order and oriented towards bureaucratic centralism. In a way one-party rule and 'National Party Government' are simply post-colonial terms for the same phenomenon. Also the role of the party in the freedom movement has helped to facilitate one-party development, giving 'The Party' an aura of legitimacy. The Party was regarded as the champion of nationalism, national unity and new African revolution. India under British rule has a different experience and, as we have discussed earlier, the traditional authority was not effective at the national level and a protracted collaboration with the colonial authority for a comparatively longer period undermined bureaucratic authoritarianism and paved the way for supremacy of popular authority.

The impact of the West on political tendencies in Africa and India are clear but in India the political elites, in their formative period, came under the influence of liberal Europe which accepted and respected plural society. While African leaders were inspired by 'Socialist' Europe, the concept of class struggle and party as a revolutionary organisation were most attractive. European parties of the left gave support and guidance to African parties on organization, strategy and tactics. This was welcome as it helped to create parties with monolithic and penetrative character appropriate for launching an attack upon the colonial regime (e.g. the SFIO, CPP, PDG, PCDI.).

Consolidation

This background facilitated the tendency of one-party system which was furthered by situational factors like the highly fragmented and unintegrated character of most of the African states, which was favourable for the plea for strong and effective government. Absence of structural and psychological restraints upon the arbitrary use of the relatively unlimited governmental power enjoyed by a party commanding a parliamentary majority, which in turn was disproportionately favoured by electoral and institutional innovations—for example 'single-vote-one-

candidate' electoral system or single list system has also consolidated this system. Further, the prevalence of one-party pre-
dispositions in the governing party elites has proved a decisive
factor in this direction compared to the Indian situation.
African leadership was also not inclined to believe that the
absence of opposition would end in the demise of democracy.
While the political culture (i.e. attitudes, beliefs, values, orientation towards authority and self-images of the leaders regarding their political role and capacities), was largely elitist, statist
and nationalist, all inter-related and mutually reinforcing and
each supportive of one aspect or another of the one-party
syndrome.[20]

At this point, it may be appropriate to assess the several
factors which helped to consolidate the one-party system in
African states. The elitism of African leaders was nourished
mainly due to illiteracy of the masses in Africa, where the "educated" could easily establish their special claim to leadership, as
well as their capacity to handle the complex affairs of the modern
state having a access to the "white man's magic" (art of reading and writing). Elites were accorded deference on this ground
by the masses and their legitimacy was accepted. From this
followed the elitiat-view that opposition, if recruited from non-
elites, is incompetent and illegitimate and if recruited from the
same social strata either frivolous and irrelevent or dangerously subversive and prompted by lust for power.

In India, though opposition elites were attacked as incompetent, frivolous and irrelevant, people chose their representatives on the pragmatic considerations of the services they gave
or could give and not because of educational achievements
only.

Statism in the African elite was reflected in the socializing
framework of society whose private sector was extremely under-
developed and the state consequently dominant in all modern
sectors of society (e.g. education, economy, public works) and
the main employer; in a word, it was statist and socialist. This
system was inherited from the colonial power and in the
absence of other agencies, served as the instrument of rapid
modernization; coupled with this the ideologically socialistic
orientation of the leadership helped to fortify this attitude.

The nationalist tendency was the result of a commitment to

national unity against parochial sentiments and this helped to rule out all opposition or stigmatize them by linking them with external or sub-national forces or influences and go for a 'parti Unifie'. As Prof. W.N. Chambers observes in his book, *Political Parties in a New Nation: The American Experience, 1776-1809:* "This is not a novel phenomenon and every new nation passes through this phase, but unlike USA, in the new African states parties existed before national independence and their existence was presumed in constitutional norms, procedures institutions, and as sources for the recruitment of political leadership. This posed a new problem for African leaders, they had not to deal with the problem of preventing the emergence of political parties as in the case of Hamilton or Washington but consolidate the dominance of one-party and establish the primacy of one party over all others."

The technique of consolidating the primacy of one party differs; but the aim is to convert, neutralize or eliminate the overt political opposition by rewarding the supporters or punishing those who oppose. This is possible in Africa because of the primacy of the state in various fields which provides the capacity to provide patronage. They have also absorbed various associations in the party or manipulated with the electoral system by legal changes or fusion of executive and legislative functions of the state in one office, consolidating the dominance of the party; and providing a theoretical defence for a one party system by broadening the concept of nationalism, by including in it the urge for progress, just distribution and the need for rapid modernization, at the most some of them like Nyerere are prepared to concede intraparty democracy.[21]

The Future

The African situation is yet unstable and fluid; in this situation we should be cautious in propounding a general theory or treating the present structure as final. However, it is interesting to examine the futuristic projections of some scholars about the one-party systems of Africa. Coleman and Rosberg[23] predict that it may take two directions: one culminating in a no-party state, what Wallerstein has called the trend towards *inanition*, i.e. progressive decline[24] of the party as the centre of power and decision making. This would mean that it has either moved in the direction of bureaucratization or a shift has occurred in the role of parties from being an instrument of liberation to that of coercion and repression; in other words, loss of a revolutionary ideology and emergence of a purely administrative state, or a dominant personality (Fuehrerism) ruling through an oligarchic party, which in turn may degenerate into military rule if the army becomes capable and is predisposed to capture power. The second possible pattern, as envisaged by Coleman and Rosberg, is that of 'Party-State' in which the dominant party remains supreme and structurally effective fusion between party and government hierarchies, at all levels, is achieved (not incomplete as in Ghana). However, they accept the probability of pluralistic-pragmatic one-party states either moving in the direction of variant forms of the "no party" states—or loosing their revolutionary momentum, or catapulted by new militant leadership, towards the 'party-state'.

However, modernization is bound to produce new classes and functional groups, which may get oriented to and motivated by liberal ideology; in that case demand for participation would increase. It is true that, as Apter[25] has argued, it is most unlikely that African one-party states will enter an industrial phase in the predicatable future. But one should not disregard the force of ideology and its capacity to influence the backward nations, as it is evident from the rise of nationalism which put the tribal, fragment and backward countries of Africa on the path of independence. This clearly underpins that idea has the capacity to work as a catalyst among various elements and bend the structure or institution and manoeuvre them to produce an altogether different effect than deducted from the functioning of the formal syndrome. Idea may be the product of culture and societal structure, but, it is also the creator and motivator of them, and exists in its own right as an independent variable and affects political development. Binder observes that "It seems evident and hardly arguable in these days of the communication revolution that ideology is one of the keys to development."[26] Further, looking at the African situation we can see that parties in Africa are far from monolithic unity and ideological cohesion, a characteristic of the communist party, and, it seems that, looking at the problems and resources at their disposal African leaders have to go in for pragmatic policies though their aim be revolutionary transformation of the African system; but without a totalitarian ideology and system, it is not possible to move in the direction of revolutionary centralization. The experiences of Ghana, Guinea and Mali are illustrative reminders. Thus it seems that it is difficult for African states to move in the direction of the totalitarian system which champions'unitary, hierarchical and scientific' truth. Looking at the diversified and multitribal African society, with an urge for progress, they have to go for 'multilateral, segmentary and existential' truth. Hence, they have to adopt or change, both the ideologies, in accordance with their indigenous traditions and thereby produce their own ideology,[27] combining revolutionary and particularistic truth. President Nyerere's efforts to evolve African Socialism is perhaps a pointer in this direction. This may result in a 'third way',[28] a synthesis of liberal values and revolutionary organization. How, and to what extent, the leaders in the Third World can achieve this combination may indicate an alternative to the two courses predicated by Coleman and Rosberg.

REFERENCES

[1] Maurice Duverger, *Politics Parties* (London, 1964). (English translation by Barbara and Robert North) p. xxiii.
"In the United States although modern parties appeared in the 1790's with the Federalists of Hamilton and Adams and the Republicans of Jefferson and Madison, it was not until the era of Andrew Jackson in the 1830's that party organization developed to include strong centres of local power on a substantial mass base."
Joseph LaPalombara and Myron Weiner, *Political Parties and Political Development* (Princeton, N.J., 1966), p. 6. See also, V.O. Key, *Politics, Parties and Pressure Groups* (New York, 1958) and William N. Chambers, *Political Parties in a New Nations: The American Experience, 1766-1809* (Oxford University Press, 1963).

[2] LaPalombara and Weiner, n. 1, p. 6

[3] Differentiation between party and movement is significant—Sigmund Neumann (see S. Nuemann, "Toward a Comparative Study of Political

Parties", in S. Neumann, edor *Modern Political Parties* (Chicago, 1956) classified parties as parties of 'aggregation' and 'integzation'. Though movement closely resembles Neumann's party of aggregation it is not aggregative; it works as also ideological persuader. However, in colonies main concern being independence and striving for independence, its main ideology was nationalism and anti-colonialism, within which various factions, groups and interests united; it was a loose 'Congress'.

[4] Thomas Hodgkin, *African Political Parties* (Harmondsworth 1961), p. 16

[5] Sekou is the grandson of Samory Toure, the founder of this empire and Samory-Warrior tradition.

[6] The Action Group Party in the Nigeria's Western (Yoruba) region illustrates such a party. See James Coleman, *Nigeria Background to Nationalism* (California, 1958).

[7] For theoretical and illustrative discussion of "Colonial Dialectics" see C.H. Moore, *North Africa*: Chapter II (Boston, 1970), Chapter II.

[8] J.H. Price, *The Gold Coast Elections West Africa 1955*. quoted by Hodgkin, n. 4, p. 29.

[9] Ministry of Home Affairs, Government of India, *The Nature and Character of Representation in the Democratic System* (Mime) pp. 47-48.

[10] James Coleman "The Emergence of African Political Parties", in C.G. Haines (ed.) *Africa Today* (Baltimore, 1955).

[11] Jayanti K. Patel, "African Strategy for Development," *Vidya* (Journal of Gujarat University) Humanities, Vol. XVIII No.1, January 1975, pp. 105-6.

[12] Ruth Schachter, "The Development of Political Parties in French West Africa", Unpublished doctoral thesis, 1958, quoted by Hodgkin, n. 4.

[13] Kenyatta was also influenced by Pan-African leader, G. Padmore; he also visited the USSR.

[14] The characteristics, according to Dr. Coleman, are:
  (a) a broad nationalist objective, the elimination of the existing colonial system;
  (b) looseness of structure—taking the form, often of local and functional associations, grouped around a central junta which has entire control over policy;
  (c) emphasis on the idea of representing 'all the people'; and
  (d) an aggressive strategy, associated with the lack of constitutional mechanisms for the realization of the nationalist objective.

[15] LaPalombara and Weiner give the classification under the head of Competitive systems as:
  Hegemonic — Ideological
  Turnover — Ideological
  Hegemonic — Pragmatic
  Turnover — Pragmatic
  See n. 1, p. 29.

[16] Coleman-Rosberg's typification of one-party system into Pluaralistic-Pragmatic and Revolutionary-Centralizing could be useful here.

[17] LaPalombara and Weiner, n. 1, p. 416.

[18] *Ibid.*, 426.

[19] Jayanti K. Patel, "African Nationalism—A functional interpretation," *Vidya*, 1977.

[20] Coleman-Rosberg (ed)., *Political Parties and National Integration in Tropical Africa* (Berkeley and Los Angeles, 1964), pp. 662-4.

[21] Nyerere says, "Where there is *one* party provided it is identified with the nation as a whole the foundation of democracy can be firmer, and the people can have more opportunity to exercise a real choice, than where you have two or more parties." Quoted in Tom Mboya, "The Party System and Democracy in Africa", *Foreign Affairs*, July 1963, p. 655.

[22] Carl Beck, "Bureaucracy and Political Development" in Eastern Europe", in J. LaPalombara (ed.) *Bureaucracy and Political Development* (Princeton, N.J., 1963), p. 270 and William J. Foltz, "Building the Newest Nations: Short-Run Strategies and Long-Run Problems,"in Karl. W Deutsch and William J. Foltz (ed.), *Nation Building* (New York, 1963), p. 124.

[23] J S. Coleman and C.G. Rosberg, Jr., *Political Parties and National Integration* (Berkeley and Los Angeles, 1964), pp. 676-80.

[24] Here it would be interesting to note the opinion of Ruth Morgenthau. She observes that "at the start of 1960's most political parties appeared to be at their low point and except in few countries, insignificant in comparison with the 1950's". This suggests that political parties are under eclipse in Africa. Ruth Schachter Morgenthau, "African Politics, Background and Prospects" in Frederick S. Arkhurst (ed.), *Africa in the Seventies and Eighties* (New York, 1970) p. 35.

[25] David Apter, "Political Religion in the New Nations," in Gerty, (ed), *Old Societies and New States* (Glencoe, 1964).

[26] Leonard Binder, "Ideology and Political Development" in *Modernization, The Dynamics of Growth* (VOA Lectures) (Higginbotham, 1967), p. 220.

[27] *Ibid*, p.225.,

[28] "Modernity is not a fixed quantity, and development is the term for diverse paths by which it may be attained. Probably it can be attained only by diverse paths, each suited to the conditions and the traditions of the people in question" *Ibid.*, p. 232; also, p. 226.

APPENDIX 1

Type of Party Configuration

	Competitive System	*Non-Competitive System*
HEGEMONIC	(a) Ideological	(a) Authoritation
	(b) Pragmatic ONE-PARTY	(b) Pluralistic
TURNOVER	(a) Ideological	(c) Totalitarian
	(b) Pragmatic	

Source: J. LaPalombara and Myron Wiener (ed), *Political Parties and Political Development* (Princeton, N. J., 1966), pp. 33-41.

ONE-PARTY COMPETITIVE SYSTEM

(a) PRAGMATIC-PLURALISTIC

e.g. Senegal, Ivory-Coast, Sierra-Leone, Cameroon.

(b) REVOLUTIONARY-CENTRALIZING

e.g. Guinea, Mali, Ghana.

Source: J.S. Coleman and C. G. Rosberg, Jr., *Political Parties and National Integration in Tropical Africa* (Berkeley and Los Angeles, 1964).

APPENDIX II

Tendencies among Uniparty and One-Party-Dominant African States

Differentiating factor	Pragmatic-pluralistic pattern	Revolutionary centralizing trend
I. Ideology		
A. Degree of ideological occupation, declamation and rationalization	Limited pre-occupation	Heavy preoccupation, constant and compulsive
B. Scope, depth, and tempo of modernization objectives	Adaptive; aggregative of a tolerated but controlled pluralism.	
C. Degree of insistance and commitment to consummation of Africa—nationalist objectives		

Differentiating factor	Pragmatic-pluralistic pattern	Revoiutionary centralizing trend
1. Neutralism	Pragmatic, formally neutralist but tolerant regarding continued unbalanced dependence on West	"Positive neutralism"
2. Pan-African Unity	Pragmatic, functional cooperation	Political unification
3. Tempo and degree of decolonization and "Africanization	Pragmatic	Immediate and total.

II. Popular Participation

A. Degree of political mobilization and expected popular commitment	Partial/intermittent	High/constant
B. Mode of individual participation	Direct and indirect	Direct; only between individual and party-state.

III. Organizational Aspects

A. Degree of interparty hierarchism, centralism, and discipline	Variable; hierarchical and centralized by tolerated and controlled pluralism	High, monolithic; concentration; conformity sanction severe
B. Degree of associational monopoly and fusion	Variable, looser relationship	High/total monopoly and fusion
C. Degree of party-government assimilation	Limited assimilation	Total assimilation.

J.S. Coleman and C.G. Rosberg, Jr., ed., *Political Parties and National Integration in Tropical Africa* (Berkeley and Los Angeles, 1964), p. 5.

APPENDIX III

The Functional Load of the Polity in a New African State

Function	Character of Functional Load
Interest articulation and aggregration	Unaggregable character of most interests and nonexistence, weakness, or ethnicity of interest associations, dispose governing party unilaterally to identify and to determine interest satisfaction in terms of its concept of national interest as well as the state of public opinion.
Political recruitment	Monopoly over political arena and hostility to alternative structures or channels of recruitment dispose governing party to develop, routinize, and regluate recruitment processes within all authoritative and non-authoritative structures in society.
Political socialization	Widespread persistence and pervasiveness of parochial ties dispose party to perform dual function of (1) facilitating the extinction of old psychological commitments to sub-cultures viewed as terminal communities, and (2) politically socializing both present and upcoming adult citizenry into (i.e. inculcating respect for and loyalty to) new national political culture, new authority structures and new bases of legitimacy.
Political communication	Absence of weakness of mass communication media and underdevelopment and discontinuities in communication network increase need for governing party to develop a penetrative communication process both within the party and population, as well as to ensure high informational output regarding governmental plans and programmes and expected commitments from population.
National integration	Ethnic, regional, and other parochialisms, not trancended or contained by sense of national community or by habituation to national institutions, and the elite-mass gap dispose party to serve as the main instrument, singly, or through auxiliary instrumentalities it controls, for both terrritorial and political integration.

J. S. Coleman and C.G. Rosberg, Jr., ed., *Political Parties and National Integration in Tropical Africa* (Berkeley and Los Angeles, 1964), p. 657.

APPENDIX IV

African and Indian Party Systems Compared: A Causal Matrix

Element	African Context	Impact	Indian Context	Impact
Political Culture (001)	Tribal tradition of a talking out the issue in open and arriving at consensus; idea of permanently organized opposition absent.	Legitimacy of opposition absent.	Diversity of views at abstract level and existence of separate groups-sects-tolerated though, within the group 'Mahajan' tradition.	Existence of different parties tolerated; but accendency of leader respected within the group.
Conditions for Emergence of Party (002) (a) Constitutional Development	Very low-rapid in last phase (except Chana-Nigeria).	Elites and people not acclimatized to constitutional behaviours and sustaining infrastructure weak.	Fairly long and protracted development	Acclimatization to parliamentary System scope for its institutionalization.
(b) Democratic Liberal Ideology	Not evident	Predisposition of leadership authoritarian.	Impact of liberal ideology.	Prevalance of liberal idea of rights and legitimacy of opposition.
(c) Modernizing Conditions	Scarce	Atmosphere for the development of real political party lacking.	Largely comfortable situation.	Rise of real political parties possible.

Element	African Context	Impact	Indian Context	Impact
Economy (003)	Largely subsistence economy.	Commercial middle class and professional class nearly absent.	Money economy with diversification.	Substantial middle class and existence of specialized professions.
Impact of Western Ideology (004)	Leadership influenced and guided by leftist, socialist Europe.	Favour revolutionary and ideological party with authoritarian tendencies.	In the formative period leadership influenced by liberal Europe.	Tolerance for freedom of expression and opposition.
Colonial Rule (a) Direct (French, Belgian, Portuguese)	Traditional elites ignored and eradicated.	Erosion of traditional elites obstructed colonial dialectics as well as problem for new elites regarding establishing their legitimacy against modernizing colonial rule; tendency for one-party system: Hegemonic-Ideological.	Mixed System: in British India direct system and Princely States allowed with autonomy in certain sphere.	Traditional elites few, their influence comprised; new elites successful in establishing their legitimacy over large areas though, aligned with some princes in electoral arrangments after freedom; Tendency: Hegemonic pragmatic system with possible competition in certain areas.
(b) Indirect (British)	Traditional elites protected and allowed to share power.	Traditional elites discredited as collaboraters but in some		

Element	African Context	Impact	Indian Context	Impact
		case powerful enough to share power with new elites. New elites task to establish their legitimacy against them and effect integration. Tendency for one-party system; Hegemonic-pragmatic,		New elites problem limited to process integration; can tolerate opposition without fear of disintegration.
(c) Inheriting Colonial Space	Colonial space not coextensive with nation (in Sub-Sahara).	New elites have to evolve national-integration and process-integration; cannot tolerate divisive tendencies.	Colonial space coextensive with nation.	
Origin of Party (005) External	Party organized outside the legislature as a national freedom movement under the leadership of one charismatic leader.	Opposition discredited as collaborators agent of imperialists or distractors. Dominance of one person. Party not institutionalized.	Though external origin it developed from a small group, which exercised a collective influence and trained a number of leaders before it acquired the shape of a mass movement,	Party institutionalized, Charismatic leadership, yet a group of trained leaders, allowing diversity in views without any stigma.

Element	African Context	Impact	Indian Context	Impact
Elites (006)	Lack of articulated opposition and number of persons required to fill new and various roles.	Accumulation of functions amongst these elites, leading towards unification.	Adequate number of trained persons to handle various roles.	Allowed specialization and role diversification.
Bureaucracy (007)	Following the tradition of colonial authoritarian system. Bureaucracy lacking the requirement of a responsible government and not conversant with separation of powers and tradition of neutral administration.	Legislative and administrative arms could easily merge to create a party-state.	Bureaucracy conversant with separation of powers between executive, legislative and judiciary. Role of impartial bureaucracy favoured.	Legislative and administrative functions separated enough to provide for a safeguard against the evolution of a party-state.
Predisposition of Leadership (008)	Harassed by 'load', divisive ethnicselves and unable to fulfill the aspirations. Yet desirous for maintaining democratic stance before West.	Non-tolerance of opposition; maintenance of some structural device to claim democracy.	Not plagued by heavy 'load' or divisive tendencies, confident of delivering the promises.	Opposition tolerated, though emphasis on consensus but pragmatic approach leading to absorption of opposition.

Element	African Context	Impact	Indian Context	Impact
Role of State (009)	"Accelerated History". State accepted as the only agency for development and integration.	Dominant role of the state, intolerance of opposition	Need for rapid progress. Predominant role of the state yet other voluntary associations active and playing significant independent roles. Party has also assumed certain interest-articulation functions of such groups by developing an eclectic approach and composite structure.	Existences of other groups and accepted also tendency for one party dominance system which interanlases functions of certain salient societal groups.
Mode of response to (a) Legitimacy (010)	Succession from man to man, generation to generation and party to party not institutionalized.	Frequent coups or purges.	Succession crises resolved within institutional framework.	Stability of the system established.
(b) Participation (i) Repression	(a) Due to values. (Guinea, Mali, Ghana) (b) Due to absence.	Revolutionary centralizing trend. Tribal separationist		

Element	African Context	Impact	Indian Context	Impact
	of consensus (Zaire, Nigeria)	movement (Biafra, Katanga)		
	(c) Due to new elite not prepared to share power with new claimants, (Sierra Leone)	Purge leading to one party system. (Guinea)		
(ii) Mobilization	People used as tools or objects (Egypt)	Facade of popular sanction		
(iii) Limited admission	Not evident	—		
(iv) Full admission	Through existing parties.	Pragmatic-pluralistic parties.	Full admission in the party or through other parties.	Turnover-pluralistic system-evolving at centre and in states, existence of local parties leading to competitive system.
(c) Integration (a) National	(i) Parties based on narrow regional tribal or sectarian foundations;	National consciousness lacking, prospects of national integration in danger (Zaire) possibility of more repression or conflict. Leading to	Existing with limited influence.	Tendency favouring pragmatic parties

Eliment	African Context	Impact	Indian Context	Impact
	(ii) Parties based on territorial or national aims.	federal structure accommodating local autonomy and pragmatic-pluralist tendency or unitary government with centralizing tendencies. (Nigeria)	Main party system national, most of the interests also accommodated within the national party.	
	Parties having 'Pan' tendencies.	National conciousness present prospects for national integration good. Minimum repression.		
		Involment with foreign policy stressed. Revolutionary centralizing tendency.	Existing with limited influence.	
(b) Process	(See legitimacy and inheriting colonial space)			
(d) Conflict Management	Nature of cleavages where societal, basic and intense or ideological and share in power not allowed.	Open and peaceful conflict by political parties difficult, leading to hegemonic system. But if allowed a share or accommodated as in Nigeria,	Cleavages not intense and basic possibility for peaceful resolution and participation. freedom struggle peaceful.	Pluralistic-Pragmatic pattern with a decentralized system to deal with conflicts at local level also.

Element	African Context	Impact	Indian Context	Impact
		there could be a working acceptance in the hegemonic system.		
	Leadership not trained in conflict management. Also where conflict was violent (e.g. Algeria) political style of rational discussion is difficult to evolve.	Leading to one-party. system and centralization, again, creating difficulties for pragmatic, resolution; which may lead to military take-over or no-party state.		
(e) Political Socialization	Party used as an instrument for effecting attitudinal and behavioural changes.	The Mobilist party leading to a sense of popular support while effective political participation is absent. The party becomes a monopolistic institution with the tendency towards one party system.	Other independent institutions and groups also play notable role in socialization.	Monopoly of party in this field not accepted leading to pluralist and competitive system.

PADMA SRINIVASAN

Paramountcy and Indirect Rule*

Variations on a Common Theme

Both Indirect Rule—that special result of British genius in African dependencies—and Paramountcy belong to the wider phenomenon of indirect rule through indigenous institutions by colonizers. In this wider sense it goes back to the time of Moses. In Africa it was evolved as a unique philosophy of administrative policy by Frederick Dealtry Lugard at the turn of the century. As a general method, the British applied it much earlier in a slightly different form in India, Burma and Ceylon. The essence of the system is that the colonial power recognizes and uses the traditional rulers and councils as agents for certain purposes, and gives them a limited authority in a number of fields. It has at least three merits:

1. It is a conciliatory gesture to the traditional leaders and keeps down their hostility;
2. it is very cheap; and
3. the common people understand it and are not badly disturbed.

* The phrase, "Indirect Rule", here indicates the special form that the British system of administration took on the African continent.

151

British administrators were empiricists *par excellence* and there is no evidence of any conscious application of their Indian experience to their African dependencies. Unique historical circumstances in each country made for striking differences between Paramountcy and Indirect Rule. But the fact remains that both Indian Paramountcy and African Indirect Rule are variations on the same theme. Moreover, it was to their long administrative experience on the Indian subcontinent that the British looked up to in dealing with problems of governing dependent peoples elsewhere.[1] Points of direct contact were not wanting between India and Africa. There were large numbers of British officers who had seen civil and military service in both India and Africa. And, not the least among them, were F.D. Lugard and Lord Hailey. There were similarities in the administrative and judicial functions of the collector in India and Africa; and the great legal codes of India became, after a few strokes of the pen, the basis of East African administration. The two phenomena examined in this paper present interesting points of comparison and contrast. Unlike the philosophy of Indirect Rule, which emerged full-blown from the creative mind of Lugard, the concept of Paramountcy had a chequered career. Conceptually, Indirect Rule happens to be the culmination of the long evolution Paramountcy had in India from 1765 onwards. Governor-Generals like Canning and Mayo groped unconsciously towards it.

Paramountcy in India

With the acquisition of the Diwani of Bengal in 1765 the East India Company came into its own as a power to be reckoned with and second to none. Between 1765 and the annexation of Oudh in 1856 is the second period when the East India Company became a dominant power that was superior to all.

Between 1765 and 1858 are discernible three distinct phases:

(i) The phase that ends with Lord Wellesley's Governor-Generalship; marked by his ring-fence policy and subsidiary treaties. At this time the "Company defended its frontiers by defending the further frontier of the states on its own borders at the expense of those states."[2] The policy was picturesquely described by Lord Salisbury as that of defending the moon in order to ward off an attack on the Earth from Mars. The main aim was to keep away war and invasions. The army was used for securing the Company's interests in those states. The Company was not responsible for the peninsula as a whole.

(ii) The Marquis of Hastings made treaties of Subordinate Co-operation with the Indian States. They were isolated from the outside world and also from each other. After some uncertainty a positive idea of Paramountcy slowly emerged; a sense of responsibility for the condition of the whole peninsula grew to maturity. The whole of the peninsula was included in the British Empire.

(iii) This phase began in 1858. It was marked by a renunciation of further extensions of the territory of British India. If responsibility was merely felt earlier, it now came to be exercised for the whole of the peninsula. This third phase has two parts: (a) a period of relative suspicion and aggressiveness towards Indian States, and (b) a period of conciliation, relaxation and confidence. The Indian states had no international status. They were units within Britain's Indian Empire.

In 1858, the Crown stood forth as the sovereign vis-a-vis both the Indian States as well as British India. There was no 'mistaken' policy of annexation *now*, it appeared to be direct intervention. The policy was clearly put forth by Lord Mayo to the Rajput Chiefs: "If we support you in your powers, we expect in return good government." The British were no longer indifferent to misrule within the states. The case of the Gaekwad of Baroda in Lord Northbrook's time shows that the British would interfere and depose but not annex. The British Government felt its moral responsibility keenly. It was a long and hesitant journey from Lord Hastings' time to 1889, when the Indian States were not "in alliance with Her Majesty", but "under the suzerainty of Her Majesty."[3]

There are indications that the British had been groping towards a policy that was rather more than political *laissez faire* and rather less than direct rule. In other words, they were groping for Lugard's Indirect Rule. As early as 1799, Wellesley regretted, in a despatch to the Court of Directors, "the double Governments and conflicting authorities unfortunately established in Oudh, the Carnatic and Tanjore."[4] He wished "to reserve to the Company the most extensive and indisputable

rights of inter-position in the internal affairs of Mysore as well
as an unlimited right of assuming direct management of the
country."[4] Wellesley's wishful thinking wasi mplemented by
Lugard in Africa, 121 years later, as Indirect Rule.

British relations with Indian States involved a sort of defen-
sive system which eventually led to a complete breakdown of
whatever was left of the Indian system of government. Unlike
Indirect Rule, it was not a cogent philosophy of administration applied to the common people. Protection made the Indian
rulers indolent, cruel and avaricious. In 1817, Sir Thomas
Munro noted that "wherever the subsidiary system is introduced the country will soon bear the marks of it, in decaying
villages, a decreasing population."[5] For the princes, under the
system, enjoyed power without responsibility.

The African Scene

In Africa, as in India, the first concern of the British was
to ensure that no European rival would encroach upon their
possessions. It was in the final quarter of the nineteenth century that the European powers sought dominion over large portions of Africa. Britain was anxious not to burden herself
over much financially, and only hesitantly did she take possession of large tracts of African territory. The easiest solution
was the Protectorate, a conveniently vague method by which
internal administration was managed by indigenous rulers
under their supervision. Legally it was a nebulous concept
which left the protecting power's rights and duties delightfully
vague. Britain was not in a position to take administrative
responsibilities of any sort. Establishing protectorates in Africa
after the Berlin Conference was a challenge to European
powers because of the vastness of the African bush where
there had never been well-defined territories. The problem of
external security was less pressing than in Wellesley's India.
In India there were clearly identifiable kingdoms and princes
with whom clear treaties could be made. In Africa it was
often difficult to identify the indigenous rulers. Moreover,
the nominal consent of such chiefs, where they existed, was
difficult to obtain, because of a traditional type of democratic
decentralization.

Britain would have found it impossible to involve herself in the direct administration that annexation implied. The very vagueness of the concept of protection—which W.E. Hall says had "different meanings in different circumstances in the mouths of different people"[6]— appealed to Britain and made it possible for her to participate in the scramble in the 1880s and 1890s. At the Berlin Conference there was a suggestion that each signatory power should recognise "the obligation to establish and maintain in the territories occupied by it, or taken under its protection, an authority sufficient to ensure the maintenance of peace, the administration of justice, respect for rights acquired, and, in the case of necessity, freedom of commerce and transit in the conditions in which it shall have been established." This clause was so objectionable to Britain that Bismarck gave in at last, and the reference to protected territories was omitted. Britain excluded her rivals in her protectorates and decided on the nature of internal control. It was a situation similar to that faced by Wellesley in India. Annexation brought in a share of administrative headaches and responsibilities that were best avoided. But Protection went hand-in-hand with political *laissez-faire*. Britain knew how to eat the cake and have it too. For instance, one of the problems Britain would have had to face if she annexed her East African territories was the elimination of slavery in accordance with the Slavery Act of 1833. With all her genuine commitment to the cause, Britain would not have been able to do so. In India, the Paramount Power had a general right over the external relations of the states and could force them to honour its own legal obligations. Thus, in the matter of Slave Trade, the Indian Princes made effective Britain's international obligations. This was done, for instance, in Kutch, where the proclamations of the Rao imposed the necessary penalties upon Kutchi subjects, within Kutch, who were guilty of slave trade offences. The Indian States were indeed protectorates, though the word has not been generally used in the literature on Paramountcy. The "Native States of India" were also called the "Protected States of India" or the "Indian States". The Interpretation Act of 1889 referred to them as being *under* the suzerainty of Her Majesty. Protection was till the very end, a major responsibility of the Paramount Power.[7] The right of protection was infused into the entire relationship between the Paramount Power and the Indian States.

The Africa Order in Council of 1889 provided the legal framework for British administration in the East Africa Protectorates. First the Imperial British East Africa Company and then the Crown entered into various agreements with local chiefs who ceded certain portions of their sovereignty. A rudimentary system of administration was set up, establishing minimal law and order and keeping foreign influence out. Britain's role as Protector was quickly transformed into that of administrator when the Crown took over from the Imperial British East Africa Company. The East Africa and the Uganda Orders in Council of 1902 provided the constitutional framework for the administration. There were to be no limitations on the power and jurisdiction of the Crown.

Operational Levels

Under Indirect Rule, the administration reached down to the common people through their chiefs. Here the African situation presents a strong contrast to the Indian one. For, in India, British influence and Paramountcy did not operate at the local level; there were only goings-on at the upper levels between the Ruler and the Resident, which left the common people untouched, ignored and abandoned, more often then not, to the capricious whims of tyrannical rulers. Relations between them concerned external relations and obligations, protection and defence and intervention to preserve the general order, peace and tranquillity in the whole country. The Indian States had a right to be excluded from the King's Dominions. The Indian Rulers were heads of large territorial units comprising government at many lower levels; whereas the African chiefs were heads of small independent ethnic groups which, under colonialism sank to local levels.

The proponents of Indirect Rule did not concern themselves with African membership of legislative councils; the idea meant nothing to them. They concentrated mainly on the development of the so-called tribal authorities at local levels. They felt that these were the traditional, and hence the desirable forums for the development of African political life. There could be no question at all of the African sitting in the central legislative councils. Cameron felt that even with Indirect Rule at the local government level, it would take "many years, probably not

less than three or four generations," for the African to merely
sit at the centre, let alone control it. An American enthusiast
for Indirect Rule, writing in 1928, held that European control
will probably last a hundred years and that the "legislative
Council has no logical place for an elected African majority."[8]
Obviously, Buell who regarded legislatures as "European for-
mulae" that misfitted African conditions, did not know that
responsible legislatures were a part of Africa's ancient political
heritage. It is amusing today to read of Cameron's duty "to
develop the native politically." Imported institutions at a higher
level were to be used for the benefit of non-African communities. African political parties and vernacular press— where
these existed at all— were concerned with local, tribal issues.
The government was keenly aware of the need to formulate
and elicit the opinions of the African people and their leaders.
This was a vital responsibility of the district officers. The native chiefs and their councils or *barazas* aided the district officers in the two-way process. The DO's role was a vital one and
the entire governmental machine depended upon him.

Empiricism and Ideology

While Paramountcy, all down the line from 1765 onwards,
gives one the impression of empiricism, Indirect Rule started
at the outset, in the 'twenties', as a definite ideology. The
British met each situation as it arose with treaty, annexation or
conquest. Among the Indian States there were quasi-sovereign
states and dependent principalities and among the princes
there were Treaty Princes and Sanad Chiefs. As Protectorates,
their legal status was and is difficult to define; the only general-
ization possible is that all of them gave up their freedom of
action in foreign affairs. Britain's control varied from State to
State according to its size and standing; an important example
is the difference between Hyderabad (83,000 sq miles) and tiny
Kathiawad.

British policies varied and it was an obvious criticism that
the relationship of no one State with the Government was like
that of another. Three broad categories have been discovered:

i) those whose treaties entitle them to full and absolute

sovereignty within the state;

ii) those who enjoy criminal and civil jurisdiction and legislative powers only under supervision even though they
are treaty states; and

iii) those whose rights are based on grants and sanads.

We know for a fact that Sir Thomas Munro's fears only
proved too true about the conditions that prevailed for the
common people under despotic rulers they could not dislodge
through revolt—thanks to British protection. On the one hand
they owed a double allegiance to their rulers and overrulers;
but they had no rights of life or property at all, no court to
appeal to and no authority to turn to for protection. What
the British allowed down to the twenties of our century was
more of political *laissez-faire* and "we don't care" than indirect
rule. Yet, Lugard, the creator and apologist of Indirect Rule
writes of the Indian States: "In the remaining part of India we
have ruled indirectly through the native princes. . . Their
progress has been fostered by the tactful and devoted guidance
of the British Residents at their courts. . . . The institutions
and enlightened rule of some of these states rival those of
British India. Their peasantry are said to be happier and more
satisfied under the rule of their own chiefs than under the
system of direct rule."9

He contrasts these conditions with those in the British
Provinces which are, according to him, only apparently a
model of efficiency. In the latter, direct rule has destroyed
irretrievably the ancient bases of government because administrative efficiency was rated higher than education in self-rule.
But one is glad when this incorrigible advocate of Indirect
Rule feels: "It is, of course, now too late to adopt to any
large extent the alternative of gradually transforming the
greater part of British India into native States governed by
their own hereditary dynasties, whose representatives in many
cases still exist, and extending to them the principles which
have so successfully guided our relations with the native States
in India itself, and in Malaya in the past."10 The truth is that
the British stumbled towards an administrative policy approach-
ing Lugard's brilliant creation only after the turn of the
century; it approached Indirect Rule in practice if not in

theory. What Panikkar denounces as "veiled intervention" was a belated realization by the absent-minded British that they had in fact inherited the paramount position of the Mughal emperors. Far from being an attempt "to ride rough-shod over treaties" and "legitimate rights" it was an awakening to the practical responsibilities of Paramountcy.

As early as 1806, Arthur Wellesley, the Governor-General's brother, pointed out that the vey stipulation in the treaties "that the Native States should be independent in all questions of its internal government," involved the moment it was made, "the interference of the British Government."[11] In a minute of 1860, Lord Canning made it clear that he would step in wherever there were serious abuses in a native government or anarchy or disturbance. The sole judge was the Governor-General-in-Council, subject to the control of Parliament. While Panikkar calls this interference a "notorious" fact, one wonders whether it was not Lugard's Indirect Rule making a modest debut upon the Indian stage. Lord Curzon was, after all, right when he declared in the Bhawalpur speech that "the sovereignty of the Crown is everywhere unchallenged. It has itself laid down the limitations of its own prerogative."[12]

The legal position regarding the Crown's jurisdiction over a protectorate, i.e. a foreign country, is made clear by H.F. Morris, writing about Britain's East African Protectorates. "The constitutional position. . .appears to be that, in effect, although an Agreement may be the means whereby the Crown obtains jurisdiction in what remains, in theory, a foreign country, and although the measure of that jurisdiction is initially limited by the term of the Agreement, yet if the Crown thereafter exercises jurisdiction in excess of that originally ceded, even if in direct conflict with the terms of the Agreement, this cannot be questioned in a court of law. Furthermore, such excess jurisdiction, once exercised, acquires legality through sufferance or usage. The restraints which are placed on the Crown to keep to the terms of the Agreement are merely those of political expediency and a natural distaste for the commission of a breach of faith."[13] The very same position was valid for breaches of agreements with Indian Princes. Morris goes on to show how this position was crystallized only with the greatest difficulty in the highest courts, for the judges faced an intractable problem, *having neither statute nor precedent to take this stand.* The Foreign Jurisdiction Acts and the judges of the nineteenth century could not have covered the new situation of the Crown's jurisdiction over protectorates and agreements with their rulers. It is clear that they were determined to justify the actions already taken by the executive by following "an expansionist policy in the field of jurisdiction."[13] It is clear from this that the Indian Princes and their champions like Sardar D.K. Sen were kicking against the inevitable pricks. Sen's fine legal analysis falls before the Indian States Committee's stand (1929): "The relationship of the Paramount Power with the States is not merely a contractual relationship, resting on treaties made more than a century ago. It is a living, growing relationship shaped by circumstances and policies, resting, as Professor Westlake has said, 'on a mixture of history, theory and modern fact.' " By means of a broad, historical approach the Butler Committee arrived at the same position that the High Court of the East Africa Protectorate did by judicial interpretation in 1912, for the first time. The judgement of 1912, (*Ol Le Njogo and Ors* vs. *Attorney-General and Ors, 1913*) is interesting because it was based upon a judgement given in the Privy Council in the case of *The Secretary of State for India* v.s. *K.B. Sahaba*: "It may have been just or unjust, politic or impolitic, beneficial or injurious taken as a whole, to those whose interests are affected. These are considerations into which this Court cannot enter. It is sufficient to say that even if a wrong has been done, it is a wrong for which no municipal court of justice can afford a remedy."[14]

The British kept up the legal make-believe of treaties and agreements, without honestly annexing the states. Their every intervention, sometimes undertaken for righting wrongs, had to be justified. Panikkar, writing in 1927, the heyday of Indirect Rule, was able to use 150 years of legal fiction to criticize the British rule. Perhaps the British found it was too late for systematic intervention through Indian Rulers and too late for an avowed ideology of Indirect Rule. Moreover, the Indian Rulers were heads of large States, not tribal heads at the local government level; hence, dynamic policies of administration could not perhaps be put through to the people.

In Africa, Cameron (who had served in Nigeria under Lugard) defined the principles of Indirect Rule as that "of adapting for the purposes of local government the institutions which the native peoples have evolved for themselves, so that they may develop in a constitutional manner from their own past, guided and restrained by the traditions and sanctions which they have inherited (moulded or modified as they may be on the advice of British Officers) and by the general advice and control of those officers." What Lugard hated about direct rule was that, even at its best, it shirked the difficult task of educating the common people for self-government. When the time came for them to demand self-rule, "we shall find—as we find in India today—that we have destroyed the natural institutions of the country, that we have sapped the foundations of native rule, and have taught them only the duty of obedience."[15] He did not wish to impose even the most theoretically perfect form of government on the people. His aim was to evolve from their own institutions and cultural patterns a form of polity best suited to their own political genius. He knew that only a political system that grew naturally from its own roots would find the resilience and adaptability necessary for changing situations.

Lugard's policy was that the government of the native peoples by their own rulers should be a reality. The native ruler himself was to be the source of all orders. The European official, i.e. the District Officer, should only confine himself to persuasion; should pressure be necessary, it must always appear as the chief's own, free action in the eyes of his subjects. "This principle," says Lucy Mair, "implies a difference, not of degree, but of kind, from that underlying system where native rulers are used as a mere mouthpiece for the issue of orders on behalf of European interests, and are rewarded in proportion to the efficacy of those orders."[16] Lugard himself was fortunate that he happened to favour only those policies that did not need coercion.

Indirect Rule had a new turn given to it later by Sir Donald Cameron, who wanted to adapt native institutions to meet new needs in a modern world. In the early days, in Nigeria, attention was concentrated on the routine aspects of local administration, the eradication of the defects of the existing system, such as corruption in revenue collection, suppression of slavery, human sacrifice, etc. It was a special feature of Indirect Rule that the native authorities, far from being subsidiary to a programme of development, imposed by aliens, were the foundation on which all development came to be based. Cameron intended to restrict direct action by the District Officers. He was emphatic that "progress" could not be made by *forcing* sanitation or education upon the Native Authorities.

The concept of Indirect Rule was based by Cameron upon the idea of British 'guardianship' in Tanganyika, that was enshrined in the Mandate System. He resisted the pressures from the local European community to develop a political system to suit their own convenience. He was anxious that the Africans must not become a servile people. The only way to educate them to be politically self-reliant in the future and be proud of their Africanity was the method of Indirect Rule. This meant that he had to build on the institutions of the people themselves the tribal institutions that were centuries in the making. Artificially created institutions would crumble away at the slightest shock. The doctrine of Indirect Rule has a very contemporary ring when we read of Sir Donald's concern for making the African "proud of being an African. . .on the basis of a true African civilization."[17] Sir Philip Mitchell, who combined realism with idealism in his admirable personality, was anxious that the African societies must not crack up too fast under the multiple impacts of modern civilization; for this they must be given time, lest the African be cast "adrift before he is equipped with oars and rudder. . ."[18] He had remarkable insight into the demoralizing and destabilizing effects of modernization upon traditional societies. The only way to combat this tidal wave threatening Africa was the vitalization and transformation of native institutions. The silent revolution had to be wrought in far away villages in the African bush by the District Officers. Mitchell himself lived like a nomad and travelled for about 220 days a year with his "long-suffering wife." He writes: "As we were introducing as rapidly as possible, may be too rapidly, an entirely new system of administration, this peripatetic method had much to commend it."

The District Officers and the Residents

The Simon Commission's Report on Constitutional Reform in India described the District Officer's (DO) position as one which made the success of civil administration depend on the man rather than on the machine. This is true of DOs both in India and in Africa. The DO was an embodiment of effective authority to whom the countryside turned in time of difficulty or crisis. The Indian District Officer's duties were exactly like those of his counterpart, the 'collector' (changed to 'district commissioner' in 1906), in East Africa; they comprised both administrative and judicial functions. For an assessment of the District Officer's role, valid for both India and Africa, one cannot do better than quote Lord Syndenham of India: "The administration so far as the masses are concerned is mainly carried on by the District Officers,. . .upon them the maintenance of law and order largely depends. They alone represent the British Raj in the minds of tens of millions who have not the faintest idea of what a Legislative Council means. The ultimate responsibility for the welfare of the native races rests not with the educated native, nor yet with the native rulers, but in the hands of the controlling power, e.g., the District Officer, to whom the native ultimately appeals for justice. He is the exact opposite of the bureaucrat."[19]

In a memorandum, issued in 1934, we see clearly Sir Donald Cameron's interpretation of Indirect Rule. He "intended to restrict direct action by the British Officer to cases of genuine necessity."[20] He insisted that medical, technical, educational, agricultural or public works services stood in an advisory relationship to the native administrations. The District Officers were to use their powers of persuasion rather than methods of coercion. This was the aim; though in actual practice it was difficult to tell between them.

Unlike the Residents in Indian States, African DOs were in touch with the people, and deeply committed to a programme of directed social change. For nearly a generation they, the "devotees" of Indirect Rule, worked like "a sort of orgiastic order of monks".[21] They were stimulated in their work by the guidance of Cameron's *Memoranda* and fired by enthusiasm to re-vitalize African political institutions. Dama Margery Perham noted how, in the course of their researches into tribal institutions, the administrative officers discovered the old checks on the power of chiefs by groups of councillors. Miss Perham wrote in 1931: "The more Bantu society is studied, the more does it seem to contain the element of true democracy. . ."[22] The Residents of India were not impelled by any such noble ideals of guiding social change. They were not in touch with the people at all, for they operated at the highest level of the Royal Court. Indirect Rule, on the other hand, operated at the comparatively low level of local administration, for the obvious reason that these were the levels of traditional forms of government. The Indian Resident was bound by the fact that the Princes' States were 'excluded from the King's Dominions'. This made them immune to British jurisdiction, and gave them the right to enjoy internal sovereignty. Internally, they were 'foreign' territories. The Crown had specially renounced the intention to annex them. Residents usually practised minimal interference in those cases where imperial interests were involved or where anarchy threatened the peace and tranquility of the Empire. Paramountcy and Indirect Rule operated at different levels in different climes; yet, in a strange way, the Residents too, like the African DOs, were expected "to restrict direct action to...cases of genuine necessity." Tracing the history of interferences in the internal affairs of States, Palmer states that "it clearly demonstrates that in this period the Paramount Power was gradually realising its responsibilities though still trying to avoid them."[23] The British felt responsible for gross misrule and inhuman practices. Lord Northbrook observed in writing to the Gaikwad of Baroda in 1875 that the Governor-General in Council "had the right of intervention in case of misrule of which the Governor-General in Council is of course, the Chief Judge."[24] The British also interfered in cases of infanticide, *safi*, slavery and individual acts of cruelty committed by the ruler of an Indian State. There seems to be a contradiction between pure legal theory and historical compulsions—which is reflected in the haphazard responses of the British authorities and Residents to various situations. A right to intervene is vaguely insisted upon from time to time. The Paramount Power's duty to intervene ought to have been pressed; that there was a crying need for this is clearly revealed in the Memorandum of the Indian

States' People.[25] It was because this was not done that the Princes could raise legal hornets' nests on every side. There is uncertainty in the Butler Report's phrase "Paramountcy must remain Paramount." It was impossible to say how and when it would intervene and no two cases were comparable.

As interpretations of Paramountcy changed from time to time, the instructions to Residents could not have been static; though the fundamental legal position was a fixed one. Residents were normally deferential, but also "haughty, polite, impertinent and ironical" as occasion demanded.[26] The Resident was in the unenviable position of the master who had to pretend that he was not the master. The African administrative officer's position was rather similar. He was sandwiched between the native chiefs on the one hand and the Governor on the other. But, unlike the Resident, he had at least the impenetrable bush on every side to save him from the glare of publicity. Moreover, the legal positions were not so sharply defined as in India.

Often, the chief himself was a creation of British ingenuity. The DO had clear instructions from a Cameron or a Mitchell about how he should go about his job. But the Indian States often saw friction and tension and reprisals—a difficult situation for the Maharajah and apoplexy for the Resident.

Indeed, it was solely on account of a false sense of equality (or contractual 'rights') that the sense of injustice arose in the minds of Indian rulers. They smarted all the more when the Residents were tactless and rude in their behaviour. At times, the Residents appointed their own favourites as Dewans (as in Hyderabad or Travancore) and humiliated the rulers.

The Legacies of the Two Systems

The conclusion that they often reeked of paternalism cannot be escaped. Whether Paramountcy can be called a 'system' can be challenged. To the extent that it created Protectorates, it was paternalistic. To the extent that it supported and maintained in power princes who could indulge in gross misrule and tyranny against helpless people, it left only the legacy of backwardness and ignorance for modern India—not to mention a host of legal problems for the Fathers of the Constitution.

On the other hand, Indirect Rule was too perfect a philosophy for an imperfect world. There was frequent conflict between political idealism on the one hand and administrative expediency on the other. This fact is clearly borne out by the following instance. A.M.D. Turnbull, who was Provincial Commissioner of Mwanza, Tanganyika (1924-26), had, in spite of all his enthusiasm for Indirect Rule, little affection for traditional African institutions or their representatives. The main advantage of the new Native Authority instruments, Turnbull unabashedly pointed out, would be to enable "an experienced administrative officer. . .to maintain the fatherly control and discipline he should exercise and without which the native population cannot be guided aright." Though he obstensibly toed the Cameron line his two-year tenure was marked by a harsh authoritarianism which was the negation of the spirit of Cameron's philosophy.[27]

Indirect Rule was paternalistic because its entire inspiration and initiative were unilateral. The true aims of the system seldom, if ever, went home to the chiefs.[28] There was no African participation or pressure in the formulation of the policy; though, paradoxically, it was to involve African participation. The initiative in the policy (of devolving responsibilities upon African traditional authorities) lay with the district administration—an agency that was wholly committed to the perpetuation of colonial rule. Again, Indirect Rule implied decentralization and this went counter to the centralizing tendency inherent in all bureaucracies. The very presence of the Provincial Residents or the District Officers took away from the pristine dignity and self-respect of the African chief in the eyes of his people. Kenneth Bradley, the scion of a great family and a DO himself, confesses in his memoirs that, as a group, DOs were respected rather than loved by the common folk, from whom they were, somehow, always remote. After years of service he could not help feeling "that the Colonial Service, when it was nearing the end of its task, still tended to treat Africans as if they were school-boys."[29] In spite of all their lip-service to making Africans grow and develop in every way from their cultural roots, Lugard, Cameron and Mitchell regarded African life-styles and cultures as savage and primitive and immature. They were anxious to educate the African in self-rule and politics ! They were sincere bearers, like their co-workers, of the White Man's Burden. The similarity, noted by Read, between their policy and the modern African's awakened consciousness of his own identity is merely superficial if not false.[30] What the Indirect Rulers did at the district level seems a farce when taken along with their statements that African Rule at the Central Government would take more than a hundred years ! When Africans did take over at the centre, the term 'Indirect Rule' signifying rule by Africans, had long ceased to be used at the local levels; and, in not a few cases, traditional rulers became obsolete in the new set-ups. Paternalism had tainted the homage paid to African culture.

Both in Africa and India, British Protection to native rulers was marked by superciliousness, and in both, native institutions failed to withstand the tidal waves of modernisation.

REFERENCES

[1] See "The Reception and Rejection of Indian Law", Chapter 4, H.F. Morris and J.S. Read, *Indirect Rule and the Search for Justice* (Oxford, 1972), p. 109.
[2] J. Palmer, *Sovereignty and Paramoutcy in India* (London, 1930), p. 14.
[3] Ibid., p. 26.
[4] Quoted in K.M. Panikkar, *An Introduction to the Study of the Relations of Indian States with the Government of India* (London, 1927), p. 14.
[5] Quoted in Ibid., p. 23.
[6] Cited in Morris and Read, n. 1, p. 42.
[7] Palmer, n. 2, p. 71.
[8] R.L. Buell, *The Native Problem in Africa* (New York, 1924), p. 744.
[9] Lord Lugard, *The Dual Mandate in British Tropical Africa* (London, 1965), p. 226.
[10] Ibid., p. 196.
[11] Panikkar, n. 4, p. 19.
[12] Quoted, ibid., p. 30.
[13] Morris and Read, n. 1 p. 59.
[14] Ibid., fn , pp. 55-6.
[15] Lugard, n. 9, p. 219.
[16] Lucy Mair, *Native Policies in Africa* (London, 1936), p. 123.
[17] Quoted in Morris and Read, n. 1, p. 259.

[18] Sir Philip Mitchell, *African After-Thoughts* (London, 1954), p. 131.

[19] Lugard, n. 9, p. 132.

[20] Quoted, Mair n. 16, p. 25. The Memorandum was called "Principles of Administration".

[21] Mitchell, n. 18, p. 127.

[22] Quoted in Morris and Read, n. 1, p. 264.

[23] Palmer, n. 2, p. 82.

[24] Quoted in Panikkar, n. 4, p. 109.

[25] Cited, G.N. Singh, *Indian States and British India*, Benaras (n. d. 1930 ?), p. 328.

[26] Quoted in Panikkar n. 4, pp. 110-11.

[27] R.A. Austen, *Northwest Tanzania under German and British Rule* (New Haven, 1968), p. 180.

[28] Ibid., p. 187.

[29] K. Bradley, *Once a District Officer* (London, 1966), pp. 15-6.

[30] Morris and Read, n. 1, pp. 263-65.

Part II

Indians in East Africa

R.R. RAMCHANDANI

Indians in East Africa:
Past Experiences and Future Prospects

MANY THOUSAND ASIANS from the East African countries of
Kenya, Uganda and Tanzania have become a floating population in search of a 'home'. President Idi Amin had expelled
them from Uganda five years ago; only a few hundred remain
there. Kenya and Tanzania have taken a number of measures
resulting in substantial Asian exodus from there, too. The
1969 Kenya census returned the non-African population of
209,000, bulk of whom were Asians. Today the number of
Asians in Kenya is likely to be one-half of that figure. In
Tanzania, too, there may be around 50,000 Asians left at present as against double that figure about a decade earlier.
During 1975 even President Banda of Malawi expelled a
couple of hundred Goans and issued orders asking Asians to
wind up their business in the country-side and concentrate in
the three large towns of Lilognwe, Blantyre and Zomba by
March 1977. It will be remembered that Dr. Banda had cham-
pioned the cause of Uganda Asians. Thus, during the last
twelve years, the East African Asians have indeed faced
enough rough weather. They are being eliminated from East
Africa; they are unwelcome in Britain to which most of them
belong legally; nor do they expect any enthusiastic reception

171

back home, in the countries of their origin, India or Pakistan.

They are the same Asians who were not very long ago welcomed to East African territories in thousands; and had in course of time become the backbone of East African economies. Did they not play a significant economic role in the development of the East African countries during the colonial regime? Did they not provide the missing link of artisan skills, subordinate services and trading talent which the White settlers found uneconomical to supply in the economic set-up of those territories, and for which the Africans were yet to be motivated and trained? Were they not more sympathetic and responsive to African aspirations than the Whites? How do we then explain the turn in the situation with such a rapidity after the independence of those countries. Did the Africans by and large dislike their Asians? Had they been anxious to get rid of them?

I

UNDERSTANDING FUTURE PROSPECTS

In my recent study relating to Uganda Asians[1] I have systematically probed into the questions raised above. I am examining some aspects of these issues in this essay for two reasons: (1) To review the future prospects of Asians settled in East Africa; and (2) more importantly, to see whether past experience, could throw some light on the future prospects of the thousands of Indians who are presently going to several countries of Africa and Asia in search of a job or business opportunity. There is strong demand for their skills and talents. Even President Amin of Uganda who pushed out the Asians within a narrow three-month period, did not mind recruiting Indians to meet with the crucial manpower needs of the Ugandan economy. In countries like Nigeria and Ghana, where there were hardly a couple of hundred Indians before their independence, the number of Indians has already jumped up to a few thousands.

The question arises whether Indias from free India are likely to face the same problem in the countries of their destination as the Asians of the yester-years did in East Africa. After all,

the major driving force for Indians to go over to these countries is the same as it was for the East African Asians around
the turn of the century—the period that extended almost until
the Second World War. The motivation invariably comes from
the search for better economic opportunity. However, belonging to an ancient culture—inheriting deep-rooted social
commitment and religious beliefs they, like the Whites, generally do not entertain an idea of merging their identity. They
view the question of their social integration with the local
population as a personal matter. Their main interest is to
improve their economic lot and social standing among their
own community back home in India. Most of them do not
entertain an idea of permanent settlement. But, then, most
of the Asians who went to East Africa earlier also did not
think in terms of permanent settlement.

Hence, it is good for us to learn from the experience of
such earlier migratory movements of Indians to African
countries, to grasp the similarities and contrasts in the two
situations—one as it obtained when Britain ruled India and
East Africa and both the Indians and the East Africans were
British subjects; and the other when both India and the East
African countries have emerged as free, independent nations.
It is useful to have a clearer historical perspective in this
regard as it may enable us to work out a 'Code' or a 'Matrix'
which could perhaps serve as a lighthouse to the present
generation of Indian migrants to Africa, and perhaps elsewhere
too, fore-warning them of the boundaries prescribed by the
matrix. Any disregard of the matrix without caring to reconstruct its parameters, scope and operation may jeopordise their
future prospects.

II

COLONIAL EQUATION

Let us, then, firstly find out the basic elements of the
colonial situation. To put it briefly, the British colonial control
was extended to the East African territories through close
cooperation with the British Government of India. The
British Indian Government worked hand-in-glove with the

Imperial British Government because, as Robinson and Gallaghar point out: "To all Victorian statesmen, India and British Isles were the twin centres of their wealth and strength in the world as a whole."[2] One of the major motivations for the Imperial Government was the need for safeguarding their Indian and Mediterranean interests. The early British expeditions like those by Captain Smee, in 1811; Major Owen in 1922; and later Captain Burton in 1958 and 1960, and Captain Speke in 1860 were all organised from India. These British explorers of East Africa worked in the Imperial Indian Army. Zanzibar, in fact, was for all practical purposes treated as an outpost of India, and the affairs of East Africa were left to the British Indian Government. It was under the well known "Canning Award" of 1861 that the Zanzibar succession dispute, following the death of Sayyid Said, was resolved, and the Sultanate of Zanzibar was separated from the Immamate of Oman.[3] However, with the grant of royal charter to the British Imperial East Africa Company in 1888, the British India Government ceased to have direct say in the affairs of East Africa. However, the interests of British Indian subjects, were duly recognised by the I.B.E.A.C.

Indian immigration, trade and settlement received full patronage from the Company which even employed Indian troops. Its senior officers were the persons with Indian experience, while its lower cadres were almost exclusively manned by Indians. Norman Leys stresses this point when he writes: "Lord Salisbury was for some reason specially anxious to further the trade between East Africa and India."[4] With special reference to the then East Africa Protectorate (now Kenya) he writes: "The new Imperialist ideas had not yet been clearly formulated by Mr. Chamberlain. Most of the early Governors and most of their principal subordinates were men with Indian, not colonial, experience. The country, in fact, looked towards India rather than towards Europe. The currency was naturally Indian, and the Indian Penal Code was taken over bodily. . . . Indians built the railway to Uganda, and the Indian armed police were attached to every important government station. Indian traders and shopkeepers spread over the country, selling the Calico of Lancashire and buying hides for export in return."[5] The position was much the same in Zanzibar, Uganda and later in Tanganyika (Zanzibar and Tanganyika now constitute present Tanzania). So much was the impact of India and Indians that even the town streets in the East African territories were named as 'Calcutta Street', 'Bombay Street', 'Madras Street', and 'Karachi Street'. Several proposals were afloat to set up even Indian agricultural colonies. That such colonies did not materialise is another matter. But, before the White settlement gathered momentum, the Indians had already become an integral part of the economic life of Kenya. When, therefore, the White settlers moved into the Kenya Highlands in larger numbers, they were badly disturbed by the Indian presence. In the words of their acknowledged leader, Lord Delamare, they (the Whites) sincerely believed that the East Africa Protectorate would one day become a part of United South Africa, a great White colony stretching from the cape to the "Zambesi and governed for His Majesty by a true Afrikanner bond."[6] If their dream could not be realised, in Kenya, as it did for their bretheren in Southern Rhodesia (present Rhodesia), it was because the Imperial British Government could not ride roughshod over the interests of their British Indian subjects. There were atleast three good reasons for that: (1) The Indians of East Africa traced their presence in that region prior to British occupation; (2) the Indians were as much British subjects as the White settlers and the whole 'operation East Africa' was devised and conducted from India with specific assurances incorporated in the charter of the I.B.E.A.C. that the interests of the British Indian subjects in East Africa would be further promoted under the British rule. The Indians in India were very sensitive on this issue. The leaders of the nationalist movement in India were already sore over the discriminatory treatment meted out to the British Indian subjects in many other British colonial territories. The British Indian government fore-warned the Imperial government that whole of India would rise as one man, if the Imperial Government yielded to the White settler pressures in Kenya[7]; and (3) The East African Indians were neither the coolies recruited earlier for the Uganda Railway, nor their descendents. Most of the indentured labourers recruited for the railways were repatriated and only couple of thousands remained behind as I have shown in my

study mentioned above.[8] The bulk of the Indians in East
Africa were duka traders, artisans, technicians, small and big
merchants, who played a vital role in the economic development of East Africa as designed by the colonial masters
themselves.

Indian Question in Colonial Times

The question of Indians in East Africa had assumed such a
prominence in the urgent deliberations of the contemporary
East African scence, that it has gone down in History books
as 'Indian Question'. All speculations about Kenya being made
a self-governing colony ruled by the White settlers were finally
set at rest when the White Paper of 1923 on *Indians in Kenya*
specifically stressed the point that Kenya would not be granted
self-governing status "within any period of time which need
now be taken into consideration."[9] The principle of elected
representation for the Indians in the Legislative Council of
Kenya was also conceded.[10] Once the friction between the
White settlers and the Indians was thus resolved, it was more
or less taken for granted that the Indian interests in East
Africa, if they would not be promoted, neither would they be
totally ignored.

It may be noted that till then Africans had shown little
resentment, if any against the Asian presence in East Africa.
This was despite the fact, as Lord Hailey pointed out, that
almost 90 per cent of trade was in the hands of Indians. The
reason was the Africans had only recently appeared on the
commercial scene. Their functioning on the economic plane
was as yet marginal, largely complementry to that of the
Asians. No one then ever mentioned that Asians were handicapping African advancement. All the same some African
resentment over the Asians methods of trading—both buying
and selling—was noticed from early times. However, most of
the malpractices in trading practices could be traced to the
creation of vested monopoly in the industry through the
government policies. Take the case of cotton marketing in
Uganda.[11] Yet African ill-will against the Asian traders was
generated in the market place and "the racial tinge was added
to a purely economic evil."[12] It was the hostility thus generated
that was intensified day-after-day in the post-war period when

the African nationalist movements in the three territories
became an active instrument of African advancement.

Fake African Paramountcy

The reasons for the ill-will are not far to seek. One of the
casualities of the colonial system, as it evolved in East Africa,
was the African interests—much more so in this region than,
say, in the former British West Africa. Although in theory
their interests were hailed to be paramount vide the 1923 White
Paper, yet in practice the Kenyan colonial administration was
primarily devoted to the White man's interests; and even the
brown man's interests received precedence because of their
vital economic role and the backing from the British Government of India. Hence, despite the fact that Uganda was a
Protectorate, Tanganyika a Trust Territory, Kenya a Colony
and Protectorate and Zanzibar a Protectorate, the African
interests suffered the most. Let us see how the system worked
and what came by the Africans.

The highlands of Kenya and Uganda[13], the most fertile and
climatically the best areas, were taken away from the Africans.
They were reserved for the Whites despite Africans' resentment
and Asians' protests. The dislocated Africans were crowded in
the surrounding lowland African reserves from where they
trekked to work on the White planters' farms, from dawn to
dusk. It will be recalled that the land question in Kenya had
been the most irritating issue for the poor, ill-clad and illete-
rate African peasantry throughout the colonial period. Under
the African customary land law, the land is equated with
mother. It can not be owned or alienated. Dr. T.O. Elias
explains: "It is a common feature of all types of African land
tenure that "ownership" is normally never vested in an individual but in a group. . . .Within each group, however, individual members have specific portions alloted to them by the
family head, in much the same way as the local chief allots—
at least notionally—specific parcels of the village land to the
constituent family heads according to need." [14] The individuals enjoy possessory rights but not ownership rights as
known in English law. But in Kenya the Africans were dis-
possessed of their richest community lands located in the
highland region. Nor were they adequately compensated for

the loss, or properly looked after in other spheres of modern sector of the economy.

African Economic Advancement Handicapped

In the commercial sector, the early marketing legislation discouraged petty trading by the Africans. The hawking was considered by the colonial administration as an undesirable occupation by them. The Chief Secretary of Uganda viewed that "The Government cannot ignore the fact that hawking of goods about the countryside is not a satisfactory or desirable occupation for natives."[15] Even 'touting' by Africans was made illegal by 1934. Such a policy, in respect of petty trading, could hardly be expected to help the process of African advancement in trade and commerce, when African contact with the market economy was so recent and so inconsequential. In fact much of the early marketing legislation had an effect of restricting trading opportunities to Africans. To that was added the in-group and family business characteristics of the Asian trading community. Such aspects of the business practices of Asians were not discouraged by the administration. On the contrary, these were indirectly boosted up by the colonial administration which, quite often, in the words of Stephen Morris, dealt with the Indian community as a single group, and separately legislated for Asians as a group. They made regulations concerning their salaries and their schools, put a certain class of housing for them which also forced them in some sort of group characteristics "not by their own volition but by the external pressures."[16] Such tendencies and restrictive practices among Asians, like mutual credit facilities, price fixation, etc. also restricted African entry in trade.

In short, the non-African trading system, not only Asian but also European, developed an institutionalised character in which strong racial and family relationships were reflected which affected the operation of market. Consequently, the bulk of trade tended to go to non-Africans, and the African efforts at breaking this vicious circle were largely frustrated.

Similarly, whether it was manufacturing industry or plantation cultivation, Africans were left behind in wilderness.

The colonial administration in Ehrlich's words, viewed the Africans as "incapable of enterpreneurship, inexperienced, too eager to run before they walk." But, then, nothing was either done to prepare them for such tasks. On the contrary, the entire economic policy was conducted in a way which literally ruled out African participation in modern sector of the economy beyond the supply of unskilled and semi-skilled labour and the cultivation and marketing of peasant crops of elementary level. The trouble was that the early schemes of residential racial segregation had virtually thrown them out of the mainstream of the nerve centres of commercial development in the early stages of economic growth. Although such residential segregation schemes were later withdrawn in theory, the system continued in practice under the guise of strict sanitary regulations. The Africans could hardly be expected to build houses in the European or Asian quarters since the building regulations and sanitary prescriptions were beyond their means to meet with. They were thereby pushed to the peripheral surroundings of the urban centres or those who worked as domestic servants lived in the 'out-houses' of the European and Asian residential buildings.

Another key sector which badly handicapped African vertical mobility was education and training. Here, again, scant attention was paid to the question of linking up African training and education to the manpower needs of the East African economies. The colonial policy in East Africa did not envisage the supply of manpower needs of the East African economies from within the colonial territories. The educational framework was not designed to meet such needs even over a period of time. Rather the requisite skills and manpower needs were largely hired from India because the Indian supply price for such skills was the cheapest in the entire British Empire. African education was left primarily to European missionaries, who were not interested in education as such. Thomas and Scott rightly underline this aspect of missionary education system when they point out: "However useful work they did in this field and no one denies their important contribution yet the main work of their schools was evangelization."[17] Apart from the missionary education, the government spent very little on African education. In Uganda, for instance, only a

paltry sum of sh 1.70 per head was spent on African education as against shs 24 per head on Asian education.[18] The
same was true of Kenya and Tanzania, too. The Government's education policy for Africans was based on "the provision of facilities for practical education for the masses and
for advanced education for a limited number."[19] Even that was
not carried out faithfully. Consequently, the Africans were
invariably left behind the Asians in educational achievements.
In 1959, sociologists Cyril and Rhona Sofer conducted a
sample study of 1,099 African employees in Jinja, an industrial town of Uganda. It showed that 55 per cent of them
had not obtained any formal education, less than 6 per cent
had been to secondary schools of whom only 0.5 per cent had
studied upto class VI. The corresponding sample of 504
Asians returned only 6.6 per cent without formal education,
around 60 per cent of them had been to secondary schools
and 10 per cent had done, in addition to secondary education,
a formal and systematic course leading to a professional,
academic or technical qualification.[20] This then accounted
for a substantial wage-differential between Africans and
Asians, while the Europeans constituted a class by themselves.

Thus, around the time of independence, the entire socio-
economic framework was viciated, in which racial friction
had become a built-in factor. The African animosity towards
Asian settlers was the product of such disturbing elements in
the structure itself. Let us have a closer look at the economic
and social aspects of this structure.

Economic Aspects

Under the British colonial system, as it evolved in East
Africa, Africans were relegated to a subordinate position.
They suffered disparities in every walk of economic life. Let
us take racial classification of employees by occupation and
distribution of Income by Race. Table I in the Appendix,
shows occupation of Employees by Race. It is found that the
bulk of African employees in Uganda, in 1963, were unskilled
workers. A larger number of them, shown under Managerial
and Professional category, would, in the words of Walter
Elkan, "be elementary school teachers and may be a number

of Africans returned as managers are only so for name sake. In the private sector, quite often behind such managers operate a non-African. Even under the category of clerks, an African may be a copy typist while a non-African is generally a responsible cashier etc." [21] This is further proved from the wage bill of the African employees. In Uganda, for instance, an African employee on an average earned just £51 per annum in 1956 as against £497 earned by an Asian employee, and £1,133 by a European employee. The position in this regard changed somewhat by 1963 when an African employee earned £97 while the earning of an Asian and European employee improved only slightly to $588 and £1,561, respectively. Yet the wage-differential was significant to indicate the structural pattern evolved during the colonial period. The racial overtones of the structure were further highlighted by the distribution of Gross Domestic Product.

As we examine the distribution of income by race, we find large disparities of income between Africans, Asians and Europeans. This could be seen from Table 2, 3 and 4 relating to Uganda, Kenya and Tanzania. Whatever be the economic growth that was achieved during the colonial regime, it had clearly enriched the immigrant settler communities and their descendants much too disproportionately than the benefits that accrued to the great majority of the indigenous African population. The non-Africans constituted less than 2.3 per cent of the total population of the three East African countries. Yet, they occupied a pivotal position in the economic life of the three countries. Their wealth was undoubtedly altogether disproportionate to their numbers. Around the time of independence they received 26 per cent of the monetary G.D.P. in Uganda, as much as 60 per cent in Kenya and 38 per cent in Tanganyika. Throughout the 1950's the position had remained the same even though a number of steps were taken to advance African economic interests in the post-war period. The non-African immigrant communities had thus left the indigenous African population miles behind them in economic sphere. Whereas the population ratio of Africans to non-Africans, in 1963, was around 50:1, their monetary income ratio was just around 2.5:1. To be precise, we find from table II, on Uganda, that the African per capita monetary income

was just £12 per annum, as against Asian per capita income of
£288 and European per capita income of £990. On per capita
bases the African income in Uganda, was, thus, 4.2 per cent
of the Asian income and 1.2 per cent of the European income.
In Kenya and Tanzania the African per capita incomes were
even lower—around £7 per annum in Kenya and £8.7 per
annum in Tanzania.

The striking feature of this peculiar colonial system was,
thus, a wide imbalance of wealth between the indigenous
African population and the alien settler communities of Asian
and European descent. The system had badly choked for Africans the outlets for vertical mobility. Only the services sector
had recorded some African advancement—most of it after
the Second World War. The net outcome was that, around the
time of independence of Uganda, only 51 Africans under the
category of individuals, just 87 concerns in the category of
African companies, clubs and trusts, etc. and only 700
African employees were assessed to income tax. The respective figures for the other two communities were 118, 154 and
4086 for Europeans, and 2445, 1129 and 3667 for Asians. It will
be seen that the Asians paid 56 per cent of the total income
tax payable and Europeans 42 per cent, while the Africans
contributed only 2 per cent. It is not that the Africans were
exempted from this tax, but rather in their own country their
incomes were comparatively so low that only an insignificant
number of them could be assessed.

The friction was particularly acute between Africans and
Asians. It was, again, rooted in the structure. The commercial sector, from small 'duka' keeping to large-scale merchanting, was dominated by the Asians. That is why the friction
was most acutely felt in commercial sphere, although the
sectors like subordinate services and artisan skill were also
enveloped in the climate of friction. In those spheres African
aspiration for advancement directly clashed with those of the
bulk of Asians. On attaining independence the Africans
widely resented the nature of this economic order in which
they were placed at the lowest rung of the economic ladder.
'The bazaars in cities and towns were lined with Asian shops.
The fashionable residential localities were mainly occupied by
Asians and Europeans. Most of the privately-owned buildings

belonged to the Asians, and Asians held commanding position in the entire commercial set up. The racial friction was organically a build-up from such mounting tensions."[21] That in turn vitiated the entire social fabric of the East African society.

Three-tier Society on Racial Lines

The product of this warped colonial pattern of economic development was a three-tier social order based on racial lines. The Asian community occupied a middle-layer position, with precious little free mixing among the three racial communities. Apart from formal sundowners and meetings in the marketing places and scout organisations, there was no other social contact. Each community retained intact its cultural traits and taboos. The Asians with their Indian caste-conscious background looked down upon Africans as socially and culturally inferior to them—a situation resembling in some respects the worst aspects of the caste problem in India.

In such a situation, the least that the Africans expected from their nationalist governments was to provide them racial justice. That implied not only doing away the racial structuring of society but also active and positive policy to promote African interests and African advancement—to provide ample scope for their vertical mobility, a ladder with sufficiency of steps to take care of their smooth upward movement. The expulsion and elimination of Asians from East Africa is, therefore, to be explained in the context of this type of colonial equation.

III

FUTURE PROSPECTS

There has recently, however, arisen a new situation. As mentioned earlier, the Asians have gone out of Uganda. They are also moving out of Kenya and Tanzania, too. But alongwith this outflow, there is a noticeable fresh inflow of Indians to those very countries as well as to some other developing countries of Asia and Africa. This should not normally concern us. The market forces and the immigration policies of the countries concerned take care of such inflow and outflow of migratory processes. But, the question is if we can not learn a few lessons from the past experiences. The future is after all built on the present, and the present on the past. Persons like Brintley Thomas have, of course, written books on *Economics of International Migration*.[23] But such studies do not explain the economics of expulsion of the alien settler element.

We have stated above some of the basic economic and social factors that led to the expulsion of Asians from the East African countries. And we argue, now, whether that kind of elimination process, has not left behind sufficient trail of events which, when properly analysed, could throw some light on the future prospects of our people in the countries of their migration. There is no denying about the rising demand for certain categories of Indian manpower resources the world over both in the advanced countries and in the developing countries. That should be welcomed, but we must take care that the fear of their expulsion at some future date is removed from the mind of the Indian immigrants, as far as it can reasonably be helped. We must also see that the Indians do not cause any embarrassment to the countries where they seek economic opportunity, so that instead of earning goodwill for their country they become a liability. It is in this context that I suggest whether the past-experiences in the matter of Asians expulsion could not enable us to construct a broad framework of a matrix, or a code of conduct, whose parameters could provide a guide line to the Indians residing overseas, particularly those living in the developing countries where political instability is greater and sensitivity of the local population is understandably higher. The exercise could perhaps also have a practical utility. It could help the administration to have a proper rationale in formulating immigration—emigration policies of their respective countries. For example, in India, we could have better grasp of our policy goals in the matter of Indians seeking economic opportunities outside India—how far and to what extent this trend should be welcomed and encouraged. At what point of time it would need proper probing and the application of breaks and so on.

My findings are based on the East African experiences. Similar excercises pertaining to countries like Ceylon and other

South East Asian countries could be further helpful. I give
below five broad parameters of this matrix.

Indian Nationality

In the past, migratory process was conditioned by colonial
system. The system had helped in accelerating Indian migration in the early years of British occupation of East Africa.
The Indians were then British subjects. That position has now
undergone radical transformation. India is no more a British
subjected country nor are the East African countries. An
Indian with Indian nationality does not carry any colonial
symbol carried by most of the East African Asians, most of
whom are technically British citizens. My personal experience
in East African was that the Africans by and large did not
bear any hostility towards Indians from independent India. I
think the fresh Indian migrants, therefore, will do well to retain
Indian nationality when they seek jobs in developing countries.
But, later, if they want to settle down in those countries they
must obtain local citizenship, and also be prepared to socially
integrate with the local population. They should be willing
to join the national mainstream and become part and parcel
of the social order of the country of their settlement. Since,
ordinarily an Indian, with a highly developed sense of his
cultural commitment and traditional taboos is unlikely to
merge his social identity in a cultural pattern of even advanced
countries, it is highly unlikely if he would do that of his own
volition in the other under-developed countries with different
cultural backgrounds. It is, therefore, better that he retains
his Indian nationality, rather than change it for, say a Kenyan
nationality, or for that matter a Tanzanian or Iranian nationality and the like.

Non-Racial Equilibrium

The second parameter of this matrix is the non-racial equilibrium. This is particularly important in respect of East
African countries. My structural analysis of the colonial East
African situation shows that the African dislike of the Asians
was not rooted in the wilful avoidance of social integration
by the latter as some would like us to believe. The basic cause

was the warped colonial pattern of economic development in the working of which the Africans had become an insignificant entity in their own country, while the Asians had emerged as a middle-class in some one else's territory. This class formation process in the East Africa worked on distinct racial lines. It looked as if East Africa was doubly colonised by the British masters and white settlers on the one hand and the Indian settlers on the other. Hence, until the non-racial equlibrium is restored and fully reflected in the East African socio-economic order, the tinge of racial friction will continue to haunt the East African peoples. As the colonial equation at political level has now become a thing of the past, it is equally urgent that non-racial equlibrium is established without much loss of time. It is only then that the significance of Indian enterprise in the developmental effort will no more be clouded by the tensions generated by the colonial system and its racial overbearings in East Africa.

Prominence of Africans in Economic Development

Thirdly, in an East African country, it is very important that the gross national product is not so disproportionately distributed that it retains its colonial racial cvertones. The point is that ostentious life-style of a tiny racial minority vibrates racial signals all around which deeply undermine the morale of a common African. Racial consciousness in such a situation precedes class consciousness. It is, therefore, necessary for the reasons of racial justice, in an African country, that the bulk of national income is shared by the indigenous Africans and only a relatively small part accrues to the alien settler element, whether Asian or European. It is an absurdity to permit indefinitely economically dominant position to an alien element. The middle-class constitutes a backbone of the society in a free-enterprise economy, and no respectable independent country in the world could be expected to permit an alien settler element to enjoy that position indefinitely, even if we assume that the country concerned wants to follow broad traits of 'laissz-faire' economy. It would, therefore, be in the interest of the alien settler elements to help African advancement whenever and whereever this balance has been badly disturbed under the colonial system. It is most urgent that Africans occupy prominent position in the economic development of their own countries.

Complementary Economic Role

A corrolary to the above proposition would be to evolve a new pattern of economic development which takes care of much faster African advancement than achieved in the past. We are not concerned with the nature and essential components of this pattern. But, from the point of view of Asian settlers, our structural study suggests that the role of Asians in the development process should be rendered complementary to that of the Africans. In the early years of colonisation there was little friction between Asians and Africans as long as African advancement was not hindered by the Asian presence whether in trading sphere or the services sector. On the contrary, there is evidence which suggests greater understanding between the two communities. The friction then prevailed between the European and Asian settlers. Lord Delamare, the acknowledged leader of the White settlers complained of this friction when he wrote: "In all new countries the backbone of the country is the small man, the white colonist with small means, but there is no place for him in a country when once the Asiatic is there. . . . All the vegetables grown for the town is done by Indians, all the butchers with one or two exceptions are Indians, all the small country stores are kept by Indians and most of the town shops, all the lower grade clerks are Indians, nearly all the carpentry and building is done by Indians. They thus fill all the occupations and trades which would give employment to the poor white colonists, specially those arriving new in the country. That is what Indian immigration means in the early days of a very new country in Africa. It means that if open competition is allowed the small white colonist must go to the well."[24] By the end of the Second World War this friction was replaced by the one between Africans and Asians because by the then African advancement was hindered or handicapped by the Asians as explained above. Hence, the significance of complementary economic roles in independent East African territories without which tensions are likely to persist and non-racial equilibrium cannot be obtained.

No Interference in Internal Politics

Yet, the fifth parameter of this matrix is to keep off the internal politics. The African countries are by and large convulsing under the pressures of political instability and economic dependence. The conflicting situations are the bane of several independent African states. Adda B. Bozeman rightly points out that: "Conflicts in Africa have become intensified in the last decade both within each state and in relation between states."[25] Almost half of them have witnessed military *coup d'etats*. There could always be a temptation to fish around in such troubled waters. The conflicting situations in Southern Africa, the Horn of Africa, the Western Sahara and Arab-Israeli postures are the matters of deep concern the world over. These have already sharpened East-West interaction. The new Indian migrants and early Asian settlers will, under these circumstances, be well advised to keep away from internal tensions and external pulls and pressures. They must keep on the right side of the African cause in the liberation struggles. To my mind, one of the great happenings of historical significance of the post-World War II period has been the assertion by Africans of their identity. The African personality could no more be disregarded as it was in the past. The people of Indian origin in these parts will particularly do well to remember this.

Thus, the future prospects of the Asians in East Africa both those who are settled in those countries as citizens and the fresh Indian element is likely to be largely conditioned by this five-sided matrix or five-pointed star. As long as the Asians operate within the parameters of the matrix, and observe the code of conduct indicated by it, they could still play a significant economic role in the future development of the East African countries—the development largely designed by the Africans themselves. Out-stepping the matrix without reconstructing its broad cantours may be disasterous, not only for the Asian settlers but may be for those Indians, too, who are being presently recruited by the African countries to supply the missing factor in-puts in their development effort. India maintains most cordial relations with African countries as also most of the other developing countries, loosely referred to as the Third World countries. These countries—most of whom have attained independence after the Second World War—gene-

rally recognise that India has a great asset in its trained manpower resources, and that she has also attained an intermediate
level in the matter of technological and industrial development.
They, therefore, look to India for the supply of appropriate
technology and certain category of manpower resources. There
is, thus, a great potential for economic collaboration and technical cooperation between India and other developing countries. That could also be an important factor in building up a
new economic order to free the newly independent countries
from their total dependence on the former imperial powers.
But there are pitfalls, and those must be identified and avoided.
One such problem is the economic role played by Asians in
the economic development of the former British East African
territories of Kenya, Uganda and Tanzania. It is shown in
this paper how this role was reflected in the structural imbalances of those countries that undermined African advancement.
It was, of course, a product of colonial system and situation
peculiar to East Africa. However, learning from that experience, it is urgent to take care that such a situation is not repeated there or elsewhere, which apart from causing deep fissures
in India's relations with those countries, could prove to be
disasterous for the resident Indian community.

An attempt to construct the matrix is to avoid such pitfalls
in the future. The matrix provides only a broad guide-line,
which may be found useful not only by the Indian residents
of East Africa, but also by the Indians residing in other parts
of Africa and Asia.

REFERENCES

[1] R.R. Ramchandani, *Uganda Asians: The End of an Enterprise*
(Bombay, 1976).
[2] R. Robinson and J. Gallaghar, *Africa and Victorians* (London,
1961), p. 13.
[3] McDermott points out that "The arbitrament of Lord Canning was
an acknowledgement of the paramoun intetrest and influence of the
British Indian Empire in East Africa ... " P,L. McDermott,
British East Africa or I.B.E.A. (London, 1895), p. 2.

[4] Leys Norman, *Kenya* (London, 1924), p. 70.

[5] Ibid., pp . 76-77.

[6] Cf. Elspeth Huxley, *White Man's Country*, Vol. I (London, 1953), p. 206.

[7] The Government of India impressed upon the Imperial Government that the Indian intelligentia without regard to political divisions or party aims, stood as one man to resent the slight cast upon thelr country, and to demand in the strongest terms the vindication of what they regarded as the elementary rights of their nationals in Kenya". See Government of India, *India in 1924-25*, (Calcutta, 1926), **p. 49.**

[8] Ramchandani, n. 1, Table 2.1, p. 49.

[9] Great Britain, *Indians in Kenya: Memorandum* (London, Cmd., 1922, 1923), p. 11.

[10] Loc, cit,

[11] See Ramchandani, n.1, Ch. IV on the Development of Cotton Industry, Particularly pp. 120-39.

[12] Ibid., p. 137.

[13] Uganda's highlands adjacent to Kenyan border were transferred from Uganda to Kenya in 1902.

[14] T.O. Elias, "Some Current Problems of African Land Tenure", *Tropical Agriculture*, Vol. 33, No. 4, (October 1956).

[15] C.S., Uganda, to Indian Association, Kampala, No. 2288, 14 November 1924, *E.A. File 2288 I*, pp. 368-69; Cf. Ramchandani, n. 1, p. 106. Also see in this book "Factors Handicapping African Advancement in Trade", pp.105-9.

[16] S.H. Morris. '*Social Structure with Particular Reference to Asians in Uganda*, Makerere Institute of Social Research, Box 20.2/23, p. 22.

[17] Thomas and Scott, *Uganda* (London, 1935), p. 313.

[18] Ramchandani, n. 1, p. 214.

[19] Thomas and Scott, n. 17, p. 315.

[20] Cyril and Rhona Sofer, *Jinja Transformed* (Kampala, 1954), p. 50.

[21] Walter Elkan, *Migrants and Proletarians* (London, 1960), p. 49.

[22] Ramchandani, n. 1, p. 247.

[23] Thomas Brintley, *Economics of International Migration* (London, 1958).

[24] cf. White Mans Country, n. 6, p. 206.

[25] Adda B. Bozeman, *Conflict in Africa* (*Concepts and Realities*) (Princeton, N.J., 1976).

TABLE 1

Uganda: Racial Classification of Employes by Occupation, June 1963

Occupational Category	*Africans	Europeans	**Asians
1. Professional and Technological	10,438	1,853	1,104
2. Administrative, Clerical and Managerial	5,656	1,051	1,545
3. Secretarial and Clerical	9 143	491	2,610
4. Sales Staff	1,686	73	1,149
5. Carpenters, Masons, etc.	6,148	19	500
6. Metal Trades (Mechnical)	2,612	52	808
7. Electrical Trades	1,077	42	222
8. Other Skilled Workers	10,088	31	516
9. Semi-Skilled Workers	18,913	13	176
10. Unskilled Workers	1,15,959	2	47
11. Other Occupations	17,952	10	129
Total	1,99,322	3,637	8,806

*African Adult Males
**Asian Males

Source: UgandaG overnment, *Enumeration of Employees*, June, 1963.

(Entebbe: Statistical Division, Ministry for Planning and Community Development, December, 1964).

TABLE 2

Uganda: *1963 Monetary Income by Race*
(*in pound sterling*)

1. Monetary G.D.P.	128.7mn
2. Total African Monetary Income	85.4mn
3. Total Non-African Monetary income	33.7mn
4. Total European Income	9.7mn
5. Total Asian Income	24.8mn
6. Non-African per capita Income	345
7. Asian per capita Income	288
8. African per capita Income	12
9. European per capita Income	990*
10. (8) As percentage of (7)	4.2
11. (8) As percentage of (9)	1.2

Source: R.R. Ramchandani, *Uganda Asians: The End of An Enterprise* (Bombay, 1976), p. 241.

TABLE 3

Kenya: G.D.P.: African and Non-African Income
(in pounds sterling)

	1954	1962	1963
1. Gross Domestic Products	158.0mn	244.1mn	260.0mn
2. Monetary G.D.P.	112.5mn	180.9mn	193.3mn
3 Subsistence Sector	45.5mn	63.2mn	66.7mn
4. African employment income	24.5mn	44.9mn	48.3mn
5. African marketed product	6.6mn	11.7mn	12.4mn
6. Non-agric. African enterprise	2.4mn	4.5mn	5.0mn
7. Total African Monetary Income	33.5mn	61.1mn	65.7mn
8. Total African Income	79.0mn	124.3mn	132.4mn
9. (8) as % of (1)	50.0 %	50.0 %	50.9 %
10. (7) as % of (2)	29.8 %	33 8 %	34.0 %
11. African population ('000)	6,572	8,325	8,575
12. African per capita Income	12.0	14.9	15.4
13. African per capita monetary income	5.1	7.3	7.7
14. Non-African income	72.4mn	100.0mn	115.3mn
15. (14) as % of (2)	64.4	59.7	59.6
16. Non-African population ('000)	215	270	272
17. Non-African per capita Income	337	400	424

Provisional

Source: Dharam Ghai, *Some Aspects of Income Distribution in East Africa,* E.D.R.P./51, 24 November 1964.

TABLE 4

Tanganyika: G.D.P. African and non-African Incomes
(in pound Sterling)

	1962	1963
1. Gross Dometic Product	211.4mn	231.3mn
2. Monetary G. D. P.	136.8mn	154.6mn
3. Subsistence Income	74.6mn	76.7mn
4. African employment income	36.5mn	41.9mn
5. African peasant monetary income	30.0mn	32.5mn
6. African non-agricultural enterprises	9.4mn	9.8mn
7. Total African income	150.0mn	160.9mn
8. African monetary income	75.9mn	84.2mn
9. (7) as % of (1)	71.2 %	69.6 %
10. (8) as % of (2)	55.5 %	54.5 %
11. African population ('000)	9,419	9,654
12. Africa per capita income	16.0	16.7
13. African per capita monetary income	8.1	8.7
14. Non-African income	52.3mn	59.0mn
15. (14) as % of (2)	38.2	38.2
16. Non-African population : ('000)	141	121
17. Non-African per capita income.	371	413

Source : Dharam Gahi, *Some Aspects of Income Distribution in East Africa* E. D. R. P./51, 24 November 1964, p. 16.

R. V. RAMDAS

Indian Settlements in Mauritius

MAURITIUS WAS UNINHABITED only four centuries ago. From times immemorial India has established contacts with her west-shore neighbour, Africa. On their way to East Africa Indian sailors and traders must have known and touched this island. The Dutch who were the first to occupy Mauritius, found the Indian crows in Mauritian jungles. It was an ingenious practice of the early Indians to carry with them trained birds with strong wings on their voyages to guide them to the shores in case of difficulty. This instinct of birds particularly of crows is common knowledge. There are references to shore finding crows in the Digha Nikaya and the Baveru Jataka as having been carried by sailors in their trading expeditions.[1]

Andre Scherer noted in *History of Reunion* that the Dutch who settled in Mauritius in 1598 saw 300 pounds of wax on which something had been written. The historian does not admit that the language used was Greek. His opinion is that it is more probable that Sanskrit or some other ancient language of Asia had been used.[2] This view corroborates with that of the Mauritian historian, Guimbeau, who remarks that when the Arabs had not christened Mauritius every name given to it in old maps was Sanskrit.[3]

A map which the Portuguese seized on a Moorish vessel gave

195

Arab names to the various islands of the Indian Ocean. Mauritius was known as Din-e-Arabi. The Portuguese called it "Ilha do Cirno", perhaps because of the huge birds known as Dodo, which then swarmed this island and which may have been mistaken for the swan. The Dutch gave the name of Mauritius in the honour of the stadholder Maurice of Nasau, son of William of Orange.[4]

The strategic importance of Mauritius has given the island some symbolic names: "The Gataway of India," "The Key to the Asian Colonies," "Gibralter of the East," "Malta of the Indian Ocean" and "Pearl of the Indian Ocean". During the Portuguese period Mauritius remained a mere refuelling station to vessels going East. From a refuelling station, Labourdonnais turned it into a spring-board of attack against India. It contributed to the Anglo-French conflict in India. Ultimately the English annexed Mauritius to the British Empire.

An Indian is known to have gone to Mauritius with the Dutch from Madagascar. He embraced Christianity and was named Lawrence.[5] A man named Calcutye accompanied the Dutch when they finally withdrew from Mauritius in 1710. Calcutye is the inflected from a 'Kalkatiya,' i.e. a person from Calcutta.[6]

It was Labourdonnais who brought artisans from South India and employed Africans as apprentices under them who became good machanics. In 1740 there were 137 Indian artisans, masons, carpenters and blacksmiths, 67 African artisans and 72 apprentices. After the departure of the French engineer, an Indian even acted as an engineer and was in-charge of the constructions.[7] Some Indian traders also settled down in Mauritius during the French period. Saint Pierre dwells on the customs and manners of the Indians settled in Mauritius not only in Paul and Virginia but also in Etudes de la Nature. Saint Pierre was pleased to find the flora and fauna of India in Mauritius.[8]

Shortly, after the end of the French rule convicts were brought from India in 1815 to rear silk worms. The Mauritian silk industry came into being with the help of Indian convict labour. R.T. Faraguahar, the first British Governor of Mauritius, employed Indian convicts for road building. They built public roads, and many a private one as well, in Mauritius.

Charles Darwin was in Mauritius in 1836. He notes:

Convicts from India are banished here for life, at present there are about 800 and they are all employed in various public works. Before seeing these people, I had no idea that the inhabitants of India were such noble looking figures.

These men are generally quiet and well conducted, from their outward conduct, their cleanliness and faithful observance of their strange religious rites, it was impossible to look at them with the same eyes as our own wretched convicts in New South Wales.[9]

Mauritius was, by and large, a colony of slaves till 1835. Slaves outnumbered free Mauritians. It has been estimated that Mauritius had 87,000 slaves in 1815. The number of slaves progressively declined to 80,000 in 1817 and 77,000 in 1826. It further went down to 69,000 in 1827, and 76,000 in 1835.[10]

The emigration of Indian labour began with the abolition of slavery in the British Empire in 1834. During the first four years the emancipated slaves had to remain with their former masters as paid labourers but as soon as they were able, the freed slaves left the plantations for the towns or set themselves up in villages as small planters or artisans.

The abolition of slavery in the British Colonies was followed by a serious labour problem in Mauritius and thousands of Indian indentured labourers were imported to work on Mauritian plantations. Mauritius, by the way was the first British colony to import free labour on a large scale from another part of British Empire. Transportation of labour into long distances had been limited hitherto to convicts or slaves. The introduction of Indian 'coolies' or 'labourers' was to proceed and prosper in Mauritius at such a rate as to constitute an absolutely novel phenomenon in economic history.

Mauritian planters considered Indians very useful and under proper treatment extremely tractable labourers. Emancipated Negro slaves, on the other hand, were described by Franco-Mauritian planters as idle, lazy and drunkards—set of beings prefering to work by jobling or lash work. The planters preferred Indians to Negroes for carting work as Indians were more temperate or trustworthy.

Indian immigration began in 1835. During that year 1,160 men, 61 women, 22 boys and 11 girls were landed in Mauritius under contracts of indenture to planters. Immigration continued till 1907. During this period over 450,000 Indians were brought to Mauritius. The influx of Indians brought a radical change in the composition of Mauritian population. In 1835 the Indians constituted only a minute proportion of the population. By 1846, one third of the population was Indian. In 1861, two thirds of the population was Indian— a proportion maintained to the present.[12]

Mr. Dawson, one of the members of the inquiry committee set up in Bengal Presidency, observed in his minute in 1840 that the continuance of this system is indispensible to the existence of the island as a commercial colony.[13] The introduction of 25,468 immigrants between 1834 and 1839 saved the colony from ruin. Had it not been for Indian immigration, the sugar industry would almost certainly have disappeared altogether in the period of severe competition with slave-grown sugar after the equalisation of duties in 1846.[14]

It is due to the Indian indentured labour that Mauritius became more and more prosperous. The prosperity of the colony is to be attributed, mainly, to the expansion of sugar cultivation made possible by Indian labour. Mauritius produced only 11,200 metric tons of sugar in 1823. The growth of the sugar industry since 1823 as shown by S.B. Mukerjee in his book on *The Indentured System in Mauritius*[15] speaks for itself.

Year	Sugar production (metric tons)
1823	11,200
1843	35,580
1863	129,210
1883	112,800
1903	161,120
1923	225,040
1943	310,720
1953	500,000

On his way to South Africa, Gandhiji visited and stayed in Mauritius for ten days. In reply to the reception accorded to him by the Indian community at Port Louis, Gandhiji said that

the sugar industry of the island owed its unprecedented prosperity mainly to Indian immigrants. He stressed that Indians
should regard it their duty to acquaint themselves with happenings in their motherland and should take interest in politics.[16]

It was Adolphe de Plevitz, a Prussian who had settled in
Mauritius, who espoused the cause of Indian immigrants. He
toured the country and obtained 9,401 signatures to a petition
which he submitted to the Secretary of State along with a
pamphlet setting out their grievances. He demanded a Royal
Commission. Plevitz was publicly assaulted by Louis Lavoquer,
a planter, who later became the Mayor of Port Louis.[17] A
Royal Commission was appointed. The recommendations did
not improve the condition of Indian labourers.

Manilal Doctor began to practise as a barrister in Mauritius.
He was moved by the plight of Indian labourers and planters.
With the help of Mohammedan and Tamil merchants, Manilal
Doctor was able to acquire a press. He started his billingual
weekly paper, *The Hindustanee*, on 15 March 1909. The paper
was in English and Gujarati, but later he changed Gujarati
into Hindi. With consistency and courage, he fought the battle
of the underdog and was unsullied by the jeer and jibes of the
white oligarchy. His paper stood for the "liberty of individual,
fraternity of men and equality of races."[18]

Gandhiji published the accounts of the sufferings of Indians
in Mauritius in the *Indian Opinion* dated 26 November 1909
and added, "Those who read about these sufferings will be
convinced of the need to put a stop to the system of indenture.
The all too numerous incidents of this kind prove again and
again that this system is indistinguishable from slavery."[19]

The indenture system was abolished by the Emigration Act
of 1922. Rev. Beaton said in 1859:

These swarthy Orientals, so thinly clad, are the muscles and
sinews of Mauritius body politics. They are the secret
source of all the wealth, luxury and splendour with which
the island abounds. There is not a carriage that rolls the
macadamised chaussee or a robe of silk worn by the fair
Mauritian, to the purchase of which, the Indian has not by
his labour indirectly contributed. It is from the labour of

this swarthy body in the canefields that gold is extracted more plenteously than from the diggings of Ballarat. Respect that swarthy stranger, for without him Mauritius would soon be stripped of its wealth and left with scarcely sufficient exports to produce food for its rice eating cigar smoking inhabitants.[20]

All Indians settled in Mauritius were not labourers. In 1829, Dr. Mallappa Sinnapoulay, a South Indian was among the few doctors Mauritius had. In 1870 Prof. Rajarathnam Mudliar taught Tamil at the Royal College, Port Louis. In 1879 Taleb Hussein was the Professor of Hindusthani at the same College.[21]

The Muslim traders probably first came when Tipu Sultan was negotiating with the authorities of Il de France. The next to arrive were the Cutchee Memons from Cutch, the Hallaye Memons from Kathiavar and Soonee Surtee from Surat. One of the Soortee firms, that of Ibrahim Bahemia, was established in 1845. Hindu merchants came from Madras and Pondicherry. They were Pillays and Chettiars and being wealthier than the immigrants they naturally had more political consciousness. Some of these came earlier than the Muslim traders because one of them Vellivahel Annaswamy had bought the estate of Bon Espoir as far back as 1826. In 1852, the same estate was sold to Tirumondi Chettiar. These merchants built the first temple and first mosque on the island and made their culture respected by Europeans. They also gave to the colony its first Indian politicians and members of the legislature and of the municipality.[22]

Among the Hindu merchants who came later from the Bombay Presidency were the jewellers from Kathiawar and Brahmins from Gujarat. Many of the Gujaratis came as clerks of Muslim merchants but have now set up firms of their own. The Indian merchants imported most of the food-grains and are still among the biggest in the textile trade.

As the Indian population became stabilized a generation of Mauritian-born Indians grew up. By 1898 Mauritian-born Indians outnumbered those born in India. The economically successful began to educate their children for the professions and employment in the Government Civil Service. In 1851,

Indians contributed 43 per cent of the population but only 4 per cent of professionals and 27 per cent of the civil service. By 1901, 70 per cent population was Indian and Indians cons- tituted 23 per cent of professional and 28 per cent of civil service. In 1952 Indians constituted 67 per cent of the popula- tion. The Indian percentage in the professions had risen to 27 per cent and in the civil service to 53 per cent.[23]

A large proportion of Indo-Mauritians are engaged as farm hands on the sugar plantations of Mauritius. The breaking up of the large estates into small holdings has afforded them opportunity of owning or leasing sufficient land which they cultivate themselves. The steady rise in the number of Indian peasant proprietors, and the system of cultivation adopted by them have contributed to the general prosperity of Mauritius.

Nearly 55,000 acres of cane land, 95 per cent of land under vegetables, 90 per cent of all the carts in colony, 95 per cent of all the milk cows, the whole milk trade, the poultry and the egg trade, hnd the important manure trade are handled entirely by Indians. 80 per cent of the buses, taxis and lorries also belong to the Indian population.[24]

In the following table the rise of the Indians in the medical, legal and teaching professions over the past hundred years is noted.

Percentage of Indians in the Medical, Legal and Teaching Professions, 1851-1952[25]

Year	Medical		Legal		Teaching	
	Indian	Non-Indian	Indian	Non-Indian	Indian	Non-Indian
	%	%	%	%	%	%
1851	3	97	—	100	1	99
1861	2	98	—	100	10	90
1871	—	100	—	100	17	83
1881	2	98	—	100	18	82
1901	2	98	1	99	18	82
1944	14	86	15	85	26	74
1952	29	71	25	75	26	74

There is a tendency for certain groups to be associated with certain occupations. Thus there is a predominance of Chinese among sales men, a predominance of Indians in agricultural pursuits and a predominance of the general population among craftsmen and related workers. More of the top positions are still held by the Franco-Mauritians; more of the lower positions are still occupied by the Hindus.

The population of Mauritius today is 845,000 of which 52 per cent are Hindus and about 20 per cent are Muslims. More than 70 per cent of the population are of Indian origin. Another important group Creole—a mixed race—number nearly 2,00,000. There are 20,000 economically all-powerful French, known as Franco-Mauritians, and about 25,000 Chinese.[26] The Franco-Mauritians control the economy. They own 17 of the 21 sugar factories.[27] In the economic pyramid the Franco-Mauritian is at the top and Hindus are at the base.

Mauritius is sugar. It is the sugar that is the basis of the prosperity of the island. It produces nearly 70,000 tons of sugar exported mostly to Britain. It has a very delicate relation with South Africa. Mauritius earns its foreign exchange from South African tourists and buys some food from that country. It has no diplomatic ties with South Africa, but there is a trade representative from that country.[28]

In Mauritius, the people of Indian origin are in power. The Labour Party led by Prime Minister, Sir Seewosagar Ramgoolam is an alliance of Hindus and Muslims. The leader of the opposition in Parliament Mr. Gaetan Duval leads the Parti Mauricien Social Democrate (PMSD), which is a party of Creoles and has its main supporters from Creoles and Franco-Mauritians. Paul Berenger, leader of Movement Militant Mauritians (MMM) is a Marxist. Mauritians of Indian origin will positively influence course of events in Mauritius.

REFERENCES

[1] *The Indian Review*, August 1961.
[2] B. Bissondoyal, *The Truth about Mauritius* (1968), pp. 9-10.

[3] Ibid.

[4] J.N. Roy, *Mauritius in Transition* (1960), p. 21.

[5] S.B. Mookherji, *The Indenture System in Mauritius, 1837-1916*, p. 11.

[6] Ibid.

[7] Ibid., p. 26.

[8] Bissondoyal, n. 2, p. 1.

[9] B. Bissondoyal, "Mauritius to England", Chapter XXI, *A Journal of Researches*, n. 2, p. 17.

[10] Mookherji, n. 5, p. 13.

[11] *Parliamentary Papers, India, 1841*, XVI, (45), p. 87.

[12] B. Benedict, *Indians in a Plural Society*, p. 17.

[13] Gen. Dept., (Engg.) 4 November 1840, Nos. 15-20.

[14] Saha Panchanan, *Emigration of Indian Labour 1834-1900* (1970), p. 157.

[15] Mookherji, n. 5, p. 66.

[16] *The Standard*, 15 November 1901; *La Radical*, 15 November 1901.

[17] Roy, n. 4, pp. 216-7.

[18] Ibid., p. 228.

[19] *Indian Opinion*, 26 November 1910.

[20] Roy, n. 4, p. 187.

[21] Bissondoyal, n. 2, p. 160.

[22] Roy, n. 4, pp. 231-32.

[23] Benedict, n. 12, p. 27.

[24] Bissondoyal, n. 2, p. 79.

[25] Benedict, n. 12, p. 28, Table II.

[26] *The Financial Times*, 26 June 1974.

[27] *The Financial Times*, 18 June 1976.

[28] *Commerce*, 27 December 1976, p. 21.

A.S. KALA

The Role of 'Asians' in Kenya's Nationalist Movement

AS ELSEWHERE, IN Africa too, nationalist movements began as a revolution against colonialism. Africa entered the age of nationalism quite late. It was only after the Second World War when the British and the French colonies in South and Southeast Asia had become independent that nationalist movements in Africa gathered momentum. The Africans bitterly resented the European racial arrogance. As Prof. K.A. Busia puts it: "The fact that African nationalism is, in the first place a demand for racial equality, is its most conspicuous attribute. Africans demand acceptance as equals in the human family."[1]

One important feature to be remembered while discussing Kenyan nationalism is the existence of a large white settler population in Eastern Africa, and more prominently in Kenya. Along with these white settlers, there were a large number of Asians in Kenya. mostly the people from India, who came there as early as the beginning of the 19th century. The growth of nationalism in Kenya illustrates the trend of politics in the twentieth century in those areas of Africa, where the colonial system was all pervasive and where non-Africans dominated the economic and political scenes.[2]

Due to the dominance of the alien races in the economic and political spheres, the Kenyan Africans always remained at

204

the bottom and as a result, there was a continuous tension and racial friction in Kenya during the colonial rule. In this respect, nationalist aspirations of Kenyan Africans were not always the same as in the countries of other parts of Africa.

The role of Asians in the African nationalist movements in the former British East African territories of Kenya, Uganda and Tanzania has been significant. It has been particularly marked in Kenya. In order to have a proper appraisal of the role played by the Asians in Kenya's nationalist movement, it is necessary to examine the background of the influx of Asians into Kenya and their economic and political status vis-a-vis that of the white settlers and the Africans.

By the middle of the 19th century, the Asians, i.e. largely the people of Indian origin, had well established themselves as traders and middlemen. They had indeed come to play a vital role in the economic life of Kenya. Gradually, they entered the political arena too and rendered a valuable service in the cause of African nationalist movement. For obvious reasons, the white settlers considered themselves as belonging to the ruling element. As such, the question of their participation in any nationalist movement did not arise. On the other hand, the Asians had to fight for their own rights and survival. Like the Africans, the Asians too were the victims of discriminatory practices of the colonial administration. It is as such that the Asians shared some thing common with the indigenous African population. Another important factor in this context is the fact that India was the first non-white British subjected country to emerge from the clutches of foreign rule. This became a starting point in giving a boost to the nationalist movements elsewhere. In Kenya, therefore, the African leaders were influenced not only by the political activities of the Kenyan Indians, who all along fought for their equality of status with the white settlers, but also by the nationalist movement in India.

To begin with, it is important to know how the Asians became a sizeable community in Kenya? How and why did the Asians obtain a better social, political and economic position than the indigenous Africans? How did their struggle against racial discriminatory practices of the colonial adminstration help the Africans in their struggle for independence? Did the

Indians play a substantial role in the African nationalist movement or they merely sat on the fence? In this essay, an attempt
is made to answer these querries.

Influx of Indians

The Indians have been trading on the East coast of Africa
from ancient times. From the 10th century to the middle
of 18th century, the East Africa coastal trade was mainly in
the hands of Arab and Indian dhow traders. However, the
Indian contact with East Africa substantially increased since
the 19th century. Sir R. Coupland has drawn attention to
the long standing Indian attitude for trading in these parts.
"Much of the ocean shipping," he writes, "was Indian owned
and Indian manned and since Arabs in general seem never to
have shown much aptitude for the technique of business, it was
probable that Indians were from the earlist day, the masters of
finance, the bankers, money changers and money lenders."[3]

Kenya was declared a British Protectorate on 1 July 1895
and it was made a Crown Colony in 1920. The Indians had
settled there long before the British came to East African territory. They had established themselves mainly as traders, who
maintained financial transactions and business. They invariably operated behind the Arab trading expeditions with the
interior by supply of funds and finance. Sir Edward C. Buck,
Secretary of the Department of Revenue and Agriculture in
the Government of India, who visited the Protectorate in 1905
remarked, "the first thing that struck me was that the whole
country had an Indian complexion, it was run by Indians and
financed by Indians."[4]

With the coming of the British, the Indian immigration
gained further momentum. This time, a new Indian element
was injected in the economy. This was the Indian artisan
skills, subordinate services and also coolies for the Uganda
Railway. Over 32,000 Indians were brought from India as coolies, almost 30,000 of whom were sent back home. Gradually
the Indians emerged as the prominent operators in trade and
commerce of the colony and they served as a link between the
virtually illterate Africans and upperclass Europeans. "It was
the Indian trader" wrote Winston Churchill, "who penetrating
and maintaining himself in all sorts of places to which no

whiteman could not go—has more than any one else developed
the early beginnings of trade."[5]

Prior to 1895, there were proposals to Consul-General
Kirke by wealthy and influential Indians like Jairam Sewji of
Zanzibar regarding the establishment of an Indian capital. By
the end of the 19th century, the Indian community had increased
very much and mostly they were traders and artisans. Being a
dynamic and resourceful people, the Indians established themselves in the economic sphere. As a result, the Europeans,
who had arrived in Kenya in large numbers feared that not
only the activities of the Indians would influence the Africans,
but it would also be a hinderance to the progress of the settlers
in the matter of establishing a self-governing white colony for
themselves.

The Indians played a conspicuous role in the country's development in the early years of colonial rule. They laid a foundation for a retail economy and provided a basis for the Kenyan
currency and they were also responsible for the creation of
adequate transportation within the province. Thus they played
a vital role in opening up trade in the remote areas, in building
the railway and in financing development.

White settlers resent Indian presence

By the beginning of the 20th century, the European settlers
started a bitter campaign against the Indians and their role in
the country's economy. They wanted to keep the Indians out
of the country altogether. In order to restrict the flow of
Indians into Kenya, numerous immigration regulations were
introduced.

From the beginning, the settlers were hostile to the Indian
presence and this hostility increased as the time progressed.
This naturally made the Indians cooperate with the Africans
in their joint struggle against European racial domination. The
Indians did not enter the Kenyan political scene for a long time.
It was only when the white settlers started resenting their presence that aroused the Indians to fight for their rights. Being so
long confined only to the economic sphere of Kenya, they now
registered their protests against discriminatory measures which
affected them as well as the Africans.

The colonial administration, being under heavy pressure

from the white settler community was significantly influenced by the interests of the white settlers. As a result, several discriminatory regulations against non-whites were introduced. The Crown Lands Ordinance of 1915 gave powers to the Governor to veto land transactions between different races. Under that, the Indians totally lost access to the highland areas. That is how the highlands became the white land by completely excluding the Asians and Africans: Before 1920, the grievances of the Indians centered around: (1) their exclusion from the highlands; (2) their representation in the legislative council; (3) their segregation on racial grounds both in commercial and residential areas; and (4) the restrictions on their immigration to the territory.

The political opposition by the Indians to the discriminatory practices, adopted in Kenya, seriously began when prominent Indians like A.M. Jeevanjee took the lead. He wrote articles in the Indian newspapers to draw the support of the Indian nationalist opinion against the anti-Indian policies of the Kenyan colonial administration which were formulated at the instance of the European settlers. The British Africa Indian Association, formed in 1907 appealed to Winstons. Churchill during his visit to Kenya. In 1909, A.M. Jeevanjee became the first Indian to be nominated as a number of the Legislative Council of Kenya. The Indians were naturally not satisfied with the mere token representation. They expected to be treated on par with the white settlers in this matter of representation in the Legislative Council. The struggle intensified when Jeevanjee retired in 1911. The Government declined to appoint any Indian in Jeevanjee's place on the grounds that there were "no prominent Indians of sufficient educational qualifications for appointment to the Legislative Council."[6] Meanwhile, "An appeal on behalf of Indians in East Africa"—was published by A.M. Jeevanjee, which put forth the grievances of the Indians in Kenya. This appeal mainly aimed at obtaining the elementary human rights that were denied to the Indians.

Indians Struggle for Equality of Status

Till the First World War, Indian political activity in Kenya was not systematically organised. It became more organised when the East African Indian National Congress (EAINC) was formed in March 1914. When India shifted her attention to Kenyan affairs after the War, a real political feeling was created among the Kenyan Asians. Indian nationalists demanded compensation for Indians' contribution in the war. They wanted equal rights for the Indian subjects of the Crown. This gave a fillip to the Asians in Kenya, who now pressed with greater vigour their case for equality of status and treatment with the European settlers. In the words of Gregory, although unsuccessful in efforts towards equality of treatment, the Indians were able to achieve a substantial modification of imperial policy. Their situation improved considerably as the period progressed.[7]

The Indian government was also approached by many leading individuals and organisations in India. In June 1920, Motilal Nehru, President of the All India Congress Committee cabled the Viceroy, a condemnation of the East Africa Government's attitude and asked that the Imperial Government intercede to "ensure Indians full status as British subjects." C.Y. Chintamani, Secretary of the National Liberal Federation, forwarded resolutions criticizing British policy towards Indians in Kenya, Uganda and Tanganyika.[8] It should be observed here that the Indians in Kenya never aspired for an Indian colony in Kenya or elsewhere in East Africa. May be some locally settled Indians were misdirected in this regard when the question came up with regard to territory of Tanganyika which was snatched from Germany during the war and placed under the British control as a mandatory territory. Some influential Indian leaders like Gandhiji, C.F. Andrews and others agreed that if Indians accepted an exclusive previleged position in East Africa, it would be morally wrong since Indians always struggled for equality of treatment throughout the British empire.

The friction between the Asians and the Europeans reached its peak in the early 1920's. This tussel between the alien races had pushed to the background the needs and grievances of the Africans so far. Now the Asians and the Europeans by blaming each other started their show of support for the Africans. The Europeans commented that the influence of the Asians on the Africans was morally degrading and corrupting. In January 1920, a petition was submitted by the Committee of European settlers in Nairobi. This called upon the Government to 'encourage European colonisation' and restrict Indian immigration, since it was detrimental to the European settlers and also the native Africans.[9]

During this time, there was a change in the leadership of the Indian community in Kenya from the old merchants to the newly-arrived immigrants, many of whom were professionals. M.A. Desai became more prominent among the new leaders. Other Indian leaders like H.S. Virji, L.J. Amin, B.S. Varma, Mangal Dass also joined him. Uuder their joint efforts, an organised campaign was launched. They sent deputations to the Viceroy of India and also laid a petition to Lord Milner, the Colonial Secretary. They could bear it no longer when the new Governor, Sir Edward Northey, made it clear that even though Indian interests were safeguarded, it would be the European demands which will be given primary concern. As a result of the Indian campaign, they were granted two elected seats in the Legislative Council, while the Europeans were given eleven seats. This intensified the Indian anger.

As the "Indian question" in Kenya became a major political issue, the Government of India began to take serious interest to find a solution to the controversy. As a result, the Indian protest gathered momentum. In 1921, Rev. C.F. Andrews, one of the most respected missionaries in India and a close associate of Gandhiji, came to Kenya to assist the local Indians.

In the Imperial Conference held in London during the summer of 1921, the Prime Minister, Lloyd George, praised India's war efforts and said that "she had proved her right to a new status in our council." One of the Indian delegates, Srinivas Shastri, asked that the Indians domiciled in the Dominions and Crown colonies should be admitted into the general body of citizenship with no deductions made from the rights enjoyed by other British subjects.[10]

The Indians also received encouragement from leading Europeans like Sir Harry Johnston, an early British administrator in Central and East Africa. Writing in *The Times* dated 22 August 1921, Sir Johnston referred to the injustice of the settlers' attitude. "The excess of their influence", he wrote, "revolts me, who strove before they were born to open up East

Africa to knowledge, by the help of Indian troops, Indian doctors and Indian clerks." He pointed out that it was the presence of the Indian traders on the East African coast, which was the main excuse and justification for British interference in those regions and that without the help, the bravery and the discipline of Indian soldiers, it was doubtful whether Britain would easily have got the better of Arab hostility, have suppressed slavery and slave trade or have acquired the 'mangificent empire' over East Africa, which she now possessed.[11]

Britain Recognises African Paramountcy

To bring out a compromise, the Winterton Agreement of 1922 provided for a common electoral roll for all British subjects with a property qualification and an educational test. This gave the Indians four seats in the Legislative Council. The immigration was to be unrestricted and segregation was to be abolished. This arrangement dissatisfied the white settlers.

To find a solution to this aggravated controversy, the European and Indian delegations were called to London. Following that, a settlement was made on 25th July 1923 in respect of the long pending 'Indian Question' in Kenya. The White Paper *Indians in Kenya: A Memorandum* was issued. One important aspect of the 'White Paper' was that it gave prominence to the African cause, while trying to find a solution to the European and Indian controversy. Thus, a first step was taken in giving expression to the doctrine of African paramountcy. It stressed that the British must safeguard the interests of the Africans since Kenya primarily belonged to the Africans. In part II of the White Paper, the following statement of policy appears: "His Majesty's Government cannot but regard the grant of responsible self-government as out of the question within any period of time, which need now be taken into consideration."[12]

The White Paper granted five seats to the Indians in the Legislative Council, elected on communal system as against common franchise. The Europeans were given eleven elected seats and one seat was reserved for the Arab community. In addition, one member was to be nominated to represent native interests. The segregation in townships was done away with and this aspect was not liked by the white settlers. However, the Highlands were owned by the Europeans only and this provision was naturally resented by the Indian community.

The White Paper of 1923 was a turning point from the point of view of Indian outlook. Till the early 20th century, the Indians were rather preoccupied with their economic interests. They were more concerned with improving their business opportunities. Their role in the political sphere seriously began only when the white settlers started competing with them. Prior to 1920, the African nationalist feeling in Kenya remained completely suppressed. And the politics in Kenya mainly centered around the white settlers and the brown settlers. The African had his grievances ever since the seed of colonialism was planted on his soil. But the lack of education, the lack of able guidance and the utterly bad conditions in which he lived did not enable him to open his mouth. While watching the white-brown conflict their political instinct was aroused and with the emergence of the 'educated elite' among them, nationalist sentiments were now boldly expressed with every passing day.

The Indians played a unique role in laying the foundation of the East African economy. The most impartial and authoritative opinion on the Indians' contribution was probably the Imperial Government's report to the League of Nations on the administration of Tanganyika during 1937. "The Indian trader is an essential part of the economic structure of the territory (the government stated) as he forms the link between the native purchaser and the wholesale importer. In the more remote areas of the territory he performs the double function of buyer and seller". After citing the Indian role in the economic life of the country, the report says, "all the evidence indeed goes to show that native and non-native trade are complementary and not antagonistic."[13]

Just as they laid the foundations of the Kenyan economy, the Indians, although not always aware of it played an important role in initiating the Africans in their struggle for freedom. The Indians were fighting for their own interests as the Europeans did for theirs. However, the political activities of the Indians gave a fillip to the African sense of nationalism. The net outcome of the widespread Indian agitation in East Africa and India, as Dr. R.R. Ramchandani mentions, was that,

Kenya ultimately did not go the same way as the Union of South Africa or present Rhodesia.[14]

Indians Support African Paramountcy

When the African interests were pronounced to be paramount vide the White Paper of 1923, the Indians were urged by the leaders of the EAINC to improve their relations with the Africans. Early educated Africans like Harry Thuku started asserting their demands. They received constant encouragement from the Indian leaders in Kenya. It should be emphasized that the Africans then considered the Indians as their good friends and the Indians too established contacts with the emerging African organisations like the young Kikuyu Association led by Thuku. Thuku recieved help from Indians like M.A. Desai, Hussein Suleman Virjee, G.B. Tadwalkar, K.N. Jani and others. Desai, being the editor of the *East African Chronicle*, gave prominence to the Kikuyu grievances in his newspaper.

On 8 May 1923, a letter appeared in the *Times* from C.F. Andrews: "In India today, there is an unanimous desire to recognise the interests of the African native in Kenya as of the first importance, to which Indian and European claims alike must always give way."[15]

Some of the active Indian leaders like J.M. Nazareth, A.B. Patel, M.A. Desai and others aimed at bringing the Africans and Asians together in their joint nationalist struggle against the racial discrimination by the Europeans. The EAINC supported the African cause to a great extent and all the Indian leaders showed absolute sympathy towards the issues that caused grievances to the Africans. Apart from this, the Africans were highly influenced by the nationalist movement in India. As Mangat observes, that the Indian political agitation and the support extended to their demands by the Government of India had far-reaching significance both for the initial declaration in favour of African paramountcy in 1923 and its subsequent reiteration in 1930. Similarly, their political disaffection in East Africa was of crucial importance in initiating Indian attempts to associate politically with the Africans in so far as this was made possible by the underprivileged status of the two communities vis-a-vis the Europeans.[16] The Indians assisted in printing the newspaper *Muiguithania*, which was edited by Jomo Kenyatta, on behalf of Kikuyu Central Association. In 1929, Isher Dass, an eminent Indian leader, accompanied Kenyatta to London.

Prior to 1945, none of the Indian leaders ever showed any resentment towards the Africans and the African causes. On the contrary, the Indian leaders actually supported their cause. In 1927 Tyeb Ali said: "The interests of the Africans and our own are indissolubly bound up together. In protecting our own interests we are also protecting the interests of the Africans."[17] In a similar vein, A.B. Patel said in his 1938 Presidential Address (15th session): "The bitterest opponents of the Congress will have to admit that at no time during its career, the Congress has considered it necessary to advocate any measure which will prejudicially affect native interests."[18]

In India, the interest in East Africa was rather more political and social than economic. There were three groups of thinking in this regard. One was the imperialist led by people like Aga Khan, G.K. Gokhale, Sir P. Mehta, Sarojini Naidu and others. They advocated for an Indian colony to serve as an outlet for India's surplus population. The second group was a large group which stressed the Indians' right to equality of status and treatment throughout the empire. Some principal organisations like the Imperial Indian Citizenship Association, the Indian Merchants Chamber and Bureau and the Federation of Indian Chambers of Commerce and Industry led by eminent leaders like Jehangir Petit, Sir Purushottamdas Thakurdas, G.A. Natesan, T.B. Sapru, V.S. Srinivas Shastri and others supported this group. The third group was humanitarian which gave prominence to African interests and it advocated that Africa belonged to Africans. This view was held by people like Tilak, B.P. Pal and others. After World War I, Gandhiji and Andrews also began to advocate the doctrine of native paramountcy. Later on many exponents of the second group joined the humanitarian group including Shastri and Thakurdas. C.F. Andrews was intrumental in persuading the Indians in East Africa to drop their demands for an exclusive Indian settlement and to compaign for equal treatment under a doctrine of native paramountcy.[19]

Further Advances in African Nationalist Movement

By the end of the 1940's, the Africans had made considerable progress in the political field. After his long stay in London, Kenyatta returned in 1947. Every African was disgusted with the colonial rule and the spirit of nationalism was mounting. It became more intense when Kenyatta assumed the leadership of Kenya African Union. At this critical juncture, very few Europeans sympathised with him, but most of the Indian leaders considered him to be a great leader and cooperated with him in various matters. To quote Mangat:

> The political chess game between the two important communities in which the Europeans had held a commanding position, needed only an African checkmate to end it and the arguments and the counter-arguments which the Europeans and the Indians had used against each other were to provide the Africans with a ready-made political weapon against both of them.[20]

The Second World War influenced Kenyan nationalism to a great extent. Most of the Kenyan Africans served outside Africa during the war, especially in the Middle East, Burma and India. The experience they obtained during the War broadened their outlook and increased their political conciousness. After the War, there was a violent nationalist upsurge in almost all the colonial territories. Independence movements in Africa and also in other parts of the world gathered momentum. India set an example by achieving her independence in August 1947. Kenya naturally aspired for the same goal and the African leaders were now not satisfied with piecemeal redress of their specific grievances.

It was only after the Second World War that the contact between the KAU and the Indian Congress was more firmly established. The main political issue facing the non-White communities of Kenya after the war was the fear of White domination. When the government was reorganised, the prominent European settler, Major Sir Ferdinand Bentinck, was appointed as the member of Agriculture Department. This provoked much criticism from the African and Asian populations, for they feared that this was a sign of European settler control over the future of Kenya.

By the end of the war, when the native "reserves" became over-crowded, prominent Indian leaders like A.B. Patel advocated that the Africans should be provided with additional land from the uncultivated parts of the White Highlands.[21] Both the KAU and the EAINC interchanged speakers at their annual meetings. A "fraternal delegation" from the KAU also took part in the proceedings of the 1948 EAINC session. A resolution sponsored by the great trade unionist Makhan Singh supported the KAU demands. Makhan Singh organised the trade union movement in East Africa in 1936 and he is rightly regarded as the founder of African trade unionism. He initiated the Membasa Dock Strike in 1939. His activities inevitably strengthened the morale of African labour.

The cooperation between tne Africans and the Asians was so great during this period, that even a British M.P., Fenner Brockway observed: "There is closest cooperation between the leaders of the Indian and African communities and a realisation that they must act together in the interest of both the peoples . . . Because of the close cooperation between the Indian and African communities in Kenya . . . I believe that racial equality may yet be established in the colony. Indians have a great responsibility in Africa and in Kenya, they are fulfilling it."[22]

It should be noted that in the later days of the colonial period, the growth of African nationalism was very rapid; and this factor in itself was mainly responsible for the declining political role of Asians in Kenya. As the political activities of the Africans increased, the Asians began to realise that Kenya was after all African territory and the Africans would achieve their independence soon. Although they themselves gradually moved back from the political sphere, the Asians continued to give further support to the African nationalist movement. As Mangat rightly puts it: "Indian political activity after the war was marked by its increasing subservience to African nationalism—for much of the political disaffection that had inspired Indian agitation in East Africa seemed to provide a basis for a common cause with African Nationalism."[23]

India's Concern for Kenya

There was a closer political collaboration between the African and the Indian leaders, when India achieved her independence in August 1947. The Government of independent India had a sympathetic outlook towards the African cause. The first Indian High Commissioner to Kenya, in 1948, Sri Apa B. Pant, actively supported the African freedom struggle. His contacts with African nationalist leaders and his outspoken and fiery comments were deeply criticised by the Europeans. Together with the other leading Indian lawyers, Apa Pant participated in the defence of Jomo Kenyatta at the Kapenguria Trial. The Kenya Government strongly objected this move. Appa Saheb also made possible for Mbiyu Koinange to have an official visit to India in 1949.

The Indian Government financed scholarships for African students in Indian universities. This was highly appreciated by African leader Koinange, who said: "Africans are grateful to pioneer Indians in Africa who had fought for the rights of the native Africans, even when they did not know how to do it."[24]

During the early 1950's, African nationalism in Kenya became intese and the political activities of the Africans increased. On the other hand, Indian political activity faded into the background. When the 'Mau Mau' erupted and the emergency was declared, in Kenya, in October 1952, the Asians were caught in a difficult position. They were looked upon with suspicious eyes by Europeans on the one hand and Africans on the other. Some of the Africans were rather sceptical about the Asian support to their freedom struggle. The Europeans on the other hand thought that the Asians were involved in the 'Mau Mau'. The African-Asian relationship at the leadership level deteriorated gradually. Some of the moderate Indian leaders, especially the older generation hesitated to give full support to the African 'struggle, suspecting that in free Kenya, they may become inconsequential in the political arena. However, it goes without question that there were some Indians who continued to give full support to the African cause. As Mangat observes: "In fact the Indians generally regarded the Mau Mau movement as an orthodox nationalist struggle on the lines of India, and they sympathised with its aims, if not its methods."[25]

Asian newspapers published the African grievances. In 1951, P.G. Pinto, the Secretary of Kenya Indian Congress, strongly supported the African demands. When the KAU was banned, there was no single political party in existence. In the absence of a strong political leader like Kenyatta, who was imprisoned for seven long years, the government was trying its hand at dividing the different tribes and disuniting them, so as to make the achievement of the common national cause difficult. At this critical juncture, the extremist Asian leaders like Pinto assisted the new African leaders, which resulted in his imprisonment.

The 'Mau Mau' gave a shape to the Kenyan nationalist movement. The real changes that took place in quick succession after the emergency could be rightly attributed to the 'Mau Mau' uprising. Some steps were taken to improve the conditions of the Africans. The colour bar began to disappear. In 1955, the Lidbury Report did away with the major traces of racial discrimination. When the Coutts Report of 1956 suggested a qualitative franchise for the Africans, the African members of the Council questioned this move. In this regard, the Asians supported universal adult franchise for the Africans.

In April 1959, the Constituency Elected Members Organization (CEMO), which was formed by the African, Asian and Arab elected members and also one European elected member, demanded a self-government for Kenya on a democratic basis. The Asians also brought forth vigorously in the Council the issue of the release of Kenyatta and other detainees. The great African leader, Tom Mboyba, said: "The overwhelming majority of the Indian community in Kenya supported the African stand and wanted to adhere to the standards set by Nehru and Gandhi as friends and allies in the struggle for freedom and democracy."[26] The Asian leaders in Kenya sincerely supported the African demands and the issue of the release of Kenyatta in the beginning of the 1960s. In March 1961, Ibrahim Nathoo, the Ismaili leader, resigned his ministership over the Kenyatta issue.

As the emergency in Kenya ended in 1960, two great political parties emerged in Kenya—The Kenya African National

Union (KANU), which represented urban nationalism—constituted mainly by the Kikuyu, Luo and Akamba tribes—and Kenya African Democratic Union (KADU) which was an alliance of minority tribes. In the Lancaster House Conference held in London in 1960, a decisive constitutional step was taken. The Africans were to form the majority in the Legislative Council. A common electoral roll was to be established for the first time in Kenya. The executive council was also reconstituted in favour of the Africans. Campaigning largely on the issue of Kenyatta's release, KANU won the election held in February 1961. After his release in August 1961, Jomo Kenyatta, the leader of KANU, soon brought the whole country under his command. In the General Election of May 1963, the first-ever held on a full franchise in Kenya, KANU was returned with a overwhelming majority. On 12 December 1963, Kenya became a fully independent republic. If the Indians wished to live in Kenya, they could do so either as full-fledged Kenyan citizens if they so desired, or like an alien element as any other foreigners could. The chance was given to them and many preferred to settle there as Kenyan citizens.

Conclusions

To sum up, the Asians in Kenya did play a role in boosting up the African sense of nationalism. Even though some writers assert that most of the Asians supported the Africans only in so far as that helped the Asian cause, we cannot deny that the early Asian political activity significantly motivated the Africans in the fight for their basic rights and previleges. If it had not been for the Asians in Kenya there was the real danger that White settlers would have taken the full control of Kenya as their brethren did in Southern Rhodesia (present Rhodesia).

When the European settlers were consolidating their position in Kenya, it was the Asians who challenged their supremacy. These early efforts of Asians resulted in the White Paper of 1923, which pronounced the prarmountcy of native interests in Kenya. This was a turning point in the then Kenyan political scenario.

The political struggle which was so far confined to Asians and Europeans, now became three-cornered, the Africans emerging out as the major contenders in the power struggle against

the British colonial rule. Inspired by the Asian political activities, the early African leaders like Harry Thuku encouraged
organisations like the Young Kikuyu Association way back in
1921. Once the Africans started voicing their grievances, they
generally received moral and material support and encourge-
ment from the Asians, who invariably worked for equal rights
for all races.

After the 1940's the Asians in Kenya were by and large re-
luctant to plunge deeply into the political arena. Gandhiji always held the view that Africa belonged to the Africans. Kenya
was after all an African country. In order to avoid any clash
with the Africans, the Asians cooperated with the Africans
and helped them in their cause. "To continue in the political
field, even on a non-racial basis is wrong" was the common
view of most of the Indians in Kenya.[27]

However, it should not be forgotten that the Indians did
play their part in initiating the African freedom movement in
Kenya. Indians in large numbers mostly came to Kenya for
economic interests. They were traders and businessmen and
they worked for the prosperity of the land. They were not politically motivated to set up their kingdom in Kenya. The European colonisers looked at the Asians just as they looked at the
Africans. As the Asians were better educated and well placed,
they first deeply felt the effects of the discriminatory practices
of the colonial administration. They started voicing their
grievances and fought for their political rights so that the white
settlers were not enthroned as masters over this territory.
These activities of the Asians encouraged and influenced the
African people to a great extent and paved the way for the
emergence and growth of African nationalism in Kenya. Sail-
ing on the same boat, the Asians and Africans cooperated
in several ways in their joint struggle against colonial
domination and racial discrimination.

It was however good on the part of the Asians to realise
their position and moved back from direct political involvement in any significant scale, at a proper time. Whether the
Asians supported the African cause with full faith in African
destiny or they had their own axe to grind is a question open
to debate. Yet, the Asians did play a role of some consequence when Kenya was ripe for independence.

REFERENCES

[1] K.A. Busia, *Challenge of Africa* (1962), p. 139.

[2] O. Adewoye, "Nationalism in Kenya, 1920-1963", *Tarikh*, Vol. 4, No. 1, 1971, p. 28.

[3] R. Coupland, *East Africa and its Invaders* (London, 1938).

[4] Cited from Robert G. Gregory, *India and East Africa. A History of Race Relations within the British Empire 1890-1939* (Oxford, 1971), p. 66.

[5] Winston S. Churchill, *My African Journey* (London, 1908), pp. 49-50.

[6] J.S. Mangat, *A History of the Asians in East Africa, 1886-1945*, (Oxford, 1969), p. 108.

[7] Gregory, n. 4, p. 496.

[8] Ibid., p. 192.

[9] Mangat, n. 6, p. 98.

[10] L.W. Hollingsworth, *Asians in East Africa* (London, 1960), pp. 85-6.

[11] Cited from ibid., p. 90.

[12] Great Britain, Colonial Office, *Indians in Kenya* (H.M.S.O., 1923), ed. 1922, cited from R.R. Ramchandani, *Uganda Asians. The End of an Enterprise* (Bombay, 1976), p. 61.

[13] Gregory, n. 4, pp. 498-500.

[14] Ramchandani, n. 12, p. 61.

[15] Cited from R.K. Tangri, "Asians in Kenya: A Political History", *Africa Quarterly*, Vol. 6, 1966-67 p. 109.

[16] Mangat, n. 6, p. 167.

[17] Tangri, n. 15, p. 111.

[18] Ibid.,

[19] Gregory, n. 4, pp. 503-4.

[20] Mangat, n. 6, p. 171.

[21] *East African Standard*, 12 October 1945, cited from Tangri, n. 15, p. 112.

[22] Fenner Brockway, "Racialism in East Africa: Where the colour bar works three ways", in *Forward* (Glasgow), 13 January 1951, p. 7.

[23] Mangat, n. 6, p. 176.

[24] *Times of India* (Bombay), 17 September 1949.

[25] Mangat, n. 6, p. 176.

[26] Tom Mboya, *Freedom and After* (London, 1963), pp. 112-3.

[27] *Mombasa Times* 23 July 1962, cited from George Delf, *Asians in East Africa* (London, 1963), p. 41.

Part III

Economic Dimensions

P. R. PANCHMUKHI

Education for Equality:
East African and Indian Experiments

HAVING ACCEPTED EQUALITY as an overriding goal of socio-economic policy making, it is necessary to consider different dimensions of this goal so that appropriate policies can be introduced to achieve it. Most of the newly developing countries in the Asian and African subcontinent have given a priority treatment to the objective of equality. Such an approach becomes inevitable because in the course of economic growth equity is found to have been adversely affected. There is a trade-off between growth and equity, and if future of the country has to be shaped with socio-economic justice and with a greater degree of harmony of interests then the objective of equity cannot be relegated to the background.

The objective of equity has mainly two dimensions if it is translated in terms of concrete policy. First there must be a provision of minimum standard of living to all the people in the country and if this requires re-distribution of income and economic power, then, an appropriate redistributive policy has to be introduced. The second, is reduction of the inter-unit disparties in respect of income and wealth at different levels. While the first objective refers to the increase in the absolute levels, the second refers to the reduction in the gaps between the relative

225

levels. In the time scale, these dimensions may refer to the existing situation or to the future situation. The policy for equality has to address itself to both of these dimensions in the present and future contexts. In the course of development, it is the second objective referring to the reduction in the disparities, that assumes a real significance, for, the minimum consumption standards may be automatically achieved, as the economy grows, assuming that the country's distributional mechanism is not entirely privileged-oriented only.

The relation between growth and equity is not always as simple as that depicted in the previous paragraph. The relation depends upon the particular stage of development of the country, also the kinds of change taking place, and the nature of policies introduced. The stage of development and equity has a U-shaped relation as Simon Kuznets has hypothesised.[1]

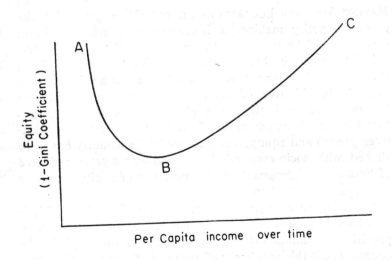

Hence, in the AB phase of equality income schedule, i.e. in the initial stages of development, there is a particular need for equity-oriented policies.

Tax transfer mechanism mostly affecting the current incomes, of the affected families, would be reducing only the current disparities; but they do not necessarily control the potential disparities, unless they influence the causative factors for such disparities. The inequities in the wealth and property ownership, inequities in the distribution of the factors causing individual's capacities to earn, and the possibilities to get employment, should be the target of equity policies if they are to be effective in the intert-emporal sense. In a system where the rewards are largely dependent upon the efficiency, skill and knowledge of the individual, the factors contributing to these should be part of the policy instruments. It is in this sense that the role of education as an agent of inter-temporal equalization needs to be recognized particularly in the context of developing countries. The objective of this paper is to briefly examine the measures of equality in education introduced in some of the African countries (especially Tanzania) and to compare them with the measures introduced in India. In the light of this brief discussion, it is intended to raise some issues of fundamental nature with regard to the relationship between education and equality.

East African Experiments

If education has to be the main policy variable to influence the distribution of income and economic power, then it is necessary that education itself should be equitably distributed. Equitable distribution in the context of current inequities (both, absolute, in the sense that minimum level of education is not available for many, and relative, in the sense that the interunit disparities exist with regard to education), would not obviously mean identical or the same distribution of education. By and large, there should be both equal treatment of equals (in case of persons with the same educational levels at present) and unequal treatment of unequals (in case of persons with unequal educational levels at present). Further, the policy has to consider the inter-sectoral (rural-urban), inter-regional (different states in a federation), inter-personal, inter-sex group (male-female), inter-community group (caste-wise, or race-wise) and inter-income group inequities.

To tackle all these dimensions of educational inequities, the developing nations in the East African region and also in India have adopted a number of policies which may be broadly grouped into: (a) global measures and (b) specific measures.

That global measures of educational expansion in general have been introduced in these developing countries can be clearly seen from the following statistical data (in Table 1 and the subsequent paragraph),

TABLE 1

Average Annual rate of growth of Enrolments
(during the 1950's and around 1960's)

East African countries	Enrolments in Primary	Secon-dary	Higher	Public exp. on educa-tion as % of total public exp.	Public exp. on education as % of GDP
Ethiopia	10	18	26	12.1	—
Kenya	8	11	15	15.9	3.6
Mauritius	6	18	8	11.6	3.0
Tanzania	9	9	—	17.0	2.2
Uganda	9	14	13	25.2	3.9
Zanzibar	9	13	—	13.1	—

These rates of growth are generally found to be higher than the rates in the previous decades. In Uganda, for instance, during the 1940's primary education enrolment increased at 5 per cent, and secondary education enrolment increased at around 15 per cent. During the 1960's and 1970's also further expansion in education has been witnessed in almost all the countries. In Tanzania, for instance, primary education enrolment increased from 7.1 lakhs in 1965 to 15.9 lakhs; in 1975, more than 200 per cent increase during the last decade. Secondary education enrolment in Tanzania increased from 31.4 thousand in 1967 to 53.2 thousand in 1975, an increase of 69 per cent during eight years.

One may also note that a fairly large percentage of the GDP of these countries is being spent on the provision of the facilities for education. Two to four per cent of GDP is not an insignificant amount looking to the other pressing needs of these poor countries. Education expenditure from the govermental sources has shown a continuous increase. In Uganda, for instance, public expenditure on education (central and local) increased from £8.2 thousand in 1922 to £9600 thousand during 1964. Hence, the major responsibility with regard to the provision of educational facilities on a massive scale was shouldered by the government even though the private agencies like the missionary and other organisations did take a fairly significant interest in the educational development in the country.

While such global measures of system expansion are partly useful for equity objective, they cannot be completely relied upon. Given the current inequities in the institutional structure, system expansion is likely to perpetuate and aggravate these inequities, for, the more privileged among the population are likely to exploit the expanded facilities more than others. This is very clearly seen from the several empirical studies in the Indian context.

In India also great stress was laid on the system expansion for meeting several objectives including the objective of equality in educational opportunity. Educational expenditure increased from Rs. 1,144 crores in 1950-51 to Rs. 12,500 crores in 1974, a nearly ten-time increase during two and half decades. As a proprtion of national income, education expenditures increased from 1.2 per cent to 3.3 per cent during the same period. Enrolment in primary classes increased nearly four times, that in secondary classes nearly 6 times, in higher secondary classes nearly 8 times and in higher education stage enrolment expanded nearly 24 times during the same period. While in 1950-51, there were only 27 Universities and 695 colleges in the country, by 1971-72, their number had increased to 86 and 3,896 respectively. Thus, even though there was no uniform expansion at all levels of education, the different levels did experience expansion of significant magnitudes. It is also worth noting that the higher education experienced expansion to the maximum extent. This is very much similar to the expansion in enrolment in a large number of the East African countries also. The highest rate of growth in enrolment in majority of the East African countries is seen in case of higher education (Table 1). Since in the developing countries, not all levels of education are free and higher education involves payment of fees and other ancillary expenditures, only socio-economically

better-off can avail of the expansion of higher educational facilities. In fact, one may also argue that in a set up where there
exist inequities, perpetuation of inequities is facilitated without
much reaction or disaffection, by expansion of higher education
and hence the elites of such a society advocate expansion of education in general and of higher education in particular. Hence,
a great need is felt for the specific measures, in contrast to the
global measures, to help the really under-privileged units in
respect of education.

This would involve the identification of the really under-privileged or backward units and unequal treatment of unequal units
in education (e.g. protective discrimination).

Specific Measures

In concrete terms this policy would mean that in educationally backward regions larger educational effort should be made,
for educationally backward communities access to education
should be made easier, participation in the education process
should be made less complex and less cumbersome, more
concessions in respect of educational attainments should be given
to the economically backward people in job allotments, stipulation of conditions of work, etc. Only when special protective
discriminatory measures in access to education, participation in
education, and utilisation of education in jobs, are introduced,
there is likely to be some equity in economic status through the
instrument of education. Both in East African nations and in
India such specific measures are introduced with greater or lesser
degree of imaginativeness.

In Tanzania, for instance, President Nyerere's directive on
education, known as Education for Self-Reliance announced in
February 1967, is a package of specific measures and general
measures. Even though it emphasized the importance of manpower development and productivity implications of education in
Tanzania the policy had great relevance for the equity objective.
President Nyerere did recognize that inequalities of wealth, income and status that were observed in Tanzania were the product of colonial administration which perpetuated heirarchical
division of the Tanzanian society in terms of African and non-
African groups. It is also clear that in most of the African countries there were serious inequities in access to education. Urban

children in Tanzania had disproportionately larger representation in secondary schools even though the urban sector occupied a very small place in the country. Since the provision of education is generally highly correlated with parental education, and other indices of modernisation, groups having an earlier historical access to education, a higher socio-economic status, maintained their comparative advantage. Since as per Nyerere's estimates only 14 per cent of primary pupils in Tanzania proceeded to secondary schools, the entire educational enterprise remained elitist in character, more and more elitist at higher and higher levels of education in view of the powerful filteration process through dropouts. The policy of expansion of education under colonial administration was also biased against the African natives as can be observed from the Ugandan experience.

TABLE 2

Percentage increase of Enrolment of different races in Uganda during 1930's to around 1960's

Race	Primary Schools	Secondary Schools
African	83	878
Indian	1523	3423
European	—	4609

TABLE 3

Government Expenditure on Education according to race in Uganda (% to total Education Expenditures,)

Years/Race	African	Indian	European
1922	100	—	—
1933	92	7	1
1943	86	10	4
1953	78	16	6
1959	78	16	6

TABLE 4

Education by Races in Tanganyika,1946

Race	Enrolled students as % of race	Net expenditure on education by government—per student in £
African	2	1.9
Asian	30	4.4
European	10	38.0

Another inegalitarian feature in education observed in many developing countries is the inequities in access to and participation in education in case of boys and girls. Normally propensity to educate girls is very low in the African and Indian families. In Uganda hardly 35 per cent of girls (of the age group) were enrolled in primary schools and this percentage declined to 23 for secodary schools.

Also, educational inequities are promoted and education is found to be a less effective means of economic equalisation if the type of education that is provided is not relevant to life situations and there is a discrepancy between work and education proper in the school curriculum. One tends to feel that the economically backward families cannot afford to receive the education which is not relevant to their work and their life problems.

It is these aspects of racial inequities, inequalities as between rural and urban sectors, and inequities born out of curricular deficiencies, which became the targets of Nyerere's education for self-reliance policy.

The racial integration of schools was attempted through the revised policy about the medium of instruction, fees and selection or admission policy. In most of the African countries, there exist separate schools for Europeans with English as the medium, Indian schools with largely Gujarati as the medium and African schools with Swahili as the medium. The standards of teaching, equipment, and performance are far better in English medium schools and in this ordering African schools stood at the lowest levels. Nyerere's solution for this problem of inequity was to devise a common syllabus and a common medium of instructions, viz. English. After 1963, Asiatic medium-schools were derecognized. How far this solution has really removed inequities is not clear. Also how far this policy has a sound logical-basis is open to question. (Incidentally, in India, the policy was reverse, as, the mother tongue was adopted as the school medium, to facilitate enrolment of the children of first generation leaders. However, this, contrary to the expectations, has, created a further gulf between the elitist English schools and mass-based vernacular schools.)

The Tanzanian government also tried to lower fees in European schools while making the access to these schools open for all races. Thus, in the English medium schools fees were £21 p.a., in Asian schools £6 p.a. and in the Swahili medium schools annual fees were £0.5. This obviously does not guarantee equal access to all, as, access to good education still depends upon fee payment. Hence, Nyerere abolished fees in all government-aided schools (secondary) with effect from 1963-64 and thus put an end to economic discrimination. In respect of admission to schools, preference was given to Tanzanian citizens and Africans. In government-aided schools, non-citizens had to pay fees.

The integration of schools and curricular reform were proposed to reduce the rural-urban inequities also in education. In case of school education, for instance, inclusion of 'self-help projects' — with all subjects related to agriculture, in the curriculum was a major step. Each school has a school farm where local cash and food crops are grown, and the latest farming techniques are employed. The teaching sessions are so adjusted to fit with the agricultural seasons. Greater degree of vocationalisation and rural bias has been introduced at the levels of higher education also.

East Africa and India: Similarity in Approaches?

A close observation of the experiments in equalisation in Tanzania and India suggests that there is an essential similarity of approaches to the problem of inequity in these countries. In India, also, the protective discriminatory measures in education for sechduled caste and scheduled tribes free education to the economically and socially backward communities, preference to

SC and ST people or stipulation of the quota in the award of jobs, etc. are some of the specific measures introduced for equalisation. The experiments with regard to basic education, multipurpose schools, and the recent attempts at introduction of 'work experience' in the curriculum at all levels of education, which are similar to curricular reform through self-help projects are some of the measures of curricular reforms to reduce sectoral inequities in education and to raise the relevance of education to life. As stated before, tremendous expansion of the entire system of education at all levels in India was partly guided by the objective of equality.

Even though a complete evaluation of Tanzanian experiments is not possible, as enough time has not passed since these experiments were introduced, and also because enough data are not available about the consequences of these experiments, a fairly reasonable evaluation of the Indian experiments suggests some insights into the problem. The system expansion has helped only the haves and the disparity between the haves and have nots has widened with this measure. Even with regard to the caste-based protective discrimination, the benefits have accrued to the better off among the backward communities. A survey conducted in selected districts of Uttar Pradesh in India would illustrate this point.[2] Table 4 presents the relevant results of the survey.

Thus while the Chamars and Khatiks are over represented in U. P. schools, Balmikis, and most of the other Scheduled Castes are seriously under-represented.

It is also noticed that a fairly large percentage of these depressed class-people are ignorant about the various concessional measures. And of those who are aware of these advantages, very few have actually utilized these special concessions.[3]

That the basic education reform and the multipurpose school reform have unfortunately proved to be a failure needs no further elaboration. Hence the egalitarian measures through generalised approach or the specific approach nave not achieved the success in proportion to the faith placed in them.

Education and Equality in a Traditional Society : Some Questions
The above account of East African and Indian experiments

TABLE 5

*Use of Educational Facilities by Different Scheduled
Caste Students, U.P. (selected districts)*

Name of the caste	Percentage of population of caste group to total SC population in the selected districts	Percentage of students of a particular caste group to total SC students
Chamar	63.1	88.1
Dhobi	4.4	4.2
Khatik	1.5	4.2
Balmiki	7.3	1.4
Shilpkar	0.8	1.0
Other Castes	22.9	1.1
Total	100	100

would pose certain questions of a fundamental nature. Neither global measures nor specific measures have been found to achieve educational equalisation. Since educational equality itself is not achieved education cannot be relied upon as a measure of economic equaliastion in the long run. The questions posed therefore are:

1. Is education an absolutely ineffective method for achieving social mobility under all situations ?
2. Is effectiveness of education less in backward but developing societies ? and
3. Is the effect of education on equalisation an extremely slow process ?

While not attempting to provide conclusive answers to these questions one may make the following observations. In a traditional society with several bases for stratification and with marked socio-economic inequities, education is likely to be a powerful device for filtration, further aggravating the educational and consequently socio-economic inequities. For, it is not simply the access to education but also participation in education which is an important criterion for social mobility, and both these are the functions of socio-economic status of the student and the family. Since the institutional structure is the determinant of the socio-economic status'[4]. manipulating education while holding the institutional framework is not likely to bear fruits as the Indian and African experiences have shown.[5] How well the institutional structure can be changed, how quickly can it be changed, and through what measures can it be altered, are different questions.

If institutional framework can be changed so as to have equal socio-economic opportunities for all, then education's role as an equaliser would be redundant, for, assuming education to be a function of the current socio-economic status, and the future socio-economic status to be the function of current education, provision of educational facilities would be merely a medium and not an effective instrument of future socio-economic equality.

If the institutional framework cannot be changed, then are the various measures for equal educational opportunities, the effectiveness of which is doubtful, a luxury that the poor developing countries can ill afford. We come back to the equity-efficiency (equity-growth) quandary that was posed tn the opening section of this essay. With larger number of abortive attempts at equalisation, the efforts at growth automatically get slackened. What weightage should one give to the objective of equity relative to efficiency ? Should social justice be interpreted as the provision of minimum socio-economic status and not the reduction of the disparities in the status, particularly in the context of developing societies ? These are obviously wider questions beyond the scope of this short essay. They are, however, crucial in any meaningful educational policy-making in developing countries.

REFERENCES

[1] S. Kuznets, "Economic Growth & Income Inequality", *American Economic Review* 1955, pp. 1-28.

[2] Brij Raj Chauhan and G. Narayana, "Problems of Education among

Scheduled Caste students in Uttar Pradesh", *Social Change*, Vol. VI, No. 1 & 2, 1976.

[3] K. K. Premi, "Educational Opportunities for Scheduled Castes", *Economic and Political Weekly*, 9 November 1974.

[4] Coleman Committee also arrived at similar conclusions in the context of the United States.

[5] Detailed empirical study of this problem for India was attepmted by this author in his *Inequality in Education* to be published by the Centre for Multi-disciplinary Research, Dharwar.

PRIYA V. MUTALIK DESAI

Transfer of Technology:
A Rationale for Economic Cooperation
between India and Africa

It is now generally recognised and agreed that the course of development cannot be explained satisfactorily by the factor augmentation emphasis of traditional analysis and has to take cognisance of the possibilities of technological borrowing and assimilation. Economic development is thus dependent on technological progress. One fact of the advance of the developed countries of the world which has contemporary relevance is the speed and the spread of economic growth. The situation of coexistence of a typically less developed country with developed countries has also been characterised by possibility of technological transfer from the latter to the former induced by the technological gap.[1] A progressive rise in the rate of growth of each "late comers" has as its basis the growth of the world's stock of transmissible knowledge. But for the developing countries of the world this advantage of late comers has not been an unmixed blessing. It has created a situation of dependency harmful to the process of economic development of these countries.

The echoes of this situation were heard in the United Nations when in June 1974 the General Assembly made a call

238

for a New International Economic Order.[2] The essence of the new economic order demanded by the developing countries is simply their "full and complete economic emancipation". And the way to achieve this, they agreed was "to recover and control their natural resources and means of economic development." The new approach to negotiations would involve common action to strengthen their bargaining position, more economic activity among themselves and a strategy based on "the principle of relying first and foremost on themselves." It is a blueprint for a comprehensive change of which transfer of technology forms an important part with an emphasis on the wide recognition that the common crisis could only be solved by cooperative action mainly aimed at self-reliance.

India's emergence as an industrial leader of the countries of the Third World and more importantly as one of the biggest donor country in the international transfer of skills, a measure of reverse transfer of technology are the two events of far-reaching significance. India has also assumed a leading role at the United Nations, IMF, and many other international organisations as a spokesman of the Third World. This role has its part to play in terms of responsibilities towards her partners who are on the lower rung of development. It is in this context too that the transfer of technology assumes importance as a phenomenon of significance particularly with reference to the concept of collective self-reliance.

The first section of this essay therefore reviews the recent thinking on transfer of technology and the state of technological development in African countries and the need for technology transfer as a catalytic agent in economic development of the region. The second section then surveys the relative significance of various machanisms of transfer to technolgy between India and African countries and brings out their relative significance a rationale for promoting closer inter-regional economic cooperation. Their role, effectiveness and future prospects also form a part of the discussion in this section.

I

Major Issues

Technological dependence of developing countries

In the growth of production in both advanced and developing countries, technological change has been a crucial factor. It is important to note that technical change in developed countries has been generated indigenously for most of the part and whenever technologies have been imported, rapid integration of these processes into the general process of technological advance has taken place. Thus every round of technological change was worked as basis for further advance. But in the newly independent countries this very process of cumulative, endogenous technological change is lacking particularly in the case of African countries because of short duration of colonialism and the speed as well as abruptness of decolonisation process meant that myriad changes imported by the Western technology had to be telescoped in a short span of five to six decades.[3] The dualistic structure of the colonial type of economy did little or nothing to generate technological advance. In the later period of monetisatian of economy, the new demand generated for consumer goods was met by imports. Additionally, as a free nation, the demand for modernisation has become a status symbol for most of these countries. Modernisation being deeply affected by the technological change in the developing countries it is equated with the importation of technology from the advanced countries. Basically the problem is that the economic organisation of developing countries being mainly structured on western models did not generate ability to create new technology or the skills required to operate them.

The transmissibility of modern technological knowledge has enormously increased the inter-dependence of countries. But this has as its consequence the connivance of the need for major innovative efforts in the developing countries. Rather a shift has taken place whereby transfer of technology from one country to another has become of overriding importance in place of indigenous technological evolution. The issue at stake for developing countries is to what extent it can help reduce the present assymetry in the consumption pattern, trade bondage, and technical knowledge which itself is a burdensome colonial legacy.

Mechanisms of transfer

Traditionally the technology transfer to developing countries has occured largely in the form of direct foreign investment in the extractive sectors like petroleum, mining and export agriculture. This is an indirect method of transfer to technology and direct investment by multinationals could be a classic example of this. National enterprise can also buy the requisite technology elements from various sources and put them together to organise industrial production and distribution. The degree of packaging of technology and degree of control exercised by the foreign technology supplier over the technology recipient will distinguish one method from the other.

Technology is also transferred in an informal and upspecific ways such as exchange of books, journals, trade journals and sales literature, informal personal contacts and relationships and attendance of meetings and conferences, training aboard of technicians from developing countries, etc. Direct transfer of technology by way of direct contracting of individual experts and consultant companies, engaging engineering design and plant construction enterprises, transfer of the process technology embodied in capital goods by importation of equipment can also take place. A lot of technical knowledge used in investment projects in developing countries is transferred directly. Agreements on patents, licensing and know-how is also transfer of technology. However, the most modern knowledge is obtained through contractual agreements, foreign investments and multinational corporations. The developing countries use simultaneously most of these ways, either individually or some mixture of it so that the needed elements of technological knowledge becomes available to set up the production of facilities.

Cost of transfer

In developing countries, in the post-independence period, the industrial policy has rested on two alternative strategies namely inward orientation or outward orientation. Whichever policy the country may follow, it is normally assumed that while the impact of the transfer may differ with the policy but the effect will be concentrated on three major issues regarding the foreign exchange cost of the transfer appropriateness of technology and the possibility of further technological development.

The cost of technology transfer represents a considerable burden on balance of payments of developing countries. An estimate of the direct foreign exchange costs of the transfer of technology to the developing countries covering only payments for patents, licensing, know-how and trademarks and consultancy services indicates that by the end of 1960's they may have reached as much as 6 1500 million. If the targets of the Second United Nations Development Decade are to be attained, these payments might grow sixfold by the end of the 1970's.[5]

Appropriateness of technology

When technology transfer takes place, one of the important questions relates to the selection of techniques suited to the abundant labour and scarce capital situation, typical for a developing country? Less developed countries are faced with a problem of labour utilisation. There is also a continuous drift of population from the rural to the urban areas thereby adding to the growing problem of urban unemployment. One may therefore be justified in asking as Michael Todaro does: "Is it sensible for LDCs to be passive recipients of production techniques whose very design was the result of a rational response to a diametrically opposite resource configuration?"[6]

Under the situation of disguised and open unemployment together, rapid expansion of industrial output where capital intensive methods are employed in its production is not enough and efficient technology using a high ratio of labour to capital becomes necessary. Under such circumstances a strong case may also exist for the choice of labour-intensive techniques even though they may be inferior to others in terms of productive efficiency. Only requirement to be met would be that they are acceptable to the workers and suit the local institutions and traditions. But contrary to all this, as one of the UNCTAD studies has brought out, industries in developing countries have tended to employ techniques which have not led to adequate utilisation of domestic resources. Moreover they have displayed a pronounced tendency for capital intensity to increase over time.[7]

In this context Chudson maintains that in many if not most large scale manufacturing operations, the opportunity for choosing among the available technologies a more economically efficient and at the same time labour intensive techniques is extremely limited.[8] Disaggregation of production function can provide scope for modification and handling of materials in a plant may be a case in point. Technologically unsophisticated form of food processing, pharmaceutical packaging being repetitive operations are amenable to successful modification. It has also been pointed out in an UNCTAD study on Kenya and Jamaica that local firms replacing the foreign firms would also use much the same technique of production.[9] Of course, it cannot be taken as conclusive evidence with regard to the shape of production function, i.e. the limited scope for major substitution of capital by labour without loss of productivity. The reasons might be wrong price signalling by the domestic economy both to the local and foreign producer, irrational emulation of the latest technology available abroad due to the working of the demonstration effect and the aversion on the part of the international firms to put to use their technological capability to explore alternatives and to innovate.

It is equally true that actual range of available techniques is largely dictated by capital equipment specifications. Labour intensive techniques are by no means infeasible from a technical point of view but because they are inefficient from an economic point of view in the advanced nations that they are not produced.[10] As a qualification to this view it could be pointed out that technical adaptation to local conditions may not always lead to a more labour-intensive process, this being particularly true of some agricultural processing industries catering to the world market which demand high and uniform quality standard. This is illustrated by a capital-intensive technological adaption for a mechanised cashew manufacturing plant recently developed in Tanzania by Oltremare Ltd., an Italian firm.[11] Acceptance of this design has not only radically improved Tanzania's position in the world cashew market but altered the structure of its international trading relations particularly with India, a monopoly buyer of raw cashew nuts and one who used mannual processing. It is important to note here that a labour intensive process was replaced by a capital intensive process even in a country of low wage rates from both a private and social point of view. A study on Kenya by Malcom Harper maintains that the selection of new products inappropriate in terms of raw material production, industrial processing and nutritional value to the consumption pattern of the country can also result into the inappropriate technology acceptance.[12]

The appropriate technology problem is thus a very complicated problem. The use of any particular technology is not an end in itself but it needs to be linked with the goals of development.[13] Developing countries also face a basic problem of the incapacity to adapt foreign production techniques and equipment to their own resources endowments. The social, intellectual and physical environment of developing countries is not conducive to the efficient utilisation of very modern technologies. It is beyond doubt that they need the techniques which use less of capital, more of labour, which can be upgraded with the availability of more skilled manpower. This amounts to greater indigenous efforts to modify, adapt and innovate or a more intensive effort at developmental research.

Assimilation of skills

The case of historical Japan is cited as a unique example in that the technology borrowing had the catalytic effect in terms of inducing domestic innovative processes.[14] According to the historical view of the technology shelf labour is not a homogeneous entity and the improvement of the quality of labour through education or learning by doing is essential for the society to master advanced state of technology. But when an LDC tries to borrow from this technology shelf, it is constrained by the education and skill attainment level of its own economic agents. Consequently the progress it is capable of making in improving indigenous skill and education level really constitutes a basic constraint on its rate of progress in this field.

Developing countries lack a labour force attuned to the unique requirements of specialisation. If they try to borrow ahead of their skill level, they find it difficult to assimilate that technology. However, the present system of transfer of technology does nothing to equip the recipient country to work out its own technologies in the future. So there is in operation a process of perpetual dependence rather than progressive reduction in dependence. Prevailing model of industrialisation based on the introduction and application of rich country technology, both the production and the consumption technologies is both expensive and ill-suited to the satisfaction of basic material needs of developing countries.[15] It also imposes a variety of other limitations which discourages not only the process of skill formation but undermines the possibilities of self-reliance in development.[16]

Cooperation among developing countries

To reduce the perpetual dependence of developing countries on advanced countries it is urgent to devise certain measures and to adopt certain practices that would encourage and help the developing countries to develop technology at the national level. Secondly, the imported procedures and technological knowledge should be useful for the purpose of development policy. For instance, the high level of unemployment in developing countries needs that industrialisation should not only aim at increasing the production of manufactured goods but as well result into creation of greater employment potential. Similarly, the overwhelming rural character of the developing countries demands that special technologies are developed for rural areas as well as village crafts and small scale industries. Technologies should have an additional function in that they should not exacerbate dualism between modern and traditional sectors in developing countries.[17]

In the context of the above requirements and the various limitations as well as disadvantages from which the less developed countries suffer, there is need to seek for measures which will create a suitable technological base domestically. The first and formost of such measures is the implementation of schemes which would bring about greater economic cooperation among the developing countries and increase the realisation of direct and indirect benefits from them. The VI and VII Special Sessions of the General Assembly of UN have again and again emphasised that LDCs cannot wait any more for more developed world to act but will have to learn the importance of cooperation among themselves.

The Conference had spelled out as early as in 1972, the concrete steps necessary to foster co-operation in the field of technology among developing countries. Paragraph 15 of resolution 39 (III) states that developing countries will have (1) to assist the transfer of technology to themselves by exchanging information concerning their experiences in acquiring, adapting, developing and applying imported technology and in this regard to set up regional and sub-regional centres, (2) to make appropriate institutional arrangements for the training and exchange of technical personnel, (3) to establish joint technical research centres for projects of regional interest and for exchanging adapted and recently imported technology between developing countries, (4) to promote the study of scientific and technological projects between LDCs with common technological requirements arising from similarities in their sectoral structure of production, (5) to set up machinery to facilitate dissemination and exchange of technology in LDCs so that the comparative advantage and specialisation offered by each sector of the activity is fully utilised, and (6) to endeavour to co-ordinate their policies with regard to adaptation of imported technology.

The outlining of these measures has not resulted into concrete steps to improve the atmosphere of collective self-reliance. In fact after a gap of a quinquenium one finds that the entire atmosphere for taking decisive action is vastly more propitious now. At a number of international forums, LDCs have exihibited their desire to work as a solid group of 77. Some of them have now built for themselves a strong technological domestic base and display conditions of surpluses regarding skilled manpower and engineering capabilities. Unfortunate part of the situation is that these surpluses are flowing to developed countries instead of being deployed in developing countries for the betterment of their conditions. In fact as one of the Reports[18] suggests the outflow of trained personnel from LDCs to developed countries has reached massive proportions in recent years. In this process of reverse transfer of technology, i.e. brain drain, the technologically backward poorer countries pass on a substantial part of their technological assets each year to richer countries which have incomparably greater technological capabilities. India is one of the biggest donor countries in this international transfer of skills.

In fact, this development, if properly channelised, could as well herald a period of strengthened bargaining power of LDCs vis-a-vis the developed world. This implies the reduction of their dependence on the West while simultaneously increasing inter-dependence among themselves. As suggested earlier a number of developing countries have developed capabilities in one or the other area vitally needed for socio-economic advance. The growth of a large range of complimentarities among them have created the basis for developing decisive action for promoting collective self-reliance.

The scope for co-operation among developing countries in specific sectors such as pharmaceuticals, agro-engineering, food processing, fertilisers, pesticides metal manufactures, paper manufactures, etc. is vast and these are areas where some developing countries have clearly developed a degree of technological competence and these sectors also closely approximate to the needs and the conditions of others. Such a transfer would help the developing countries to build up their own technological potential, so that they have enough indepen-dence and insight to be able to make their own decisions on technological alternatives and gradually also be able to deve-lop their own technologies.

Development of science and technological capacity in Africa

One of the solutions for rapid economic developement in Africa is a more systematic exploitation of natural resources potential. But as the Executive Secretary of ECA put it, very few African countries are in a position today to say what their national resources are and what could be them. Even fewer could undertake the conversion of more than a modest amount and variety of such national resources into semi-finished pro-ducts. And although Africa rightly joins Latin America, Asia and the Middle East in pressing the advanced countries to reduce and remove tariff and non-tariff barriers to exports of processed agricultural products and manufactures from deve-loping regions, yet there is hardly any evidence of the capa-bility of the region to organise the package of capital, technology, finance, transport and marketing involved. Economically, the external dependence of Africa has been increasing during the past decade.[19] This situation has another aspect namely the scaracity of the required skills in the region. It is one of the most paralysing constraints on the economic advance in Africa that there has been lack of African skilled personnel, technologists, project designers, analysers and evaluators, scientists, chemical engineers, site development specialists, etc.

Africa's post-secondary educational institutions are not designed to produce the above mentioned skills. Science instruction is not widespread in school teaching, even at secondary level. Where it is taught in school it is primarily an option for those who are going into professional training for which science constitutes an entry requirement.[20] It is, therefore, feared that Africa's dependence on external expertise is likely to grow at an exponential rate unless immediate and decisive steps are taken to correct this imbalance.

Recently there has arisen a widespread recognition of the role of science and technology in the economic development process. But its reflection is not seen either in policy making or in development planning. The government officials lack the understanding of the ways to use science and technology for promoting development. Majority of the countries in Africa have not established a section or department of the government administrative apparatus entrusted with the specific responsibility for dealing with the science and technology as a regular and integral part of the government business.[21]

In a number of fields in African countries, science and technology has a very useful role to play. For instance, science and technology can eliminate causes which have resulted into inadequate development of agriculture. Deterioration of soil due to traditional cultivation practices, low yield from local varieties as well as loss of crops caused by insects, animals, disease can be avoided by advances in science and technology.

Similar is the case with the mineral resources whose potential estimated on the basis of existing data is so vast that Africa is sure to become one of the leading continents in universal output in future. Discovery and use of these minerals is of great importance for economic development of these

countries. They provide the raw materials for the establishment of a variety of industries such as building construction
and cement industries, steel plants, etc. For instance, building
construction industry absorbed a substantially high percentage
(58.8 per cent in 1966) of the total investment in the region and
accounted for a large proportion of non-agricultural labour.
It is easy to see the dominant position of this industry in the
economic and social framework of these countries and the
significant control of this industry on the pattern of national
development. But the design of urban houses has been con-
ceived with imported materials which are expensive for the
majority of the people and this has left undeveloped the traditional use of locally available materials. At present African
industrial development has been extremely limited and one can
not seriously speak of even "foundry industry" in most countries of the region and it is better not to mention "engineering
industry".

Development of industries is crucial for African development because they remain the carriers of technology and a
medium for invention, innovation and diffusion. Industrialisation, therefore, is not an option but an imperative for African
countries. There is every possibility that if the African countries
do not take effective and planned steps to industrialise, many
of them might find themselves sitting, in a decade, in the
middle of mineral resources which they do not know how to
use and cannot sell due to lack of demand to those who do.
The foundations of industry are to be found in technology
based on empirical knowledge or derived from science. The
technogical foundations of industry are still largely non-existent in African countries and the whole range of structures
necessary to acquire and utilise such technology have to be
created in many countries.

II

ECONOMIC COOPERATION: INDIA AND AFRICA

Emerging Pattern

Africa as a continent on the next shore of the Indian Ocean
has been of importance and interest to India since early times.

However, these links were mainly the product of private initiative and were established primarily through commercial contacts, immigration as well as settlement of Indians in various African countries and especially in the countries on the Eastern coast of Africa. During the period of British Empire since both India and most of the countries of the Eastern African region were the part of the empire, Indians enjoyed more or less unrestricted and at times encouraged access to African markets and African territories for settlement.

However, the wave of independence that swept the African continent not only set these countries politically free but brought about perceptible changes in the basis of economic relations of these countries with the outside world. The changed context of their existence as independent nations was enough to bring about a shift in their attitudes and requirements. A greater desire for indigenisation was reflected in the attempts at reducing the role of foreign settlers by way of restrictive immigration and specially through barriers to effective operation of foreign settlers in certain priority fields and this brought about a virtual end to the process of migration which was the basis of the kind of economic pattern and relations promoted in the earlier period, a factor that promoted and strengthened economic relations.

In fact, by the middle of the 1960's, one finds a more or less complete overhauling in the basis of economic relations between India and African countries geared to the new situation. A pattern seems to emerge wherein India's economic links with North African countries were fostered by entering into effective bilateral trade agreements with those countries, specially Sudan and the UAR, [23] while the trade relations with East African countries were based more on free trade, promotion of joint ventures and other methods of economic cooperation. With West Africa, India's economic relations are on a significant scale mainly with Nigeria and Ghana and are taking a more concrete shape only recently. In other words, transfer of technology was utilised more effectively in the latter regions to create a more secure and lasting basis for economic ties with these countries. It, therefore, appears reasonable to separate out the factor of technology transfer as an effective agent in building up economic relations with developing African countries in the coming years mainly as an attempt at creating viable basis for cooperation among developing countries, specially in the context of the concept of "collective self-reliance".

Foreign trade pattern

Though normally not discussed, trade is a mechanism to transfer the technology embodied in goods and services. India's trade with African countries has not been very large and during the period 1960 to 1970 it showed signs of stagnation. It is during last some years that a marked improvement, as far as absolute value performance is concerned, has been observed and it is only during last two years that we may have turned the corner in our commercial relations with Africa. If one glances at the percentage value of export-import trade with Africa, there is a definite and marked fall in our performance. As compared to 1970-71, when India's export and import trade amounted to 9 and 10.4 per cent of India's total export-import trade, in 1974-75, the percentage declined to 7.1 and 3.4 per cent respectively. This indicates a measure of the improvement in trade performance that India needs to attain in the coming years.

Another characteristic of trade with Africa is the concentration on a few countries. Nearly 60 and 32 per cent of India's export-import trade respectively in 1974-75 was with North Africa alone and the UAR and the Sudan have been the predominant trading partners from this region. The respective shares for East Africa were 23 and 28 per cent and Kenya, Tanzania and Zambia were the major trading partners. To the West African region were sent 14 per cent of our exports to Africa, while hardly 3 per cent of India's imports from Africa came from this region.

The real and noticeable change was observed in the pattern of commodity exports to Africa. Export of non-traditional new goods have found expending markets in Africa, while the traditional goods exports have been the victims of import substitution in African countries. For instance, in case of our trade with Kenya, a complete restructuring of export trade has come about. The non-traditional exports now account for

76 per cent of India's total exports to Kenya in place of the same share of traditional goods in 1960-61. Since these goods are the embodiment of our advance in technology (increasing exports of these items which are more suited to the local requirements in many of the African countries) this trend indicates a satisfactory transfer of technology.

Joint industrial ventures

Last decade has witnessed constructive efforts on India's part in assisting in economic development of less developed countries and one of the major instruments for the purpose have been the establishment of joint industrial ventures and turn key projects in Asian, African and recently in Latin American countries.[24] In Africa Kenya has the largest number of joint ventures in production. The remaining joint ventures are in Ethiopia (1), Mauritius (6), Nigeria (3), Uganda (1) and there are certain ventures under implementation in Kenya (1), Mauritius (5) and Zambia (2). About eight turn-key projects have also been completed in various African countries.

India's joint ventures abroad has been a live issue during the last few years. As a form of foreign investment mostly in the developing countries it is receiving greater and greater patronage from the Indian Government in terms of more facilities. Among the African countries also there is a growing tendency, depending upon the technological, industrial and financial resources of the country, to reduce the area of foreign investment and control. In this process joint ventures become the chosen instrument.

Thus, the greater popularity of joint ventures has been due to the mutual benefits and requirements while the inadequate indigenous capital has proved to be one of the greatest deterent to the rapid industrial growth in African countries, the lack of trained technical personnel and enlightened entrepreneurship pose insurmountable hurdles. Due to these factors there appears to be considerable willingness to accept foreign investment particularly in the form of joint industrial ventures where they expect the foreign country to accept minority participation and also provide capital contribution in terms of cash, machinery and other assets. Most of the African countries are giving highest priority to the training of local skills and desire to limit the employment of foreign personnel where local skills are available.

Though a number of African countries are mainly agricultural, they are deeply interested in launching upon programmes of industrial development. In the process of industrial growth, production of consumer goods precedes the intermediate and capital goods production. A consequence of this trend is the reduction in the imports of these items from the outside world. Analysis of Indo-American trade amply reveals that changing African import structure has been one of the important factors inhibiting the growth of Indian exports to some of these countries. However, joint ventures would be a newer technique to enter the market and retain it through the exports of machinery, equipment, spare parts, etc. Additionally technical assistance provides also an important source of income in terms of royalties, fees, salaries, etc. A variation in the export opportunity depends upon the nature of the enterprise undertaken.

Markets in Africa are at present relatively small but it is important to note that they are potential and fast expanding markets. These newly independent countries are faced with a number of difficulties in catering to the internal demand by increasing domestic production. The establishment of joint industrial ventures could therefore be an exercise in partnership in development of these countries. These ventures have already gained popularity and more requests are received in this regard, because unlike multinationals in Africa, Indian investments are significantly small—Rs. 857 lakhs approximately, and intentions are neither sinister nor dubious.[25]

Image-building

However it is essential to realise that joint ventures are not an unmixed blessing as they are made out to be. It will be in the long-term interest of India that before these ventures assume an overwhelming character and result into their indiscriminate growth in the African countries, they are properly planned in certain selected countries where their impact on the development is positive. It is particularly important in the case

of those African countries where the image of the Indian settlers is still that of intruders and exploiters. It must be remembered that what happened to Indian settlers in several African
countries is not a matter of the distant past. The plight of
Asians in Uganda is still fresh in our memories. Thus our policy
regarding joint ventures calls for caution. This has relevance
since Foreign Trade Ministry has always fervently advocated
the boosting of investment abroad as a tool of export promotion. The External Affairs Ministry has also given its full
support to joint ventures in view of their role in image-building
by portraying India's industrial and technological capabilities
in a manner which any number of pamphlets cannot match.

This exercise in image-building yields indirect commercial
dividends. Once foreign business men realise that India is an
industrial power to reckon with, Indian goods will find an easy
access and acceptance in these markets. Till a decade ago transfer of capital or capital equipment to these countries was an
exclusive preserve of capital surplus, highly developed countries. But this situation has changed now and India has shown
capacity to set up the finest and up-to-date plants. This happy
transformation from pursuing a trade policy on purely commercial basis to venturing abroad in the form of industrial
plants set up in collaboration with local trade and industry
is an upshot of the emerging trends in African countries to
share with one another development experiences, technologies
and skills.

It is, however, of crucial importance that greater attention is
paid to the training of Africans and working out fade-out
arrangements so that eventually such enterprises go completely
national.[26] In the ocean of multinationals in these countries,
Indian joint ventures are like drops. But a positive and a more
constructive approach towards them along with the other
work in different fields can strengthen their impact as a
major plank in our programmes of economic cooperation with
African countries.

Certain positive aspects of this new experiment deserve to
be pinpointed. India in the last decade has acted wisely by
entering into partnerships with the African countries with a
deliberately assumed low profile. Indian ventures have put up
a very good demonstration by turning out an array of goods of

acceptable quality and price. The initial scepticism of local people, at times bordering on hostility has been now replaced by admiration for Indian technology and expertise which is more compatible to their social and economic milieu. On the negative side is the high drop-out rate of joint ventures. Again, in some countries such as Ethiopia, Kenya and Libya, these ventures have, for various reasons, met with enormous difficul ties. This may dampen the pace in this regard in the future, with an additional possibility that the flow be further affected by more inviting environment opened up in the Gulf and other West Asians countries. Indian companies have proved "giant killers" in this area.[27] A more clear-cut foreign policy towards African countries with greater emphasis on economic issues will greatly help at this juncture in working out long-term policy imperatives.

technical assistance

As observed in Section I, training of personnel in different technical fields is one of the most essential inputs for the pur- pose of industrialisation of a country. In African countries, though the fade-out arrangements in foreign investments have been worked out, scarcity of managerial and technical skills has been so acute that expatriates virtually control the opera- tions in plants, factories, etc. What these countries really want is the capital equipment and the know-how in the initial stages with increasing accent on arrangements whereby not only the production is made possible but the skills to maintain and improve the production techniques are generated. The techni- cal assistance programmes implemented so far and planned for the future are framed by taking into consideration these prere- quisites. These programmes are therefore different in their scope, content and intent. The purpose is clear, viz. to divert a larger portion of trained manpower to these countries to aid them in their planning projects and programmes of develop- ment, and also assist by providing facilities for their potential personnel training facilities in India. India has been deputing Indian experts in specialised industrial fields to these developing countries against specific requests to train personnel and for rendering advice on specific problems. Such assistance is being provided under Indian Technical and Economic Cooperation

(ITEC), Colombo Plan and Special Commonwealth African Assistance Plan (SCAAP).

The type of assistance provided could be categorised as institutional infrastructural assistance, physical infrastructural assistance and consultancy services. Thus National Industrial Development Corporation (NIDC) was associated with the establishment of Consultancy Organisation, and Machinery Maintenance Organisation and Material Testing Laboratory in Tanzania. Bharat Heavy Electricals (Ltd.) recently undertook major turnkey projects for establishment of power generation and transmission projects in Libya and Zambia.

One of the positive contributions of the Indian consultancy profession to the industrial development has been its assistance in finding solutions appropriate to the local conditions and optimisation of the use of indigenous technology, equipment, raw materials, and human skills. Indian organisations have rendered consultancy service to many African countries, viz., Kenya, Tanzania, Zambia, Libya, Sudan, Mauritius and Nigeria. For instance, Indian railways have undertaken surveying, planning and construction of railway lines in Zambia, while NIDC recently developed a road development plan for Zanzibar. NIDC is also acting as overall consultants for the establishment of first Industrial Estate in Zanzibar. The units envisaged in the estate will manufacture wide variety of products needed by the common man including bread, wood furniture, hosiery products, coconut oil, aluminium utensils, soap, canned fruits, etc. The total cost of the project is likely to be Rs. 50 mn. and the first phase of the project has already been commissioned. In fact NIDC has the largest number of assignments in Tanzania (15) covering various fields. It is important to note that as a part of its operating philosophy overseas, NIDC invariably associates local personnel, to the extent possible, in its work to bring about technology transfer and the training of local people.

A large number of Indian experts are also working in African countries. In Zambia about 3,000 Indian experts are working assisting the local authorities in various fields such as mining, industry, agriculture, public health, education and administration. The Government of India has also made available training facilities for 150 Zambians a year at the Roorkee

Engineering University in U.P. and other technical institutions. Similarly more than 500 Indian experts are working in Tanzania and a large number of Tanzanians are given training facilities in India in specific areas of studies to suit their assigned duties in various Indo-Tanzanian projects. Such examples can be multiplied, since technical assistance is being extended to a number of other African countries.

Further areas for cooperation

As mentioned in the earlier section, the extent of transfer of technology between developing countries is very small at present and so is the case with India and African countries. Yet, in spite of the inhibiting factors, there is evidence, as seen above, of greater awareness of the possibilities of such transfer and the concerte programmes implemented to bring them into reality. It is possible to specify here certain areas in which the co-operation can be more fruitful.

Agro-industries is an important area for any developing country where agriculture is the major occupation of the people. Many new developing countries in Africa are in the need of technology in areas such as cereal processing, milling, oilseeds, sugar and other food processing industries and the need is for simple machinery not commonly available in developed countries. Examples are small tractor, small engines, transport equipment, etc.

Large percentage of populations in African countries live in rural areas where there is need for developing industries relating to rural housing transport, water supply and other services based on local materials and local skills. Water purification, filtration, manufacture of bicycles and other transport equipment, road building, housing construction suggest some of the areas where transfer of technology developed for Indian villages would be appropriate and economical and could be used without much modification. National resource development is still another field where some co-operation can yield amazing results. After all what the developing countries in Africa need is the machinery and know-how which entails less automation, less sophistication, higher reliability, slowness in speed and smallness in capacity and low costs. The technology developed in India has perhaps all these major attributes.

Suggestions

The process of transfer of technology between India and African countries has started taking some shape but it still lacks the pervasiveness. It has achieved results in the case of countries where due to the presence of Indians it was easier to find local partners or in countries where the leadership was very favourably disposed towards India and took initiative in inviting Indian participation. Tanzania and Zambia are examples which easily come to mind. Establishment of the India-Tanzania Joint Commission in 1975 was greatly instrumental in bringing about a greater awareness regarding possibilities of intensifying future collaboration and identification of needs. Particularly a careful formal planning process covering immediate requirements for five years and a long term perspective over fifteen to twenty years could help to identify specific technological needs. In India such a formal planning procedure is in operation and the National Committee on Science and Technology is trying to formulate and delineate areas for local technology development, import of technology and for combination of both. Similar exercises if attempted by developing countries in Africa could identify the areas of technology transfer where developing countries like India can contribute. At the regional level, such an effort is reflected in the finalisation of a plan by ECA to establish a Centre for the "Transfer, Adaptation and Development of Technology" to help Africa to develop its national infrastructure and machinery for adaptation and development of technology. At an international conference on industrial and technological co-operation held in Delhi during January 1977, India had suggested setting up of an Industrial Technological Information Bank for pooling together the results of developmental efforts and research activities successfully undertaken in different developing countries.[28] Since the introduction of any new technology will need properly trained personnel, there could also be a manpower training institute or agency to impart training to the nationals of the participating countries.

Dissemination of information must be vigorously pursued through national and international agencies, embassies, trade missions and special agencies such as investment bank, technology cell agencies and consultancy firms.

Direct specific links must also be developed between India and African countries. Booklets, circulars, periodicals, monthly newsletters are certainly useful but ultimately only personal knowledge of requirements and of availability of new technology can ensure the success of the process of technology transfer. This is best done by extending more and more facilities for education and training to students and technologists from the African countries, exchange of personnel for long periods and through such measures as holding of exhibitions.

Conclusion

India's foreign policy towards African countries was re-oriented when the basis of that policy became irrelevant with the attainment of independence by a majority of countries in the African continent. Increasing emphasis also came to be placed on economic issues and the need for a constructive approach while restructuring the relationship. The economic cooperation policy which consisted of a three tire programme of trade promotion, joint collaboration and technical assistance was the outcome of this new thinking.

The test results of this policy were obtained by a purposeful programme of economic cooperation with Kenya, Tanzania, Zambia, Mauritius, Nigeria, etc. They have been most impressive in Tanzania and Zambia, Nigeria has also started slowly opening up and responding to the need for such collaborative efforts. Credibility of India as a country with strong industrial base, adequate trained manpower and capacity to offer industrial technology and related assistance for mutual benefit has now been established. The non-alignment policy followed by India has added strength and candour to the efforts on economic front. The various methods of transfer of technology reviewed have so far been used with discretion and selectivity. Such efforts are a measure of demonstration, to the developed countries, of the vast resources the developing countries possess and the strength of cooperative action. It brooks no doubt that the technology developed and refined in India, is of greater relevance to African countries, since India has just passed the stage of development they have entered. It is much easier now to explore common grounds for co-operation and to draw programmes for their implementation. The only limitation that I visualise is that of limited financial export capital which could be made good by the use of institutional finance. Pros perous trade and economic relations with African countries is a lever to sound political relations. To think that improvement in political relations alone can boost up the former is a negative approach, which India has shunned long ago.

REFERENCES

[1] J. Patel Surendra, "Economic Distance between Nations: Its origin, measurement and Outlook," *Economic Journal* (London), LXXIV, March 1964.

[2] In addition to the decisions of the Seventh Special Session, the main documents giving content to the new International Economic Order are (1) "The Declaration and Programme of Action on the Establishment of a New International Economic Order" (UN General Assembly, 1974 (a) adopted by the Sixth Special Session; (2) the "Charter of Economic Rights and Duties of States" (UN General Assembly, 1974, (b) adopted by the 29th General Assembly, and (3) the "*Lima* Declaration and Plan of Action on Industrial Development and Cooperation" (in UNIDO, 1975) adopted by the General Conference of the UNIDO in March 1975. Also see (4) Bhaskar P. Menon, *Global Dialogue: The New International Order* (London, 1977).

[3] D.P. Ghai, "Perspectives on future economic prospects an dproblems in Africa," in *Economics and World Order from the 1970's to the 1990's*, J. Bhagwati (ed.), pp. 257-88.

[4] A detailed discussion on this can be found in "Th echannels and mechanisms for transfer of technology from developed to developing countries." A study by Cooper and Sercovitch, UNCTAD document TD/B/Ac. 11/5

[5] UNCTAD, "Transfer of Technology," a report by UNCTAD Secretariat, in UNCTAD Third Session, Santiago de Chile, Vol. III.

[6] M.P. Todaro, "Some thoughts on transfer of technology from developed to less developed nations", *Eastern Arrica Economic Review*, Vol 2, No. 1, June 1970, pp. 53-64.

[7] UNCTAD, "Transfer of Technology", (Item 12, Main Policy issue) May 1976, Document TD/190, p. 18. For the detailed discussion of this issue see Walter Chudson, "The International transfer of Commercial Technology to developing countries," UNITAR Research Report No. 13.

[8] Chudson, n. 7.

[9] Ibid.

[10] Todaro, n 6.

[11] Chudson, n. 7.

[12] Halcom Harper, "Sugar and Maize Meal: Cases in inappropriate technology from Kenya", *Journal of Modern African Studies*, Vol. 13, No. 3, pp. 501-9.

[13] Detailed discussion on this subject is found in a recent publication by Richard S. Eckaus, "Appropriate technologies for developing countries," Washington, D.C.

[14] Japan's technological advance and excellence was mainly based on indigenous innovative effort and suitable governmental policies two vital ingredients in the process of assimilation. Due to the domestic ingenuity and skill shown by the Japanese, they were successful in borrowing the technology of the correct vintage and to 'strech' the use of that capital, resulting into reduction in the value of capital coefficient and enabling more labour to be employed per unit of capital stock. But it is necessary to remember that for the 60 years taken as a whole, Japan developed under the conditions of capital deepening and not of capital shallowing. For greater details see C.H. John, Fei and Gustav Rains, "Technological transfer, employment and development", Willy Sellekaerti, (ed.) *Economic Development and Planning: Essays in honour of Jan Tinbergen*, pp. 75-103.

[15] Harper, n. 12.

[16] For a comprehensive discussion of these limitations refer to, UNCTAD, "Major issues arising from the transfer of technology to developing countries," Document TD/B/Ac. 11/10/Rev. 1 Ch. II.

[17] K.W. Menek, "Fundamental Concepts of the transfer of technology to the developing countries," in *Economics*, Vol. 15, 1977, pp. 30-39.

[18] UNCTAD, "The reverse transfer of technology: Economic effects of the outflow of trained personnel from developing countries" (Brain Drain), UNCTAD Document TD/B/Ac. 11/25, 8 May 1974.

[19] UNECA, Statement by Mr. Abedayo Adedeji, Executive Secretary of Economic Commission for Africa, at the sixty-first session of the Economic and Social Council of the United Nations, Geneva, July-August 1976.

[20] UNECA, African regional plan for the application of Science and Technology, Document No. E 73, 11 K. 3.

[21] Ibid.

[22] UNECA—Adebayo Adebeji's n.19.

[23] L.V. Nigudkar, *Prospects of India's Export trade with Africa 1970-71*, unpublished thesis, University of Bombay, 1967, and P.V. Mutalik-Desai, "Bilateral trade agreements: Indo-Sudanese experience", *Economic and Political Weekly*, Vol. VIII, No. 19, May 1973.

[24] For details see, P.V. Mutalik-Desai, "Indo-African joint industrial ventures: A New approach", *Africa Quarterly*, April-June 1971.

[25] For a good study of intentions of multinationals in Africa see, Ann Seidman, "Old Motives, New Methods, Foreign Enterprise in Africa Today," in Allen and Johnson (ed.), *African Perspectives*, pp 251-72.

[26] Joint ventures have originally been the products of the fade-out principle which implies that, after a pre-determined period part or

all of the foreign equity participation in an enterprise is transferred to nationals of the developing country, with due compensation.

[27] *Economic Times*, 29 September 1977.

[28] *Economic Time*, "India Wants R and D Pool for Third World", 7 January 1977.

D.V. HEGDE

Indian Ventures in Mauritius

SOCIAL AND ECONOMIC ties between Mauritius and India date
back to the early years of the 18th century, when nearly two
lakh Indian labourers were indented and transported in bat-
ches to Mauritius. With a modest beginning, the workers in
sugar plantations soon constituted the life-blood of Mauritian
economy. And today the descendents of the Indian emigrants
occupy most important place in the national life of Mauritius,
not merely by virtue of their numerical strength, but more so
by their contribution to various spheres of the Mauritian
economy encompassing such crucial sectors as manufacture
and commerce. In other words, the story of the emergence of
the Indian community in Mauritius is a classic instance of the
gradual evolution of an enterprising man from the grass roots to
a position of power, economic as well as political. It is not sur-
prising, against this background, that the governments in power
at different points of time in the past, with their generous
content of the Indian element, have time and again emphasised
an expanding role, and increased participation, by India
in the development of Maritius. It is, therefore, in the fitness of
things that there exist today most cordial and warm relations
between the government of India and the present Mauritian

government headed by Prime Minister Ramgoolam. Seewoo-
sagar Ramgoolam has been in power for more than a decade
and it does not seem he will lose it in the near future. Viewed
in this context, a study of the scope for additional Indian participation in the economic development of Mauritius appears to
be quite relevant.

It, nevertheless, needs to be mentioned at the outset that
though, India has been contributing significantly to diverse
fields of the national life of Mauritius, ranging from cultural
and social institutions, such as the assistance extended towards
the construction of the Mahatma Gandhi Institute for the study
of Oriental languages and culture, to the supply of technical
skills from India under the India-Mauritius Technical and
Economic Cooperation Programme, the focus of this essay will
be on the industries set up already by Indians from India in
Mauritius and the scope for future expansion on similar lines,
thus contributing effectively in raising the tempo of development. It is proposed to discuss the position and behaviour of
the Mauritian economy in the recent past, its growth in terms
of industrialisation, the role played by Indian investment in
industrialising the country, and the scope of certain new lines
that deserve the attention of Indian entrepreneurs. Also dealt
with are the incentives and industrial schemes contemplated
and, presently offered, by the Government of Mauritius along
with some special intrinsic and specific advantages available to
the Indian industry to take advantage of the opportunities that
are available in Mauritius.

To begin with a brief description of the characteristic associated with the availability of natural resources, industries based
on that and many other factors which have an important bearing on the future pattern of industrialisation in Mauritius may
be found useful.

Mauritius, a small island occupying a total area of around
800 sq miles, is strategically situated off the East coast of
Madagaskar, bordering between Asia and Africa. It has a
population of some 8.67 lakhs, consisting of Hindus, Creoles (a
race sharing the features of Indian, African and French origin),
Moslems and White settlers descending mainly from the French
origin who are now called "Franco Mauritians". Predominant
numerically are the Hindus accounting for 52 per cent of the

total population, followed by Creoles (who now are closer to the "Franco Mauritians" in their allegiance and loyalty) and a sprinkling of Moslems, Chinese and the Franco Mauritians. However, the statistical breakup of population is rather desceptive as can be seen by the fact that the Franco-Mauritians, barely 4,000 in number, constitute the most potent economic force in Mauritius. They control 17 out of the 21 sugar factories, the most important segment of the almost mono-crop economy of Mauritius. The Hindus, have been only recently graudating from the stage of plantation workers and cultivators intro traders, and very recently have been attempting an inroad into the manufacturing sector. The Chinese are predominantly traders and have so far shown no proven skill or desire to compete with the white settlers in the field of industry. The Hindus lead in the political life of Mauritius as may be gauged from the fact that at no time during the past one decade of independent Mauritius, the cabinet has contained less than 50 per cent Hindu ministers in the total strength, besides the Prime Minister. The Creoles have recently been emerging as a political force to reckon with, due as much to their statistical advantage as the dynamism of some of their radical leaders with considerable Western inclinations. Inspite of the long period of coexistence and exposure to the sophistication of the West, Mauritians still retain their identities as dictated by their origins. This is not to say that there is no racial harmony as one may expect in such a situation. As a matter of fact, different communities following their own unique patterns of living, continue to live with a remarkable social consciousness dealing with each other on friendly terms. As the Western observers have so often in the past found to their surprise the racial disharmonies are submerged in the commercial and social dealings among Mauritians although on the domestic front they retain their separate identities so distinctly which are again reflected with considerable form in their political decisions. Another paradox of the racial life in Mauritius is the almost absolute demarcation among communities in terms of occupational distribution. The Franco-Mauritians, constituting a microscopic minority of the population, through their tight hold on a mass segment of manufacture and plantations producing sugar, control the economic power in Mauritius. Recently, goaded by the need to strengthen their base politically and socially, they have been coming down on a significant scale from the ivory towers of economic heights to weild some political power. But their march in this direction is rather slow though perceptible. On the other hand the Hindus and Creoles who are dominating together the political life, seem to have felt the need for consolidating their position further through an access to economic power. Educated Mauritians from these communities (literacy is quite high even among them), refuse to go back to sugar plantations and common place trade, but prefer to set up an industry, howsoever small it may be. This curious spectacle of the economically strong attempting to turn politically potent and the politically powerful joining in the economic race is a very significant development in the racial psychology in Mauritius and may prove to be a turning point in the growth pattern of the Mauritian economy. No less significant is the growing affinity between the Black Africa and Mauritius. Till recently and even today, South Africa is the major importer of the Mauritian sugar and tea and a major part of the tourist income derived by Mauritius is from the South African visiting the beautiful coral reefs of Mauritius. With the holding of the annual summit of the Organisation of the African Unity last year in Mauritius, under the chairmanship of Ramgoolam, the Prime Minister, Mauritius distinctly declared its determination to pursue the goal of African unity. It is quite interesting that within a short span of barely a decade of independence, Mauritius has almost found its political moorings and the political stability in evidence, and expected to continue in the foreseeable future, presents a refreshing contrast, viewed against the back drop of uncertain political situation and unsteady state policies observed in some of the countries of the neighbouring Africa. The same, however, cannot be fully said of the economic achievements in Mauritius which is still groping for a stable economic platform.

Impressive, undoubtedly, are some of the thrusts made by Mauritius in the field of economic upliftment. It is only that the march towards a fully stable economy is confronted with bottlenecks presented by natural factors. Its inevitable reliance on sugar lends it the complete picture of being a mono-crop economy so highly and desperately vulnerable to vicissitudes of the world sugar market. The smallness of population introducing the constraint of a meagre local market in conspiracy with the poor natural resources consisting of negligible mineral and modicum forest resources, has greatly curtailed the enterprising zeal in the population besides dissuading outsiders from venturing in Mauritius. Hence, any plan to spur growth of industries calls for a very attractive package of incentives and generous facilities offered to a potential entrepreneur on a scale superior to similar incentives given in any other country. In other words, the initial cost incurred by the state for encouraging industrialisation tends to be inordinately high.

In the face of constraints which, among others, relate to low indigenous market potential, inadeqaute local raw material and input base and inflation ranging at the rate of 25 per cent and more, Mauritius has still shown a commendable growth rate in terms of economic performance. Gross Domestic Product (GDP) at current prices has been staging a spectacular rise from 2.7 per cent in 1970 to 11.4 per cent in 1971 to 25.9 per cent in 1972 to 30 per cent in 1973 and to an astounding 75 per cent in 1974. In 1975, a smaller growth has been reported mainly as a result of the widespread damage to the sugar crop because of the cyclone. However, a part of the growth may be accounted for by high rate of inflation of more than 30 per cent; but even with that, at constant prices (1970-71), GDP grew at an impressive average annual rate of nearly 15 per cent over the first plan from 1971 to 1975. Meanwhile, GNP showed a corresponding growth rising at the current factor cost from Mauritian Rs. 1,281 million in 1972 to M. Rs. 1,666 million in 1973, further to M. Rs. 2, 920 million in June 1975 (which contained a staggering annual rise of 71 per cent in 1974) and to a high level of M. Rs. 3,400 million in 1977. The GNP per capital showed a consistently upward march from M. Rs. 1,550 in 1972 to M. Rs. 3, 378 in 1974, and now reportedly stands at M. Rs. 3,800. Domestic fixed capital formation has shown a five fold rise to M. Rs, 750 million in 1975 as compared to à meagre M. Rs. 120 million in 1970.

However, there are 3 important desiderata deducting a considerable portion of the achievement in terms of economic growth. Firstly, the economy continues to rely on sugar for bulk of indigenous industrial production and exports. Inspite of some serious recent efforts by the state to diversify into other areas of industrial activity, the built-in and instrinsic constraints may come in the way and sugar may continue to be the proverbial unstable king. Secondly, inflation rampant at the rate of more than 30 per cent may persist for some more time, notwithstanding the state measures including the dampering of demand pressures through the devices like: raising the bank reserve ratio, issue of commercial paper and import surcharges. As long as the import of costly food stuffs to the tune of 25 per cent of the total food requirements continues (which may continue for atleast a decade) and with the recent agreements under which higher wages have been granted to 50 per cent of industrial and plantation labour, inflation may continue. The only relieving development is the reported decline in the rate of inflation from 30 per cent in 1975 to an annual rate of 14 per cent till the last quarter of 1976. Third disturbing aspect is unemployment which partly is voluntary. Young and educated Mauritians prefer to be white collar employees rather than go back to the plantation or trade. Inspite of the labour-intensive plans undertaken during the plan period of 1971-75, absorbing around 30,000 new labour force, unemployment has reportedly not gone below the level of 16 per cent recorded in the 1972 census. The proposed gradual mechanisation of the sugar plantations and production, may further complicate the problem. No less damaging is the impact of the wage-cost-push culminating vicious circle of high wage and inflation feeding on each other.

The second five-year plan (1975-80) has ambitious projections and targets. Manufacturing sector is targetted to grow at the rate of 20 per cent per annum reaching a production value of M. Rs. 660 million in 1980, absorbing bulk of 80,000 people expected to be released in the employment market by then. Hence labour intensive projects are proposed to be encouraged. This plan also targets a significant diversification from the sugar-oriented pattern of the economy, to export oriented indurtries based on other products than merely sugar.

As has been stated time and again in this essay, sugar is the major plank on which the entire Mauritian economy rests. The fact that sugar occupies 2.05 lakh acres is an eloquent testimony of the lion's share of sugar in the national economy. It is also one of the most efficiently run industries in the world as a result of the high level of sophistication and technology injected by the Fraco-Mauritians controlling it. Sugar accounts for 65 per cent of an output value and over 75 per cent of export earnings. It earns an annual profit of £20 millions. However, of late considerable anxiety is witnessed in the performance of the sugar industry with an indifferent trend in the world market. Natural calamities such as cyclone in 1975 can mar the crops and put the country in trouble. Moreover, the world price of sugar, after reaching the peaks in 1974 is tumbling down and considering the increasing cultivation of sugar in the Soviet and Central American coutries. Africa and even the importing countries such as the US, West Europe and East Europe coupled with the development of substitutes including corn syrup, fructose, loctose, etc. grave doubts prevail with regard to the prosperity for a recovery in sugar prices. In this context, it may be noted that the exports of sugar in 1975 nose dived from 6.85 lakh tonnes in 1974 to 4.47 lakh tonnes in 1975. Hence, policy at present is to give up sugar cultivation on marginally efficient land and grow a food crop instead. It is estimated that nealy 1/4 of the retained profits of the sugar industry are diverted to other areas of manufacture each year. An additional factor encouraging this tendency is the desire of the Franco-Mauritians, controlling sugar, to diversity into a broader field, which are more labour-intensive and politically more acceptable.

Next to sugar, the important economic activity consists of the cultivation and processing of tea for export purpose. With a beginning, as recently as in 1957, with the aid of Sh. 5.2 millon from the World Bank, tea today occupies 13,000 acres of land and the production is at a level of 7.5 lakh kg. However, with the uncertainty pertaining to the future relations between Mauritius and South Africa which is the major buyer of Mauritian tea, tea industry has got a major constraint to tackle. Some of the other products of some significance include tobacco—recently introduced—a fibre whose products are employed as packaging meterial in the sugar industry, and fruits, vegetables and some food products which are not adequate for the indigenous requirements. Resources from

forest spread over an area of 1.64 lakh acres are exploited
only by a few saw-mills, small-scale paper units. As for the
mineral wealth is concerned Mauritius is poor and may
continue to be so as there is hardly any possibility of intensive
mineral exploration in the small over-populated island.

Against this background, an Indian entrepreneur has to
study the issues pertaining the position of resource availabi-
lities thoroughly. They have also to be acquainted with the
present status of an industry in Mauritius. It is pertinent to
note that industrialisation in Mauritius were confined to mainly
sugar and sugar by-products till 1960. Twenty-one sugar factories, some unite processing their by-products into molasse
and bagasse into alchohol, rum and animal feed constituted
the bulk of industry. Of course, there are some fibre-processing units, small scale foundries, workshops, bolts and nuts
units, paint manufacturing units. But the first real and purposeful policy towards industrialisation was announced in the
late 1960's. Developmental certificates were issued to investors
with liberal facilities such as tax-holiday for corporate profits
for 5 to 8 years, exemption of dividends from individual investments in securities from income tax for five years, high concessional supply of infrastructural facilities including land, building,
water, electricity and attractive long-term and working capital.
As a result, a number of industries including 8 tea factories, 10
breweries, five plastic units processing poly-propylene-poly-
ethelene products, fibre glass moulded products, razor blade
units cement and concrete pipe units, etc. came up. Nevertheless,
the most important impetus to growth of industries has delivered in 1971 with the announcement of the policy pertaining] to
export processing zone. Industries from abroad were invited
to produce for export purposes with a most impressive set of
incentives. some important incentives offered were as follows: *a*)
complete exemption of import and excise duties on capital goods,
components and raw materials needed by the units operating in
the zone; *b*) exemption from corporate income tax for 10 to
20 years; *c*) exemption from income tax leviable on dividends
for 5 years; *d*) priority and concessional treatment in the capital finance from the Development Bank of Mauritius; *e*) provision of reinforced factory buildings with provision of building
loans; *f*) repatriation of capital, remittances and dividends to

companies with an approved status. Coupled with the prospects of political stability this package of incentives is regarded to be one of the best available any where in the world. As a result, a large number of companies, nearly 66, set up units in the zone and the turnover increased from the year of inception, that is 1971, to M. Rs.140 million in 1974 and more than doubled to Rs.300 million in 1976. It is this particular opportunity offered in the form of the EPZ which may appeal to the Indian industry.

Besides an attractive set of incentives, finding very few parallels in other parts of the developing world, there are some striking factors worthy of consideration by Indian industry. Firstly, in the context of increasing cooperation in the field of technology transfer among developing countries, Mauritius may provide an excellent outlet for the intermediate technology available with the Indian industry except in the field of sugar production, in which thoroughly superior and advanced technology is already injected by Franco-Maritians. All the other fields are open to the "appropriate" type technology from India. At the present juncture when Indian technology with its simplicity and right mixture of technological ingredients is accepted all over Africa, Far Eastern and Gulf countries; there is no reason whatsoever why the labour-surplus Mauritius at the first stage of industrialisation should not appreciate the Indian technology. In this context, it may be mentioned that Indian technical personnel already working on a large scale in Mauritius may be the efficient vehicle for transmitting such technologies.

Secondly, an important factor in the successful transfer of technology is the capacity of the recipient economy to absorb the technology transferred. Here again, India is ideally placed as against the competitors from the advanced nations such as France, Britain and Japan. The most helpful factor in this respect is the large majority of Indians constituting an important segment of the entreprenurial and work force in Mauritius. An average Mauritian is quite literate and adaptable. In particular, Mauritian women, who are paid half the male wages, are known for their skills and adaptability. In other words, racial advantages in conjunction with availability of reasonably priced skilled and adaptable labour should prove a strong ground in the process of absorbtion of technology.

Thirdly, the Mauritian government its second National Plan (1975-80) has adopted a policy to encourage export-oriented labour-intensive units—with a view to employing 80,000 people in five years. In this respect, Indian manufacturers, in particular of ready-made garments and other textiles, electronic goods, etc. whose production processes are more labour-intensive than their counterparts from Western world stand good chance of favourable treatment at the hands of the Mauritian government. It may be noted that the ready-made garment units operated by the Indian units in the EPZ in Mauritius, are reported to be employing 20 to 30 per cent more labourers for the same unit of production than their counterparts from advanced countries including Germany; and 10 to 15 per cent more than the Hong Kong and Pakistan originated firms. Fourthly, for an Indian entrepreneur interested in setting up a unit in a developing country when advantage may be taken of the intermediate technology, Mauritius within literate and adaptable labour deserves the first consideration. Under the Export Enterprises Remuneration Order, 1975, the Government has fixed the minimum scales for workers operating in foreign ventures. Minimum wage rates, accordingly are M. Rs. 81 per week for a skilled worker who is more than 21 years old and the same is interestingly Rs. 49 for a female worker inspite of the reputation pertaining to the efficiency of women labourers in Mauritius. Very few African countries can boast of this cheap labour and match the qualities and abilities of the basically literate Mauritian labour ? Why, even in India, the running rate of wages is much higher in the organised market. No doubt, recently, starting from 1975, on the eve of general elections in 1976, nearly 40 per cent like in wages have been negotiated. All the same, considering the skill commanded by the labour in Mauritius, the wages are not likely to reach a level which can be deemed uneconomic.

Fifthly, for successful transfer of technology, one of the crucial requirements is the availability of middle-level executives operating as the liaison between the top hierarchy, representing the foreign management, and the local labour. In Mauritius, a large number of young men, particularly of

Hindu origin, happen to be well-educated and opt for super-visory types of jobs in organised urban factories. Besides, having racial harmony with the representatives from India, they also have the capacity to absorb technical know-how communicated to them. In other words, the problem of find-ing men with middle-level supervisory potential and then train-ing them, as found in some other developing African countries, is not present particularly for an entrepreneur from India.

Sixthly, Indian industry of late has been attempting on a large scale to capture the export potential in African count-ries. Textiles, electronics, and electricals are some such fields. Unfortunately, a number of political factors play a predomi-nant role in the purchase decisions of these countries thus reducing much of the advantage of the "technical appropr-riacy" of Indian goods with reference to the needs of these countries. In this context, Mauritius as a member of the Organisation of African Unity may serve as a fertile base for Indian export manufacturing operations. At a time when exports from India are encountered with competition from the US in electronic goods, Hong Kong and Pakistan in ready-made textiles and Japan in steel pipes and tubes in the Afri-can market, Indian exporters could contemplate an export plan under which exports could be routed to Africa through Mauritius where an Indian unit may have a production or processing unit on a "low-value-added" (say 40 to 50 per cent) basis. A classic example of such a venture is represented by the ready-made garments units currently run by Indian indus-try in Mauritius.

Seventhly, significant are the advantages emanating from a production base in Mauritius from the point of view of exports to Europe. As a member of the League of the African, Carib-bean and Pacific Countries (ACP), Mauritius enjoys some special advantages in trade with the European Economic Community under the Lome Convention incorporated in 1975. Under this scheme, Mauritian exports to the EEC countries enjoy almost an exemption from the customs tariff, and more significantly from the Indian angle, a complete freedom from quantitative restrictions. The only important condition laid down is that the exports under the scheme must have atleast 50 per cent value-added in Mauritius. At the present juncture, when the Indian exports of textiles of various types are threatened with steep restrictions of quota in the EEC countries, this facility under the Lome Convention assumes a particular appeal. Given the fact that in the field, besides their own funds, their racial and political advantages lend them a special elbow-room in their dealings with the long-term and short-term financial institutions in Mauritius. In other words, Indian industrialists besides sharing racial advantages with the Mauritian descendants, may also find financial management less problematic in collaboration with the local Hindus.

Lastly, an important ingredient for the transfer of technology is the depth of roots belonging to the transferring country in the recipient country. In this context, Indian technicians operating under various inter-governmental technical exchange schemes, notwithstanding numerous representations made by India to the EEC countries to revoke the restrictions, (going by the current trends these may continue for a long time to come), long-term planning by Indian industry in the direction of an operational route through Mauritius is considered advisable.

There are two additional very encouraging factors for the Indian industry to attempt an inroad in Mauritius. Firstly, the increasing emergence of the Mauritian-Indian community in the field of manufacture from trade and plantation to which they confined themselves for more than a century. Backed by political power, they have been making rapid strides in Mauritius, may provide a sound base. They are well-placed to play the role of the proverbial "Antenna"—an observer of gaps in technology and a judge of suitability in particular situations so essential for a successful transfer of technology. In this context, mention may be made of the historic role acted by such crucial technical experts—"Antennas"—in the eminent success of technological march of Japan. It may also be noted that the American military technicians who were in Japan after World War II, acted as the major vehicle for the transfer of technology from the United States. Reckoning with the fact that these experts had so little in common with their Japanese recipients, the position of a similar Indian expert in

Mauritius dealing with a person sharing common descendence appears almost enviable.

Another factor not to be lost track of is the interest recently shown by the Franco-Mauritians to diversify from sugar to other activities. Nearly a quarter of retained profits is invested in other industries. Considering the recent desire of these settlers to acclimatise themselves more and more to local conditions and to form a part of the normal national stream, particularly in terms of political influence, a new rapport is expected to be struck between these and the Indian community, commanding political power, in Mauritius. In this context, acceptance of industry from India is only a step forward in this direction. As these Mauritians are flush with funds, Indian industry which has planned a number of joint ventures with France in recent years may consider the increased chances of a successful negotiations with the French descendants.

However, inspite of all the advantages enumerated above, Indian industry has made rather limited inroads in Mauritius. It may mainly be attributed to the fact that most of the major advantages such as the attractive package of incentives, the Lome Convention, the African political and cultural proximity with Mauritius, etc. are only recent phenomena. For instance, the Indian industry while attempting exports to African countries some years ago found no disincentives there as they were entering almost virgin markets. It is only now, when the African markets for some items are getting congested with the invasion of a number of advanced countries, that the need to chalk out a sophisticated channel on a competitive basis through an operational base in Mauritius is viewed to other alternatives. Similarly, the quantitive restrictions by the EEC countries are rather recent and abrupt and hence not much anticipated in the past. Equally recent is the emergence of the Mauritian Hindu community to the pedestal of manufacturing industry. In other words, in the past at no time was it so opportune for an Indian industry to enter into Mauritius as it is today. Indian industry in the past was more thwarted by considerations such as limited local market commensurate with the small population in Mauritius, inadequate industrial input (raw-material) base, etc. Though these problems continue to prevail, through measures like the expansion of the export market and arranging imports of raw-materials like cotton from the neighbouring African countries and not so far Egypt, the intensity of the built-in constraints which blocked industrial growth in the past can be controlled. In other words, the advantages recently made available, far out-weigh the traditional hitches and stumble blocks.

In fact the first Indian unit to start production in Mauritius was an Ahmedabad unit in the manufacture of mosaic tiles and rolling shutters in 1969. This goes to prove how late Indian firms entered Mauritius and this is all the more striking viewed against the background of the fact that as early as in 1954 in Kenya an Indian unit was operating. The fact, of course, remains that Mauritius got independence only in 1968. Subsequent to the setting up of the tile unit in 1969, some 4 Indian industries have gone into production in Mauritius. They are: (1) a textile unit, belonging to the Orkay Group, Bombay; (2) a ready-made garments unit belonging to the J.K. Group; (3) a terry towel manufacturing unit by a firm from Ahmedabad; and (4) a steel rolling mill by the Mukund Group from Bombay. Final approval is sanctioned and pre-production operations are conducted in case of four more units including a cement plant by a Madras firm, five household cables units by a Delhi firm, a power driven pumps unit by the Kirloskar Group and a five star hotel. As can be observed, majority of units in production mainly operate in the field of textiles and ready-made garments. They cater to the export market in the EEC countries and Africa and have a value-added content of around 50 per cent in Mauritius. The basic meterial like cloth is taken from India for which again they obtain many export incentives from the Indian government. The degree of capacity utilization varies around 50 to 60 per cent in this units and they are mainly labour-intensive employing female labour to a large extent. Bulk of the labour force, that is, nearly 70 per cent reportedly is constituted by the Hindu Mauritians who also fill a large number of supervisory positions. Nevertheless, capacity utilization still remain around 50 per cent, even after a gestation of 4 years. In fact, in terms of export performance, some Pakistani, German and Hong Kong firms, which, of course, are more capital-intensive, are faring better. However, what is more disconcerting is the inordinate delay and uncertainty associated with the implementation of many projects. For instance, a cement plant to be set up by a Madras firm is faced with problems of environmental pollution which assumes particularly grave proportions in the small island and as a result the project stands doubtful of implementation. Similarly, an ambitious hotel project proposed by an Indian firm and project work on which was initiated, has been confronted with some exogenous constraints such as the currency crisis in Mauritius two years ago and indigenous problems pertaining to official transactions and has been shelved by the Indian party and returned to the Mauritian government.

These developments clearly point out the need for a planned approach to be adopted by an Indian firm. Before entering into Mauritius, a systematic appraisal of the market potential in Europe and Africa, along with a thorough study of the official policy in Mauritius governing pollution, employment pattern, etc. has to be undertaken. A casual approach often adopted in the case of ventures in developing countries may not hold water in Mauritius. In fact, a technology-mix which is slightly less labour intensive than the same in other African countries may be advisable. Because they have to compete with their counterparts from France, Hong Kong and the US. Another important feature of the Indian investement in Mauritius so far has been the preponderant reliance on their own resources and almost negligible participation allowed and that is what the Indian firms have been exploiting. On the other hand, if they plan in advance and seek partnership on a limited basis from the local parties, besides facilitating financial matters, it may also make the Indian firm more acceptable in Mauritius, in the process, making them more eligible for a special treatment by the Mauritian officials. All this amounts to stating that so far Indian firms, which went to Mauritius, were prompted more by the attractive official incentives, rather than long-term growth considerations. Hence, they neither had the will nor the time to proceed on a systematic basis. Indian firms now proposing to do so need to be guided more by pre-decision assessments pertaining to the product-mix, market and technology-mix, rather than a sudden outburst of optimism with reference to the export market in Africa and Europe. They have, however, little reason to be discouraged by the rather indifferent performance of the presently operating units from India, because these units happened to start operating at a time when the world-wide recession dampened the export market for consumer as well as industrial goods. With the recovery from recession, a more hopeful horizon looms ahead of these export-oriented units.

At this jucture, it is pertinent to assess broadly some areas of industry which may be found suitable for Indian enterprise. Sugar, the predominant industry, is ruled out as it is already controlled so efficiently by the Franco-Mauritians with an extraordinary degree of sophistication. Products based on sugar such as the processing of molasses, bogasse into alchohol, further into rum and beverages may be contemplated. However, some alchohol based chemicals which are yet to be manufactured in Mauritius deserve top priority. It may in this context be noted that 3 lakh litres of alchohol is exported from Mauritius after using bulk of alchohol for rum, denatured spirits, drugs and perfumes. With the pick-up in the export market for chemicals envisaged in the Gulf countries and Europe, this may turn an attractive proposition. Next in order is the tea processing. Already 8 factories are operating in processing and ordinary packeting. Yet improved processes of packet tea, instant tea for export purposes are not available. Given the fact that Mauritius exports nearly 35 lakh kgs. of tea in the total production of nearly 40 lakh kgs. a considerable scope appears to exist for processing and packaging of tea for marketing in the EEC countries.

Another potential field is the fibre-processing industry to meet the requirements of sugar and fertiliser units in Mauritius. Already, three units are operating in the field but an Indian unit in collaboration with a local party may contemplate the manufacture of sacks, bags of fibre grown in Mauritius. In fact, exports worth M. Rs. 1 million are annually executed to France at present, part of which could be shared by a new unit in the field.

Tobacco cultivation which has been recently introduced in Mauritius is fast catching on and it is expected that enough may be available shortly for processing into cigarattes, nicotine sulphate, etc.

The forest resources spread over nearly 1.5 lakh acres may be employed for paper board, paper and particle board units; finding a good market in the developing African market. They are some of the industries based on the raw material availability. Based on demand and export, a large range can be suggested but that involves import of raw materials. Important among these are some more textile units which at present are confined to ready-made garments and knitwear. A large integrated unit with spinning and weaving facilities may be thought of. Similarly, units for the manufacture of cement, plastics, agricultural implements (considering the enormous agricultural schemes proposed by the government) fish processing (based on a significant pick-up expected in the fish haul in the near future), footwear (in fact a reputed Indian unit is already proposing) may be considered. Equally significant are the opportunities available in activities such as construction and hotel-building to meet the fast growing tourist traffic (which rose from around 15,000 in 1970 to 75,000 in 1975).

To sum up, excellent opportunities exist for the participation of Indian industry in Mauritius. Nevertheless, a systematic planning and market survey are advised while proceeding with any project.

Considerable potential exists for the manufacture of engineering goods including mechinery, machine tools, electrical equipment. It may be seen that Mauritius imports machinery (non-electrical) worth M. Rs. 100 millions, vehicles and parts worth Rs. 50 millions, electrical eqnipment valued at M. Rs. 55 million annually. This, in combination with the abundant market in the neighbouring African countries, should help Indian industry in setting up a medium-scale unit to manufacture these items. The "appropriacy of technology" as can be guaged by the popularity of Indian trucks on the rough roads of Nigeria and many others is particularly relevant in the case of capital goods. In the context of all-round industrialisation in different African countries, often aided by Indian personnel and knowhow, a base in Mauritius is highly recommended.

RENU C. BHATIA

Indo-African Joint Ventures

THERE HAS BEEN a growing realisation among the developing countries of the need for greater economic cooperation among themselves. This realisation has stemmed, among other factors, from the growing gap between the developing and developed countries, fluctuations in the prices of primary commodities, balance of payments problems, formation of economic blocs between the developed countries like the EEC, EFTA, etc., tariff and non-tariff barriers against imports of processed and semi-finished goods from developing countries, stagflation in the developed economies, and, above all, the effectiveness of the Organisation of Petroleum Exporting Countries in raising the price of oil.

The pursuit of greater economic cooperation, however, will necessitate the adoption by the developing countries of deliberate policy measures of a multi-dimensional nature such as preferential trade agreements among themselves, payments arrangements, joint industrial ventures, producer associations, joint transport agreements, etc.

This essay deals with joint ventures as a form of economic cooperation between India and the African countries. It briefly examines the extent to which Indo-African joint ventures have contributed towards the objectives of greater economic cooperation between developing countries at different stages of technical development: and whether the establishment of these ventures has been the outcome of deliberate policy measures by India and the African countries. In order to do so, it is essential first to broadly survey the progress of Indo-African joint ventures in the context of the total picture of Indian joint ventures overseas.

The United Nations Economic Commission for Africa in its report of 1963 on *Industrial Growth in Africa* mentioned: "If political independence has been the watchword in Africa for the last ten years, rapid economic growth will no doubt be the overriding pre-occupation for the years to come."[1] Economic development has indeed become the main concern of the developing countries of Africa. This is obvious from the importance attached by most of them to their respective development plans. These plans invariably contain a programme for industrial development to enable African countries to diversify their economies and avoid total dependence on export of agricultural crops or mineral resources. Friedmann and Kalmanoff have attributed two motives to the launching of plans for industrialisation: the economic motive was to prevent the overcrowding of rural areas by providing an alternative industrial employment; and the political motive was the creation of manufacturing capacity to produce consumer goods and certain basic industrial commodities such as steel, tractors, chemical fertilizers, etc. as a means of reducing dependence on other countries.[2]

It must, however, be mentioned that the industrialisation of the developing countries pre-supposes the availability of adequate capital resources and technical know-how both of which were largely absent in the African situation. Joint ventures, therefore, were sought as one of the means to secure such scarce resources. In addition it was intended to avoid total sellout to multinational firms. Thus joint ventures were "overwhelmingly a postwar phenomenon, one of the many attempts to bridge the gap between the vast material and technological superiority of the industrially developed nations and the urgent needs and aspirations of the less developed countries".[3] However, joint industrial ventures among developing countries are comparatively a recent phenomenon.

It may be pointed out that India, having achieved comparatively a higher degree of industrialisation and sophistication
in its industrial production as well as having achieved significant
development in the matter of large, medium and small-scale
manufacturing sectors, has been soundly placed to provide and
share some of its technological and industrial achievements
with the other developing countries even though she herself is
a developing country. This is being done in a number of ways
and one of the important modes being joint ventures.

The adoption of joint ventures as a means of economic
cooperation among developing countries by India dates back to
1958 when Birla Brothers initiated the setting up of a textile
mill in Ethiopia. And after 1964 the Government of India has
adopted a positive policy of encouraging the setting up of joint
ventures abroad. In that year the Indian industrialists' goodwill delegation that visited the African countries in September-
October of 1964 reported that "we must actively participate in
setting up joint industrial ventures in as large a measure as
possible".[4]

Indian Joint Ventures Overseas: Some Aspects

India has today traversed a long way from the year 1964.
The progress that has been attained in this regard can be seen
from Table 1 on page 287. The number of joint ventures approved for setting up overseas have risen steadily from 67 in 1968 to
263 in 1976, representing an increase of 293 per cent. The
increase in the number of joint ventures that have started
production has been equally spectacular, having increased from
12 in 1968 to 23 in 1970—almost twice—further to 42 by 1974
and stood at 68 by the end of 1976 representing an increase of
467 per cent over 1968.[5]

The growth in the number of Indian joint ventures overseas
may be attributed to the somewhat flexible approach adopted
by the Government of India. The policy governing the setting
up of joint ventures has been reviewed from time to time partly
in order to encourage the setting up of joint ventures in
developing countries and partly out of concern over the non-
implementation of a large number of ventures sanctioned. In
other words an attempt is being made to adopt a more rea-
listic approach and a number of additional concessions have

been granted. For instance, the non-availability of credit facilities had been a serious constraint in the setting up of joint ventures in developing countries. The position has been eased with the availability of deferred payment facilities from the Industrial Development Bank of India for the purchase of machinery to be exported against equity.[6] Similarly the restriction on cash remittances for investment overseas has also been relaxed. However, in view of the fact that India is a developing country and is equally in need of foreign exchange resources, cash remittances against equity would be granted on a selective basis.[7]

Apart from permitting cash equity participation on a selective basis, providing credit facilities, etc. a number of fiscal incentives have been extended. Under section 80 of the Income Tax Act dividend receipts from abroad in foreign exchange have been exempted from taxation; so also the receipts in foreign exchange on account of royalties, commission, technical know-how fees, etc. Besides the above mentioned tax exemptions the Government has entered into double taxation avoidance agreements with a number of countries and negotiations are in progress for similar agreements with some countries of Africa and Asia.[8]

The product-wise position of Indian joint ventures overseas can be seen from Table 2 on pages 288-89. It is found that India has established joint ventures in diverse fields, such as textiles, engineering goods, chemicals, etc. It has even ventured into service industries such as hotels and consultancy services. Another feature revealed by the table is that more enterprises have been established in the Asian countries than in the African countries in the following fields namely, chemical and chemical products, basic metal and alloy industries, machinery and machine tools and parts, electrical machinery and appliances and parts, and automobile ancillaries and parts. Of the total number of projects that have already gone into production with Indian collaboration in Africa, thirty three per cent were accounted by the above listed industries compared to 54 per cent for Asia; and 50 per cent of the projects in the same categories were under implementation in Africa whereas in Asia the percentage was 65.

The regional distribution of Indian joint ventures overseas

reveals that (i) there has been a marked concentration in only a few countries of Africa and Asia. For instance, as on 28 December 1976, of the projects that had commenced production and those that were under active implementation in Africa, Kenya and Mauritius accounted for 10 and 9 projects respectively. Similarly in Asia, Indonesia and Malaysia accounted for 11 and 35 projects respectively; (ii) the countries where Indian investment has tended to concentrate are those countries which have a sizeable population of Indian origin. Besides the Indian entrepreneur has tended to show a perference for Indian partners wherever feasible; and (iii) there has been a change in the direction of the setting up of joint ventures. The earlier emphasis on Africa has given way to Asia (see Table 3 on page 290). Compared to 32 projects that were approved for Africa in 1968 the number for Asia was 24. The position was reversed by 1970, when the number for Asia went upto 47, while that for Africa dropped behind to 44. Since then Asia has maintained its prominence in this regard. By 1976 the number of joint ventures in Asia rose to 157 and that of Indo-African joint ventures stood at 72. Thus, there has been an increase of 125 per cent for Africa but there was five and half times increase for Asia. The same is true of the units that have gone into production.

The shift in regional emphasis has mainly been the result of a policy decision by the Government of India. The move to expand and diversify economic relations with the West Asian countries arises out of the possibility of a permanent shortage of petroleum;[9] whereas that with Southeast Asia it is largely a counter move "to China's resumption of the trade offensive after nearly a decade of economic and political hybernation."[10] The government underlined this when it stated "the Centre is understood to have decided to see that such efforts in future are concentrated in the middle-eastern and south-east Asian countries."[11] In other words the Government has been motivated by political and security considerations and not merely by economic considerations.

The neglect of Africa could prove to be unfortunate. A mere look at the ever growing investments in Africa from Western quarters is a sufficient indication of this. For instance, the United States net capital flows to Africa increased from

9 million dollars in 1957 to 108 million dollars in 1966. And by 1974 year end the amount of US direct investment in Africa other than South Africa stood at 2,233 million dollars in all industries, i.e. mining, petroleum, manufacturing, transport and communications, trade and finance, etc. "The American news magazine said that was three times what it was five years ago. . . In a report in its February 17 issue, the magazine said most big US companies once dwelt on the handicap of involvement in Africa: its scattered and backward peoples, its small markets, its sketchy road systems and utilities and its corrupt bureaucracies. . . . Now Africa is described by the US State Department's Donald Easum as a veritable storehouse of mineral wealth that is arresting attention. What the resources scanners find: bauxite, copper, cobalt, copper vast iron-ore reserves, as well as key food,"[12] uranium, chronium, industrial diamonds, etc.

Consultancy Services

Consultancy services are intimately related to the preliminary stage in the setting up of an industrial project, undertaking the study of the feasibility of the project and thereupon assisting in the design, construction and erection of it. It is, therefore, fit to look into the progress and place of Indian consultancy services.

India has achieved a considerable degree of competence in the field. It is now in a position to render engineering consultancy services in the realms of architecture and town planning, construction, cement, textiles, building of dams, electric furnace, steel plants, grey iron foundries, leather industry, light enginering industries such as bicycles, sewing machines, fasteners, fans, switches, etc., mining including ore handling and dressing, oil extraction and process, power engineering, power transmission and distribution, railway construction, re-rolling mills, roads and highways, steel foundries, structural fabrication, sugar production based on sugarcane, water supply and sewage disposal.[13] Apart from the specific fields listed above, Indian firms are also able to provide economic consultancy services, management consultancy services and management services for construction and operation.[14]

The above list is an indication of the degree of competence

achieved by India. That this ability has been internationally recognised is borne by the fact that: (a) India has been invited to UNIDO meetings as early as in 1970-71, as a potential country to offer technical and industrial collaboration, for promotion of industrial projects in Asian and African countries;[15] (b) it has a number of projects on hand in a number of countries like Kenya, Ghana, Libya, Mauritius, Sudan, Tanzania in Africa; Abu Dhabi, Iran, Iraq, Sultanate of Oman, Syria in West Asia; and Bangladesh, Indonesia, Malaysia, Nepal, Philippines, Singapore and Sri Lanka in South and Southeast Asia; and (c) the volume of its foreign exchange earnings from export of consultancy services have significantly increased to Rs. 40 million in 1975-76 from an average of about Rs. 10 million during the period 1970-71 to 1974-75.[16]

In view of the international acceptance of the competence of Indian consultancy services, the Government of India has included it as a component of India's strategy in promoting greater economic cooperation among developing countries. To this end the Government has not only created a project cell in the Ministry of Commerce to look after consultancy projects but has also extended financial assistance from the Market Development Fund.[17] The assistance provided has been multidimensional—(i) for undertaking market study abroad, assistance to the extent of 60 per cent of the net expenditure incurred by a consultancy firm; (ii) for opening foreign offices, assistance at 25 per cent of the expenditure incurred on accommodation and staff for first year and 20 per cent for the second year; (iii) 75 per cent of the expenditure for feasibility studies; (iv) 50 per cent of the expenditure after taking into account the revenue from sales and advertisements for bringing out publications for use abroad including journals, directories, brochures, pamphlets, folders, etc. and (v) 25 per cent of expenditure on brand publicity.[18]

Joint Venture as a form of Economic Cooperation between India and African Countries

Let us now take up the question of joint ventures as a form of economic cooperation between India and the African countries. The Indian overseas investments, as noted above, have been concentrated in the manufacturing sector as

against the investments in Africa by many Western Powers—
the former metropolitan countries—and even America in the
post-war period.[19] At times, investment has been made inspite
of its anticipated adverse effects on the volume of Indian
exports to Africa as in the case of textiles. Besides, of the total
of 18 projects in production in Africa as seen in Table 2,
one-third have been established in the fields of drugs and
pharmaceuticals, basic metals and alloy industries, machinery and machine tools and parts. This shows that given the
capability of Indian industry, the economic development of
Africa has been one of the foremost considerations in the
establishment of joint ventures.

The policy of the Government of India is quite specific about
this. The guidelines governing the setting up of joint ventures
overseas makes it clear that the Government is keenly interested in helping promote economic development in the countries
where it encourages setting up of joint ventures. For instance,
the Government of India permits minority participation only,
unless the host country desires majority participation. Secondly,
the Government would like the Indian enterpreneur to enter
into partnership agreements with the local development banks,
financial institutions or the host governments. Thirdly, export
of second-hand or reconditioned machinery against equity
investment is not allowed. Fourthly, in order to minimise the
involvement in foreign countries, Government of India instructs
Indian enterpreneurs to undertake turnkey projects as far as
possible. And, finally, training facilities have to be provided
for the nationals of partner countries. These guidelines further
show that the government is taking all possible measures at
the outset to prevent Indian industrialists from establishing joint
ventures overseas and taking the course similar to the one taken
by many multinational firms. Thus, while there is a clear case
for greater economic cooperation through joint ventures between India and the African countries, it is equally important
to evaluate such ventures from time to time with a view to see
that they do not violate the principle of mutual benefit which
underlies such schemes.

This is the case as far as Indian policy is concerned. As
regards African policy, the leaders of African countries have
also felt the urgent need to cooperate with the developing

countries. For instance, Kenya's Minister of Finance, in November 1972, speaking at the annual dinner of the Kenya Institute of Management said: "It was time the poorer nations realised that unless they took measures in the right direction to improve things for themselves they would for a long time remain the victims of the big powers' decisions."[20] Similarly the Tanzanian Finance Minister during his recent visit to India in July 1977 stated that the problems of developing countries could be solved through cooperation among themselves. "It is by collective action on the part of the poor that we can either confront those who have exploited our weakness to their advantage or maximise the mobilisation of the limited resources at our disposal."[21]

However, the official foreign investment policy of the African countries still do not adequately reflect the hopes and aspirations of the peoples of African countries as stressed by their leaders in their speeches. The general tendency no doubt has been to welcome foreign investments from any quarter. The incentives to that end have been provided in the shape of tax holiday, exemption from customs duties, tariff protection, etc. to all. The same concessions are available to the developing countries with no special provision added.

Further, that India signed agreements during 1975-76 for only five projects out of the 77 to be set up in Kenya, Mauritius, Tanzania, Uganda and Zambia in the realm of joint ventures, consultancy services, developement projects, technical assistance, etc.[22] indicates the absence of any special concessions offered by the five African countries mentioned above to attract Indian enterprise by way of certain special measures.

In conclusion it may be noted that although the African governments have not adopted any deliberate measures to attract joint ventures from India or any other developing country, yet the very fact that Indian joint ventures have been able to secure a foothold in some of these countries indicates that: (1) they can stand and survive on their own in the face of international competition; (2) they have the necessary potential to make a success of their enterprise in these countries and break the monopoly of Western multinationals; (3) nor do the African governments discourage their operations in terms of incentives offered to capital investment from outside. Of course, the

African countries do not offer to India any special concessions; and (4) they welcome promoting greater economic cooperation among developing countries; and the adoption of preferential policies towards each other may follow.

We believe that this spirit of economic cooperation between the developing countries will go a long way in breaking the unending self-generating vicious circle of economic dependence on the Western countries. It will generate a new climate of collective self-reliance that will in course of time help in the ushering of the new economic order.

TABLE 1

Indian Joint Ventures Overseas

	1968[1]	1970[2]	1972*[3]	1974**[4]	1976[5]
Total No. of units approved	67	105	136	171	263
No. of units in production	12	23	35	42	68
No. of units under implementation	51	46	56	107	80
N . of units abandoned	4	36	45	22	115

Notes :   * As on 15 August 1972.
        ** As on January 1975.

Sources:(1) Compiled from various issues of *Indo-African Trade Journal*.

       (2) Federation of Indian Chambers of Commerce and Industry, *Indian Industrial Joint Ventures Abroad*, 1971. Annexure III, pp. 27-47.

       (3) Indian Investment Centre, *Joint Ventures Abroad*, 1972, Annexure II, pp. 15-22.

       (4) *India : A Statistical Outline*, Fifth Edition, New Delhi, 1976.

       (5) "Vital Change in Policy on Ventures Abroad : Share Investment in Cash to be Allowed," *The Economic Times*, 13 January 1977, Table A.

TABLE 2

*Product-wise Distribution of Indian Joint
Ventures Overseas*
(as on 1 January 1976)

	In Production				Under Implementation			
	Total	Africa	Asia	Developed countries	Total	Africa	Asia	Developed countries
1	2	3	4	5	6	7	8	9
1. Food Industry	5	—	4	1	2	—	2	—
2. Textiles (cotton, wool, synthetic & allied textile products	13	7	5	1	9	1	8	—
3. Cork & cork products	1	1	—	—	—	—	—	—
4. Pulp, paper & paper products	3	1	1	1	2	—	2	—
5. Leather & leather products	1	—	1	—	1	—	1	—
6. Rubber & rubber products	2	1	1	—	1	—	1	—
7. Plastic & plastic products	—	—	—	—	1	—	1	—
8. Chemicals & chemical products								
(a) basic chemicals	—	—	—	—	4	—	4	—
(b) chemicals (others)	2	—	2	—	6	—	6	—

1	2	3	4	5	6	7	8	9
(c) drugs & pharmaceuticals	3	2	1	—	1	—	1	—
9. Non-metallic mineral products								
(a) glass & glass products	3	—	3	—	2	—	1	1
(b) others	2	1	—	1	1	1	—	—
10. Basic metal & alloy industries								
(a) iron & steel	4	2	2	—	5	—	5	—
(b) metal products	2	1	1	—	6	1	5	—
11. (a) Machinery and machine tools and parts	7	1	5	1	5	2	3	—
(b) other machinery	4	—	4	—	4	—	4	—
12. Electrical machinery, appliances & parts	2	—	2	—	5	1	3	1
13. Automatic ancillaries & parts.	4	—	4	—	5	—	5	—
14. Construction	1	—	1	—	2	—	2	—
15. Hotels & restaurants	5	—	—	5	4	2	—	2
16. Transport services	—	—	—	—	1	—	1	—
17. Engineering & consultancy services	3	1	2	—	1	—	—	1
Total	67	18	39	10	68	8	55	5

Source : Indian Investment Centre, *Joint Ventures Abroad*, 1976, Annexure VII, pp. 71-75.

TABLE 3

Distribution of Indian Joint Ventures: Region-wise

Region	No. approved	No. in Production	No. under implemen-tation	No. Abandoned
1968[1]				
Africa	32	8	22	2
Asia	24	3	19	2
South & Central America	3	—	3	—
Developed countries	8	1	7	—
1970[2]				
Africa	44	14	15	15
Asia	47	6	26	15
South & Central America	3	—	1	2
Developed countries	11	3	4	4
*1972[3]**				
Africa	52	14	19	19
Asia	68	16	32	20
South & Central America	3	—	1	2
Developed countries	13	5	4	4
*1974[4]***				
Africa	57	17	32	8
Asia	93	19	64	10
South & Central America	3	—	3	—
Developed countries	18	6	8	4
1976[5]				
Africa	72	15	12	45
Asia	157	44	59	54
South & Central America	3	—	—	3
Developed countries	31	9	9	13

Notes: * As on 15 August 1972
        ** As on January 1955

Source: Refer sources 1, 2, 3, 4, 5 cited in Table 1.

REFERENCES

[1] United Nations Economic Commission for Africa, *Industrial Growth in Africa*, (New York, 1963), p. 2.

[2] W.G. Friedmann, and G. Kalmanoff (ed.), *Joint International Business Ventures* (New York and London, 1961), p. 3.

[3] *Ibid.*, pp. 258-59.

[4] Cited in Ram Gopal Agarwal, "Joint Ventures as an Instrument of Export Promotion", *Foreign Trade Review*, January-March 1967, p. 353.

[5] The progress of Indian joint ventures overseas apart from being seen in terms of number of ventures approved and the number gone into production can also be seen in terms of investment and earnings. For instance the total investment in projects both in production and under implementation has been steadily rising: it was Rs. 160 millon in 1972, rose to Rs. 300 millon by March 1974 and reached a sum of Rs. 337 millon in 1976. Similarly, the earnings by way of dividends, royalties, etc. have also been rising from Rs. 11.4 million in March 1972 to Rs. 34 millon in 1974 and by 1976 India had earned Rs. 45 million.

[6] Government of India, Ministry of Commerce, *Report 1974-75*, New Delhi, Government of India Press, p. 37.

[7] "Ventures Abroad: Cash Equity Allowed", *The Economic Times*, 28 February 1977.

[8] *Ibid.*

[9] "Direction to Tie-ups", *The Economic Times*, 10 June 1973.

[10] *Ibid.*

[11] *Ibid.*

[12] Economic Periscope, "Increasing US Investment", *Indo-African Trade Journal*, Vol. 11, 1975.

[13] Indian Investment Centre, *Joint Ventures Abroad, 1976, Annexure* xv, p. 121.

[14] *Ibid.*, p. 23.

[15] Federation of India Chambers of Commerce and Industry, *Indian Industrial Joint Ventures Abroad, 1971*, p. 15.

[16] "Indian Foreign Trade: Surplus Trade Balance", *Indo-African Trade Journal*, Vol. 12, No. 4, October-December 1976, p. 40.

[17] Market Development Fund was established in 1963 for promoting India's exports.

[18] The assistance is available to those firms that are (a) the members of the Federation of Indian Exporters' Organisation, (b) have an annual turn-over of minimum Rs. 10 lakhs and foreign exchange earnings of Rs. 2 lakhs, and (c) the technical personnel of the firm should have sufficient experience.

[19] Of the $2,233 million US direct investment in Africa other than South Africa $1048 million or 47 per cent alone were invested in three countries, namely, Liberia, Libya and Nigeria——countries rich in mineral wealth. Thus it would not be wrong to infer that US investments in Africa have largely been prompted by its requirements of

primary products. The same conclusion can be drawn from the industry-wise distribution of US investments. That is, of the total investment of $2,233 million in Africa other than South Africa, $1785 million or 80 per cent were invested in mining and petroleum compared to a meagre sum of $165 million or 8 per cent in manufacturing. The position was no different in the countries of Liberia, Libya and Nigeria where $874 million out of $1048 million or 83 per cent were invested in mining and petroleum compared to a bare $22 million or two per cent in manufacturing. (US, Department of Commerce, *Survey of Current Business*, August 1976, p. 48.)

[20] "Kenya: Kibaki Commends Self-Help to Poor Nations", *Indo-African Trade Journal*, Vo. 8, Nol. 4. May 1972, p. 27.

[21] "Tanzania Keen to Avoid Dual Taxes", *Financial Express*, 30 July 1977.

[22] Compiled from *Africa Research Bulletin* (Economic Series) 1975-76.

V.G. MUTALIK DESAI

The City in the Third World:
A Study of Africa and India

TODAY THERE IS an explosion of cities and town both in the developed and developing countries of the world, and this phenomenal urban growth has given rise to a number of issues. Perhaps it may not be an exaggeration to say that urban problems have attained such a magnitude, and it could be considered third in importance, to have posed a danger to civilization, next in importance only to 'nuclear warfare' and the prevalence of hunger among a wider segment of developing world's population. It is rather strange that nearly three-fourths of the world's population lives in the Third World countries rather than the developed countries; and this proportion will rise considerably before the close of this century.

The purpose of this essay is to outline the important dimensions of the process and features of urbanisation in the African countries, to examine some of the burning problems that have emerged and the trend of thinking towards the solution of those problems.

I
INTRODUCTION

Process of Urbanisation
　　The future urbanisation will perhaps be mainly confined to

the Third World, though historically the process of urbanisation was initiated by the present developed countries. The acceleration in the process of urbanisation during the early 19th century was associated with industrialisation. The demand of the new industries was such that "in the long run the period of European industrialisation and urbanisation must be regarded as one characterised by shortage of labour."[1] Today one observes two vital aspects of the over-all urbanisation trend. Although developed countries are showing signs of declining rate of urbanisation, population of the new and emerging countries of Africa and Asia is playing a decisive role in the process of urbanisation more gigantic than before.[2] A combination of "pre-industrial fertility and post-industrial mortality"[3] has provided the Third World city a very high rate of natural increase in population; and the rural-urban migration continues unabated. It is rather an enigma that the rapid rate of urbanisation and the existing size of some of the Third World cities are the result of inadequate economic development rather than the result of it. Although the conditions in the cities are far from satisfactory, the pathetic conditions prevailing in the rural areas leads to a mass movement of people to the cities.

The countries in Africa are the least urbanised but today their rate of urbanisation is very fast. The countries north of the Sahara have already attained a state of urbanisation almost comparable to that of Southern Europe; and those of the South, except South Africa, are less urbanised (Table 1 on page 304). Hence, in the history of the world we are passing through the peak period of urban formation; and it is this critical period which demands considerable attention of the Third World.

An Outline of Africa

The thirty-five countries of Tropical Africa[4] are predominantly agricultural. Of the estimated population of 242 million in 1970, the urban population of this region had crossed the mark of 26 million, or 11 per cent.[5] The number is still rising at twice the rate of growth of total population. Although it is the less developed region of the world, yet one finds its new cities are assuming considerable significance in recent years.

Some pepole argue that mounting problems of cities and the

low level of urbanisation are both a challenge and an opportunity for the future development; and "Africa's very lack of development makes it the most favoured developing area in the world".[6] But the demographic outburst of the cities in Africa is basically a post-war phenomenon and a great deal of interest is being taken in the study of African urbanisation. In fact a clear idea about the demographic situation in the African countries is indispensable to realise the magnitude of the problems of urbanisation. Apart from the usual difficulties like concepts, definitions of census, etc. prevailing in the developing countries,[7] their ethnic complexity has given rise to political controversy.

II

FEATURES OF URBANISATION

Urban Inheritance

Ibadan had a population of over 100,000 in 1906; and this was the only city in the entire Tropical Africa. In the next six decades the number of cities had reached to 57. While Kinshasa and Greater Lagos had crossed the one million mark by 1970, other cities like Dakar, Accra, Ibadan, Addis-Ababa and Nairobi had over 500,000 population.[8] With certain exceptions, as in parts of West Africa, the rapid urbanisation that is emerging in Africa is the product of alien rule of the present century. Among the Yorubans of West Nigeria, there is a clear evidence of indigenous African urban tradition. Apart from this there were a number of old towns, centres of powerful chiefs, like Kumasi, the capital of Ashanti; but despite their history and long tradition they were small till the coming of Europeans, and the construction of roads and railways.

Thus, there is a high degree of concentration of the urban population in a few and important cities. But the number of relatively intermediary towns is very small and for a major part of Tropical Africa there is inadequacy of organised nucleated settlements in the rural areas. Some countries like Tanzania have emphasized the creation of such settlements, viz. Ujamaa Villages, to work together and reap the benefits of socio-economic advantages of co-operation.[9] So the enigma is the prevalence of sprawling cities co-existing with relatively unorganised and less developed village societies. As a result what emerges is "an islandic pattern of economic activity," and a bunch of "productive islands often set in vast sea of emptiness."[10]

In-migration

Another feature of the developing countries is the process of in-migration during the present times.[11] Nearly one-half of increase in urban population is mainly due to in-migration. However, it is rather difficult to study such migration processes and evaluate them. Due to their underdevelopment and uneven dispersal of population in these countries the issues emerging out of internal movement of population assumes a greater importance. The lure of cities, both real and imagined, for the rural folks, adds a new dimension to this problem. There is a dual tendency towards inter-rural movement of population and rural-urban migration. The extent to which the streams of population flow to the cities depends upon the distance they traverse to the cities.

Occupational Characteristics

The occupational characteristics of urban areas serve as focal points of attraction for outsiders. A rural migrant, who does not have skill and is unaware of the ways of the world, may be confronted with peculiar problems in the urban areas for which he is not totally prepared to face them. The marginally unemployed labour hovers around petty and scattered services. These are "made up in the main, of all the myraid hangers on and odd-job men who live on the rim of starvation in the rundown slums and miserable fringe settlements of the great urban jungles."[12] The availability of such jobs is much more than the jobs provided in the industrial sector. This is quite in contrast to the developed countries where the service sector follows the process of urbanisation.[13]

Push and Pull Factors

It may, therefore, be said that both the push and pull factors have been responsible for the migration of the rural folks into the urban areas.[14] The evidence shows that both the push factors, viz. overpopulation in villages, large rural-urban income differentials, absence of opportunity for getting the land to eke-out one's existence, land tenure resulting in the fragmentation of land, poor family conditions; and the pull factors like high expectations and the lure of city life, freedom from family restrictions, false hopes, claimed benefits and the 'feed-back' advantages to villages have all contributed to this migration.

Unemployment

It is rather dismal to see that the spectre of unemployment emerges with its attendant evils, viz. overcrowding, dilapidated houses, dirt, noise, pollution and the first set of migrants facing hostile surroundings.[15]

The main hurdle to rectify the situation is the magnitude of investment required to generate the industrial employment. A couple of hundred years back development started with elementary technology needing limited skills. Since then there has been explosion in technical know-how, level of skill and organisation, etc. But the developing countries, that see progress in the number of chimneys in the skyline belching smoke, have created an imbalance by importing sophisticated equipment at an exhorbitant cost. An effort to apply such a technology when capital is pitifully scarce and labour abundant is disastrous.

Size of Market

The installation of a modern industry is conditioned by the small size of market. The sluggishness in the countryside and joblessness in cities do not create any substantial demand for machine-made goods. The limited needs of urban middle class puts a brake for the creation of jobs in the industries and their needs could be easily met by local manufacturers. The prospect of exploring an export market too is limited. Formerly the industrialised countries had monopoly in the export but today there are multinational giants who, with their superiority and sophistication, control the market.

So the lack of technical know-how, limited size of market, inadequate capital and other factors have been responsible for creating stagnant employment situation and crisis in the Third World cities.

New Towns of Today

Nevertheless the present-day cities of the Third World as

mentioned above are essentially the product of colonial rule. A large number of cities are either transport centres or port cities spread along the rail lines. Situational factors have also influenced the growth of certain cities viz, Accra, Lagos, Abidjan and Dakar.[16] Almost all the West African coastal cities which incidentally are situated at the mouth of rivers served as vital points of trade contact for the interiors. So cities served as centres from where the natural resources could be easily tapped. They were the places from where fertile areas could be controlled, and more so if these places were situated near the sea. Quite often we see in Africa and elsewhere that the native settlement in these areas was negligible before the foreigners developed them as strategic spots for the movement of goods, military and centres of administration: for example, Mombasa and Dar-es-Salaam. They also served as transmission centres for the export of primary goods to Europe and in return import of the manufactured products. With the introduction of modern transport these centres grew in importance. But their growth unlike the cities of Europe did not take place as a result of sustained development. "They were, in a real sense, larger than and ahead of the economy sustaining them."[17]

The Interior Cities

The interior cities owe their existence to the establishment of railways, viz. Mombasa to Kisumu line started in 1896, Nairobi rail lines commenced between 1895-1930, and Accra-Kumasi in Ghana began in 1910. The growth of towns in the copperbelt area in Zambia was due to the construction of railways. In Zambia, nearly ten cities, having a population of over 20,000 are all situated along this rail line.[18] Till 1960 sixteen out of 57 cities over a population of 100,000 were port cities and the rest were connected by the colonial railway system to these ports.

No doubt that the colonial exploitation has brought about striking changes in the life of majority of Africans. "Before the present century, almost every sub-Saharan African earned his living by gathering food by cultivating crops or by herding, or by a combination of these activities.[19] But in just a couple of decades a great majority of Africans have marched from bushes to the new and attractive cities and have taken active part in the monetised economy of the industrialised society. Today the national governments have lifted earlier restrictions on the migration of people: and this has left a great impact on the socio-economic life and the demography of the urban centres.

Plight of Third World City

For a number of countries in the Third World, the programmes as laid down in their development plans remain on paper. In a few cities one comes across a few steel mills, textile industries, industrial estates, spacious and luxurious houses for the elite, a small flourishing business district which are just the islands of prosperity "submerged in a sea of urban problems," and these are represented by poverty, squatter colonies, slums, delinquency and the slowly emerging environmental pollution on an ever increasing scale. If one drives from the modern metropolis airport in the Third World to a five-star city hotel, somewhere during the journey one will have a brief sight of certain shanty areas where a large chunk of population is destined to live. Such shanty towns and slums have different names in the developing countries, viz. *bustees* in Calcutta, Zopadpattis in Bombay or 'gourbilivilles' in Tunis. It is a place where crime, delinquency, poverty, misery and human discomfort have reached the climax. These are the direct results of urbanisation.

The increasing unemployment, the miserable slum, the helpless worker, the discarded women and their hungry children are the signs of deeper malaise. Unlike the earlier cities which provided wider vistas of opportunities to the urbanites, the present Third World cities have shown their incapacity to do anything. This pathetic state of affairs has stunted the future growth of cities, and this disease in the years to come will be more harmful.

Thus, in a large number of countries in Africa nearly half of its population lives in one sprawling city—Accra, Abidjan, Dakar, etc. If one believes that the decade 1970's ends in crises, the source of this chaos could be traced in the bulging, shapeless unwieldy and uncontrolled cities of the Third World.[20]

Housing

Of all the problems confronting the Third World the problem of housing seems to be the most difficult. With the urban

growth rates ranging between 3 to 10 per cent the housiug
facilities in the cities of the Third World have deteriorated. A
large percentage of the population lives both within and on the
outskirts of cities which may be termed as 'spontaneous settlements'.[21] Varying `solution ranging from self-help schemes to
the construction of high-rise apartments as in Hong Kong have
been suggested to ease the problem of housing. As a result
Hong Kong has eliminated the squatter huts through the massive resettlement estates and vigorous penalty for new squatting.
To emulate such a pattern requires poltical will, a change in the
official attitude towards the housing of urban poor, etc.

III

RURAL-URBAN RELATIONSHIP

In the wake of urbanisation that is emerging in Africa it
would be worthwhile to see in what way the problem could be
ameliorated by establishing a close liaison between the urban
and the rural development.

Unlike the developed countries the urban development in
Africa has not been preceded by transformation of agriculture,
viz. increase in food productivity, surplus, etc. Here the spurt
in cities has overtaken the industrial growth and development
of agriculture to produce food to feed the cities. Hoselitz calls
these cities as 'parasitic' rather than 'generative'.[22] In certain
countries like Ethiopia and parts of Tanzania the prospects of
agricultural production are rather slim due to bad weather, poor
soil or barren land. But in the absence of technical possibility
of generating more surplus for sustaining the city population,
energizing rural market for consumer goods, and balanced regional development, seems to be dim. Hence, under the existing
conditions a large number of cities in Africa reveal most of
the characteristics of imbalanced and uncontrolled growth.

Perhaps in the immediate future the present trend of migration may be difficult to curb but the real issue at stake is how
to retain the economically active and vigorous age-groups in
the village for the agricultural purposes. Hence it is necessary

to evolve a strategy of development where the process of controlled urbanisation is integrated with the rural development programme. This programme could deal with a wide-ranging issues, viz. increase agricultural productivity, develop cottage and village industries, create a better environment in the rural areas, decentralise industries to create additional employment opportunities, undertake a large-scale communication schemes, start reclamation and irrigation schemes, initiate land tenure reform, set-up regional planning schemes, etc.[23] On the other hand, a comprehensive urban policy would deal with the issues like increasing the absorptive capacity of a city by providing productive jobs to the new arrivals.

The desire to have capital intensive solutions, viz. expressways and subways, without giving need to sensitive political problems, land-use road-pricing, industrial and commercial localities will add to the difficulties in the immediate future. Hence, the adoption of a rational policy embracing these and allied issues will go a long way in overcoming the various problems confronting the cities.

The Urban Politics

A word may be said about the political aspects of urbanisation which is rather peculiar to Africa. If one believes that rapid urbanisation is a novel experience for African countries, the political experience is at its infancy. In fact there is a basic dichotomy in the nature of government and their policies; and there are wide variations in the form of government and their ideology.[24] The turbulent political environment of the post-independence era is unfavourable for formulating and implementing new development programmes. On the one hand the charismatic leaders are trying to cope with economic and political crises, and on the other hand they are launching development plans.

The efforts to deal with the crisis created as a result of sudden spurt in cities lack sincerity, and it has become a political issue. And the problem of unemployment is assuming serious proportions in urban areas. This was the main theme of Kericho Conference held in Kenya in September 1966, where the problem was thoroughly discussed. It is rather a pity that the problem of surplus labour existing in the rural sector is underestimated both by politicians and planners; but the same problem in the modern sector becomes economically and politically an explosive situation.[25]

In this background it seems peculiar when one observes the African leaders talking about conferring benefits of development to the countryside by eradicating povery, ignorance, etc. They make emotional speeches and assure the villagers that no discrimination is shown to their needs. A minister says that "Developing countries are desperately short of capital, and you must realise that such countries cannot afford to spend huge sums of money in urban areas on extravagant infrastructure."[26] This compels the leaders to exhort the people 'to go back to land.' Arusha declaration elaborately deals with this aspect of the problem.[27]

The political concern for the countryside is because of their belief that rural development will put a halt for the migration of people to cities and help to ease the unemployment problem in the urban centres. The general slogan everywhere is—contain the growth of the cities, halt migration to urban areas, solve the problems of slums, etc. Some planners are less opitimistic and believe that such measures will have a marginal influence on rural migration. Harris and Todaro have suggested other alternatives.[28] Very recently efforts are being made to revitalise the rural economy to make it more attractive. There are also visible signs of other measures taken in these countries for over-all development of the economy.

IV

CONCLUSION

What is the future? The prepetual inadequate financial and physical resources to tackle the growth problems, migration, employment, lethargy of government and its incapacity to launch an action-oriented programme to deal with urbanisation are some of the main reasons that may continue in the present trend towards urbanisation.

No doubt there is a considerable awareness among the leaders about the urban problems. The national plans and programmes are launched to deal with the problems associated with them. If industrialisation and urbanisation go together then more income is generated, individuals may exert more to carve a better life in the city and produce more revenue, and these will help to deal with major problems. But the future seems to be dim because urbanisation has outstripped the pace of economic development.

"It is very doubtful", says Hauser, "that, over this span of time, the underdeveloped nations can attain economic development of adequate dimensions to meet western standards of living for their present and future city dwellers. The fundamental economic objective is... productivity; and many difficulties in meeting their efforts to attain this objective are likely to be exacerbated rather than ameliorated by present and prospective rapid rates of urban growth."[29]

These conditions accompanied by the incapacity of agriculture to solve the basic problems will create additional difficulties. The rising expectations of the people demand a better and higher standards of living than before. Even efforts to increase agricultural productivity may not go far. The fiscal and financial problems of urbanisation too will create a wide gap between the needs of urban areas and the ability of the citizen to pay for these services. Hence, it is pertinent to note that "development without urbanism is an undesirable phenomenon, but there is no worse combination than urbanisation without development, because to the lack of urban facilities is added the want of employment opportunities."[30]

If suitable measures are taken to deal with the issues related to economic development, then it is possible that some of the frightening sights of urbanisation could be averted. So far no sincere efforts are made to study the 'optimum rural-urban population balance' in these economies. It is not yet clear what form of course the future urbanisation will take. Apart from other, measures, viz. increasing agricultural productivity, decentralising industries, etc., the efforts made in some countries to decelerate urbanisation are welcome.[31]

Table 1

World Urbanisation (Selected Regions)

Regions	Level of Urbanisation (% of total population)		% of increase
	1950	*1960*	*1950-60*
World Total	21	25	17
More Developed Regions	37	41	10
North America	43	46	6
Europe (without Russia)	37	40	8
Southern Europe	23	27	16
Less Developed Regions	14	18	28
Africa	10	13	37
North Africa	21	26	23
South, West and East Africa	6	9	50

Source: Glen T. Trewartha, *A Geography of Population: World Patterns* (New York, 1969), p. 152; c.f. D.J. Dwyer (ed.), *The City in the Third World* (London, 1974), p. 18.

REFERENCES

[1] B.F. Hoselitz, "The role of Urbanisation in Economic Development: Some International Comparisons," in Roy Turner (ed), *India's Urban Future* (Berkeley, 1962), p. 168.

[2] For interesting details see Aylward Shorter, *East African Societies* (London, 1974), pp. 5-6.

[3] Ringsley Davis, "The Role of Urbanisation in the Developing Process," Cf. D.J, Dwyer (ed), *The City in the Thtrd World* (London, 1974),p. 11.

[4] The United Nations Organisation divides Africa into three major areas, viz. North Africa, Tropical Africa and South Africa. See United Nations, *Growth of the World's Urban and Rural Population, 1920-2000*, (New York, 1969),

[5] Colin Rosser, *Urbanisation in Tropical Africa : A Demographic Introduction—An International Urbansiation Survey (hereinfter cited as Tropical Africa)* (Ford Foundation, 1970), p. 1.

[6] Daniel Lerner in "Comparative Analysis of Processes of Modernisation," in *The City in Modern Africa*, p. 38.

[7] Such difficulties could be seen in the varying definitions, see Gerald H. Blake, "Urbanisation in North Africa : Its Nature and Consequences," in Dwyer, n. 3, pp. 67-80.

[8] Ibid., p. 17.

[9] A.O. Ellman, "Progress, Problems and Prospects in Ujamaa Development in Tanzania," *Urbanisation in Tropical Africa*, n. 5, p. 21.

[10] William Hance, *The Geography of Modern Africa* (New York, 1964), pp. 46-7.

[11] For details see Blake, n. 7, and John E. Brush, "Spatial Patterns of Population of Indian Cities," in Dwyer, n. 3, pp. 105-30.

[12] U.N. Committee on Housing, Building and Planning, *Housing, Building and Planning in the Second Development Decade* (New York, 1969), p. 22

[13] Wilbert E. Moore, *Social Change* (New Jesey, 1963), p. 101.

[14] Migration and its effect on the size and distribution of urban areas is effectively brought about in a report. See George Beier and others, "The Task Ahead for the Cities of the Developing Countries," in *World Development*, May 1976, pp. 377-78.

[15] For other details refer to ibid., pp. 391-2.

[16] Gerald Breese, *Urbanisation in Newly Developing Countries* (Englewood, N.J., 1966), pp. 102-3.

[17] U. N. Committee on Housing, Building and Planning n. 12, p. 16.

[18] *Tropical Africa*, n. 5, pp. 23-24.

[19] J.C. Caldwell, *African Rural-Urban Migration: The Movement to Ghana's Towns*.

[20] Ibid.

[21] D.J. Dwyer, "Attitudes Towards Spontaneous Settlement in Third World Cities" in D.J. Dwyer, n.3, pp. 204-5.

[22] Hoselitz, cf. *Tropical Africa*, n. 5, p. 50.

[23] Breese, n. 16, pp. 143-44.

[24] *Tropical Africa*, n. 5 pp. 59-60.

[25] For an interesting discussion about such a dual economy, see F.H Harbison, "The Generation of Employment in Newly Developing Countries" in James R. Sheffield (ed.), *Education, Employment and Rural Development* (Nairobi, 1967), pp. 170-74.

[26] J.S.M. Ochola, Opening remarks in Michael Safier (ed.), *The Role of Urban and Regional Planning in National Development of East Africa* (Kampala, 1970), p. 4.

[27] For details see Julius Nyerere, "The Arusha Declaration and TANU's policy on Socialism and Self-Reliance," in Svendson K.E. and M. Teisen (ed.), *Self-Reliant Tanzania* (Dar-es-Salaam, 1969), pp. 190-93.

[23] For the six policy alternatives see John R. Harris and Michael P. Todaro, "Urban Employment in East Africa: An Economic Analysis of Policy Alternatives", *Tropical Africa*, n. 5, pp. 68-9.

[29] Philip M. Hauser, "The Social, Economic and Technological Problems of Rapid Urbanisation" in Bert F. Hoseltiz and Wilbert E. Moore (eds.), n. 13, p. 203.

[80] Breese, n. 16, p. 143.

[31] Ibid., p. 144.

Index